Three Faces of God

SUNY Series in Religion, Culture, and Society
Wade Clark Roof, Editor

Three Faces of God

Society,
Religion,
and the Categories of Totality
in the Philosophy of Émile Durkheim

Donald A. Nielsen

State University of New York Press

Published by
State University of New York Press, Albany

© 1999 State University of New York

For information, address State University of New York Press,
State University Plaza, Albany, N.Y. 12246

Production by Diane Ganeles
Marketing by Dana Yanulavich

Library of Congress Cataloging-in-Publication Data

Nielsen, Donald A., 1943–
    Three faces of God : society, religion, and the categories of
totality in the philosophy of Emile Durkheim / Donald A. Nielsen.
        p.   cm. — (SUNY series in religion, culture, and society)
    Includes bibliographical references and index.
    ISBN 0-7914-4035-4 (alk. paper). — ISBN 0-7914-4036-2 (pbk. :
alk. paper)
    1. Durkheim, Emile, 1858–1917. 2. Sociology—Philosophy.
3. Religion and sociology. 4. Whole and parts (Philosophy)
I. Title. II. Series.
HM51.N49 1999
301′.01—dc21   98-24856
                                                          CIP

10 9 8 7 6 5 4 3 2 1

For Jane

CONTENTS

PREFACE

This book is the result of a lengthy rumination over Émile Durkheim's work. It emerged from a sense of puzzlement about certain striking passages in his writings, for he seems to advance a world view reaching far beyond his familiar and more limited sociological analyses. These sentences have been largely ignored by previous commentators, or treated as either mere metaphors, or stylistic ornaments irrelevant to his main concerns. However, when coupled with remarks about the Durkheimian agenda by members of his school, as well as some critical observations made by his contemporaries, they provided the initial clues for my investigation and led to a new reading of Durkheim. His metaphors, especially those concerning the whole and part relation, are the gateway to his social philosophy. I saw them as hints of a much broader perspective which placed the forces of human society at the epicenter of reality and gathered the realms of religion, knowledge, and nature itself into a unified fold. The result has been a reconstruction of his social thought around the philosophical problem of totality and an image of his work as the embodiment of a sociological monism whose central features are strongly reminiscent of Spinoza's philosophy. This comparison also places Durkheim in the longer civilizational tradition of Jewish thinkers such as Philo, Maimonides, and Spinoza, who responded to the challenges posed to inherited religious culture by the modernizing forces of their respective ages with the creation of distinctive forms of religious philosophy.

My thinking about Durkheim has been far from an unchecked, imaginative excursion through his writings. It has been tempered by his texts and linked at every point to a careful, if not entirely "orthodox" reading of them. This interpretation, like all others, is open to question, but its claims to plausibility emerge from the fact that it extracts philosophical implications from Durkheim's writings, yet remains close to his actual texts. I have not wanted to speculate about his meanings without first reading his words. Much of what follows is a commentary on the implications of some of his most striking and suggestive passages.

The heart of the book is found in chapters 4–10, where I trace the chronological development of my central themes from Durkheim's earliest reviews and essays through his final writings. These chapters form a selective commentary on Durkheim and assemble the evidence supporting my case. I have attempted to unravel the tangled skein of concepts, images, metaphors, and concealed assumptions which actually inform his writings, especially those connected with the metaphor of whole and part, the notion of totality, the images of social substance, social forces and social concentration, and the central categories of understanding. I discuss not only his four books, but also his shorter monographs, his main lecture series, and many of his other briefer essays and reviews. Indeed, several of these shorter pieces are of enormous value in the interpretation of Durkheim. In addition to the analysis of Durkheim's work, I discuss key writings written during Durkheim's lifetime by members of his school, including Marcel Mauss, Henri Hubert, Robert Hertz, and Célestin Bouglé. These Durkheimian texts add a good deal to our understanding of the master's philosophical concerns.

The book's central chapters are framed by two sorts of discussions. Chapters 1–3 lay the foundation for my interpretation. Chapter 1 states Durkheim's project, asserts the philosophical centrality of the whole/part metaphor in his work, and preliminarily suggests some of its implications for other aspects of his social metaphysic, including his so-called social realism. Chapter 2 examines Durkheim's turn toward the study of religion and the categories after the mid-1890s and argues for its connection with his hopes to create a social philosophy of totality on a new foundation. It draws out the implications of several remarks by Marcel Mauss about the Durkheimian program of reseach into the categories of understanding and Durkheim's own focus on the whole. Chapter 3 lays a foundation for the later discussion by examining aspects of the work of several philosophical predecessors, notably Aristotle, Sir Francis Bacon, Spinoza, Immanuel Kant, and Charles Renouvier; their ideas had a strong bearing on Durkheim's approach to the problems of totality and the categories. Chapter 11 has two aims. It draws on the results achieved in chapters 4–10, but attempts a more systematic reconstruction of Durkheim's mature sociological monism, one reflecting the standpoint implied, if not fully developed in his actual writings. It also tentatively locates Durkheim's philosophy within the context of a wider civilizational perspective, in particular, an encounter between Judaism, and traditional religion generally, and modernity. It argues for the recognition of his distinctive achievement as a religious and metaphysical philosopher who attempted, like others before him such as Spinoza, to combine traditional religious horizons with modernizing philosophical and scientific perspectives into a totalizing theory. Indeed, this idea was suggested in passing in an essay of mine published ten years ago and provides the starting point for this book (Nielsen 1987a).

In recent years, Durkheimian scholarship has profited from a spate of new translations. Books previously available in English have seen new and often improved translations and formerly untranslated lecture series and shorter works have also appeared. However, some existing translations are less than perfect and many shorter essays remain unavailable in English. Since my work depends on a close reading and interpretation of his texts, I have compared all existing translations with the French originals. I have sometimes modified the existing English versions or provided entirely new renditions. In all instances, I have favored a literalist approach to translation, remaining close to Durkheim's own words. Wherever I have quoted Durkheim or members of his school, I have cited both the existing English versions and the French texts, wherever possible in readily available French editions (e.g. Durkheim 1969b; 1970; 1975). This will allow readers to easily check my translations. Where no English version exists, quotations reflect my own translations. However, I do not want to make a fetish of translation problems. The following treatment depends ultimately on my interpretation of Durkheim's ideas more than on the nuances of the translation process.

ACKNOWLEDGMENTS

Although this book has been hatched in considerable intellectual isolation, I have nonetheless accumulated some notable debts over the years. I owe the most intellectually to my teachers at several universities. My interest in the classical tradition of social theory and the sociology of religion was kindled at the State University of New York, Stony Brook by Guenther Roth and Benjamin Nelson in their many undergraduate courses. While studying for the master's degree at the University of Illinois, Urbana, Louis Schneider and Alexander Vucinich taught me more than I could then appreciate. When I returned to New York to work on my doctorate, completed in 1972 under Benjamin Nelson's supervision at the Graduate Faculty, New School for Social Research, I took courses with many people and learned from them all. But it is to Nelson that I owe the most. It may seem odd that a student of one of America's leading Weberian scholars should write a book on Durkheim. But many of my previous publications (e.g. Nielsen 1989, 1990, 1991) have frequently struck more Weberian chords, even while I was investigating Durkheim and his school. Those familiar with Nelson's writings will also recognize the connection between my book and some of his main themes, including the emphasis on the genealogies of ideas, the role of key rationales in intellectual life, and the civilizational perspective.

Arthur Vidich, Chair of Sociology at the New School during my graduate years, has since included me within his intellectual circle as a fellow colleague. In the process, he has stimulated my thinking and helped me become a better writer. Edward Tiryakian has encouraged me and my Durkheimian investigations ever since I participated in his 1983 National Endowment for the Humanities summer seminar on great schools in the social sciences. Other friends, new and old, have helped me more than they realize. Bill Swatos, Tony Blasi, David Preston, and Maurice Richter have read my writings, generously shared their thoughts, and drawn me out intellectually. Thanks go to all these people, although none can be held responsible for this book's contents.

I am also indebted to the cordial interlibrary loan staff at the State University of New York College, Oneonta for providing the steady stream of "Durkheimiana" necessary for the project. Special thanks go to Zina M. Lawrence of the State University of New York Press, who has been an exemplary acquisitions editor. She and the other editorial workers at the Press have seen this project from prospectus to completion with efficiency, patience, and congeniality.

Aristotle says somewhere that man not only wants to live, but to live well. My particular *eudaimonia* is dearest Jane and our *famille solidaire*, resplendent with close feline friends, nine of whom—Julius, Cleo, Mudhorn, Wah-Wa, the Pig Man, Penelope, Jake, Ellwood and Maggie—have lived, and some died with us in our wanderings over the past twenty years. As the roseate glow fades from Durkheim and all the rest, Jane and they alone remain, new with each new day.

1

DURKHEIM'S PROJECT: A CLAIM

The work of Émile Durkheim and his school represents the most sustained effort in the history of sociology to recast the central problems of the religious and philosophical tradition in sociological form. This involved simultaneously the retention of the basic truth claims of religion and philosophy, yet also the sociological transcendence of these claims. No other social theorist or school of social thought attempted or achieved as much in this area: neither Karl Marx and the Marxists, despite promising leads in their work (Jay 1984); Max Weber; Georg Simmel, despite his deep philosophical interests; Sigmund Freud and his followers; Max Scheler (1992) and Karl Mannheim, despite their pioneering work in the "sociology of knowledge"; nor even George Herbert Mead and the Pragmatists, although these latter thinkers were perhaps, as Durkheim himself sensed, some of his main challengers in this field (Durkheim 1955).

Durkheim offered a sociological theory of religion, its essense as well as its central manifestations in beliefs and rites. He and his school also attempted to provide a sociological account of some of the main problems of philosophy: moral, epistemological, and metaphysical. Durkheim sought to create a sociology of moral life which would resolve the perennial debates over both moral obligation and the nature of the good which had exercised philosophers since Plato. This very incomplete aspect of his work has received increasing attention in recent years, but it will not be my primary focus (see Durkheim 1975, II, 292–331; Wallwork 1972; Hall 1987). Durkheim's epistemological concerns included both a sociology of knowledge and theory of science, both of which have also been discussed extensively (Hirst 1975; Schmaus 1994; Turner 1986; LaCapra 1972; Bloor 1982; Berthelot 1995; S. Collins 1985). While I will say a good deal about his doctrine of categories and his sociology of knowledge, my central concerns are neither with his epis-

1

temology nor his theory of science, as they have usually been understood. My main interest is in not only the place of his theory of the categories, but also his sociology of knowledge within his larger sociological metaphysic. As I will argue in the following pages, his work does contain the lineaments of a sociological metaphysics, including a "metaphysics of knowledge," whose full range and claims, when adequately understood, are truly astonishing. Instead of rejecting the older philosophical problems and starting from an entirely new set of premises, as some contemporary philosophers and social theorists have done (e.g. Habermas; see Nielsen 1987b; Rorty 1979), Durkheim sought to retain the truths and insights of the traditional "philosophy of consciousness," and traditional metaphysics generally, including its theory of "representation" and image of a "mirror of nature," while at the same time grounding them in a social philosophy with metaphysical intentions. In the process, Durkheim created a unique sociological, religious, and philosophical amalgam.

Durkheim's sociological metaphysic has not been given nearly enough independent attention. This is true despite, perhaps even because of the interest in his so-called social realism. The term "realism," as applied to Durkheim's position, has usually been opposed to the notion of "nominalism." It seems to have gained currency in modern sociology through Gabriel Tarde and others, who labeled Durkheim's work as a form of "realism," perhaps even "scholastic realism" (Tarde 1969, 140: 15–17; Deploige 1938). Variants of this view were soon adopted with little question by commentators and already came to dominate the discussion of this aspect of Durkheim's thought at an early date (Gehlke 1915, 86–88, 94–95; Dennes 1924, 33–53; Simpson 1933; Alpert 1939). It has done considerable mischief in the study of Durkheim's work. It has terminologically misdirected the discussion by confusing Durkheim's tenaciously held claims about the "reality" of society with philosophical debates over the reality of universals, thus putting investigators off a more fruitful trail. Durkheim never doubted that universal concepts were "nominal" (among other things), but he also believed in the "reality" of society; the conflict between these intellectual orientations drove him toward the creation of a social metaphysics which would resolve the conflict.

Durkheim's interest in the "reality" of society cannot be understood solely at the level of epistemological claims. It needs to be seen from the standpoint of the problems of metaphysics. The misunderstandings over Durkheim's so-called social realism have also led scientifically oriented sociologists to doubt the very possibilty that Durkheim's work could be informed by a metaphysics (a reaction beginning especially with Parsons 1937). Indeed, many commentators continue to deny that he makes any metaphysical claims (Wallwork 1972; Schmaus 1994). The debate over Durkheim's alleged "social realism" obscures the central fact that his "realism" is, more accurately, a reliance on the whole/part metaphor and a focus on the problem of totality, terms invested by him with a certain "metaphysical pathos" (Lovejoy 1936, 12–13). As his work develops, the whole/part rhetoric becomes increasingly linked to his analysis of religion and the problem of totality, including a view of society and nature, in a way which forms the basis of a wider metaphysics. Although it has the minor advantage of gesturing toward metaphysical problems, the term "social realism" is largely unhelpful in understanding Durkheim's work, at any stage in its development. Durkheim never adopts the term as a description of his own position and, in fact, distances himself from this characterization. For example, in his rejection of Deploige's criticism of his work, he refers to the whole/part analysis, which he had adopted from Charles Renouvier, as the true basis of *what M. Deploige calls* (author's emphasis) our social realism" (Durkheim 1975, I: 405).

My central aim is to unravel the intricate skein of Durkheim's thought and demonstrate that metaphysical commitments and related philosophical assumptions are deeply rooted in his thinking and have large implications for his theories. To achieve this aim, I have had to break free from the usual divisions established in the study of his work. I focus on the points of intersection of his conceptions of religion, the categories, and society, and not on any one of these areas alone. As such, my study moves largely outside of the generally established intellectual division of labor, which tends to separate the sociology of religion, the sociology of knowledge and social epistemology, from general social theory and all of these areas from metaphysics.

It needs to be more clearly recognized that there is a peculiar and specific intellectual strategy in Durkheim. Auguste Comte (1975, 29–30) suggested a theory of three stages of human mental development, so to speak, through which the various spheres of culture passed at varying rates. Durkheim wanted to create a theory which, in effect, retained and unified the truths found in all three of Comte's stages: religion (the theological stage), the philosophical categories (the metaphysical stage), and society (the positive stage at the highest level of development in sociology). He wanted it all three ways, so to speak, and, therefore, required an approach which vindicated both his continued devotion to traditional religious (and philosophical) ideas, and his allegiance to modern science. It is this combination which makes his thought theoretically daring, yet conceptually ambiguous, with its seemingly odd juxapositions of religion, philosophy, and science as well as its simultaneous use of a variety of rhetorical figures, including those of emotion, morality, energetics, force, concentration, wholism, and so forth.

Durkheim's contemporaries had a keener sense than sociologists today of the wider challenges posed by his work, even if they were not always entirely clear, consistent, or thorough in their estimates of these challenges. The suggestive remarks by Richard, Bergson and even some of Durkheim's own followers (e.g. Mauss, Bouglé, and Davy) have not been taken as seriously as they should be for an understanding of his work. The former are usually viewed as opponents whose intellectual, practical, and perhaps personal motives unfairly colored their views of his work. While there is some truth in this view, it is not a good reason for entirely dismissing their intuitions. Moreover, the centrality of metaphysical elements in Durkheim's thinking was noted at an early date even by foreign (i.e. non-French) writers who could not be suspected of such bias. For example, in a comment made in 1912 and based on Durkheim's early work, John Theodore Merz (1965, IV:561, fn1) noted the "synoptic" quality of Durkheim's sociology, which "starts always from the consideration of a totality, a complex; considering this to be the prius and not a later product of the assemblage of its parts. And this the author lays down as a general principle applicable to the study of the phenomena of society no less than to those of life in general and even of inanimate phenomena." Durkheim's own closest followers often expressed an awareness of these wider issues and connections of his work to the philosophical tradition. At times, they even implied a certain assent to the view that Durkheim was, in some way, concerned with metaphysical problems (Bouglé's preface to Durkheim 1974a, xxxix; Davy's introduction to Durkheim 1957, xxxiv; Davy 1911, 12). This does not mean that we need to accept at face value either the defense of Durkheim by his followers or the many exaggerated claims made about the origins and implications of Durkheim's theory by his more strident critics, especially when they tried trace his thought to German influences (Deploige 1938; also now Meštrović 1988). I think Durkheim puts many of these claims to rest quite effectively himself. But it does require that we expand our intellectual horizons to include a sense of how his contemporaries perceived his work. The very fact that they found metaphysical implications in his writings at all is itself suggestive.

One of the main leads which needs to be followed in understanding the metaphysical dimensions of Durkheim's work concerns the themes of philosophical monism and religious pantheism. Gaston Richard, an early member of the Durkheim group, who later broke with them, remarked that Durkheim's theory of religion rested on both these foundations (Richard's essay in Durkheim 1994a, 230–31). While Richard hardly makes a strong case in his analysis of Durkheim's writings for his sweeping assertions, his insight is suggestive. Henri Bergson was less specific, but also thought that Durkheim's system represented a fundamental philosophy, as much as a new sociological theory (his remarks in Besnard 1983, 133; Vialatoux 1939). The sense that there was more than sociology at stake in Durkheim's work is captured in Jules Romains' provocative image of Durkheim as "the Descartes of unanimism" (cited in Bouglé 1935, 17).

Durkheim's theories are widely assumed to be highly "dualistic," nor would I dispute the strong element of truth contained in this description. A variety of dualities do permeate his work, for example, the individual and society, two types of social solidarity, four types of suicide set out as pairs of polar opposites, the sacred and the profane, and the dualism of human nature itself. On the other hand, his early attacks on those forms of metaphysical dualism, which located humankind as a privileged case outside of and above nature, already raise questions about the place of dualisms in his thinking. A close study of his work provides other reasons for thinking that Durkheim was not entirely, or even primarily, a dualist. I will argue that Durkheim's rejection of metaphysical dualism led him to develop a standpoint best characterized as a type of "sociological monism," perhaps even one with elements of a "sociological pantheism." The crucial fact at the outset was his abiding interest in the nature of the whole (and the whole/part relationship) and, as time passed, in the problem of totality. When these central interests are integrated with his persistent "sociologism" and his increasing focus on religion and the categories, they combine to provide the basic elements of a monistic theory which regularly transcends and encompasses the other dualistic tendencies in his thought.

Along with the whole and part problem, and the notion of totality, we will need to look at his changing usage of such ideas and images as social density, concentration, association, and force and how they are related to his view of society as, in some sense, a "social substance." Indeed, despite the almost unanimous rejection of the idea that Durkheim was a "substantialist," I think there are strong indications of just such a view in his writings. His central ideas circle around a philosophical core which, despite its many ambiguities, points toward a sociological metaphysics rooted in a variant of philosophical monism.

This is what I want to demonstrate in the following pages. I do so through a chronological analysis of his writings. I will focus especially on his major published works, but I also want to examine many, if not absolutely all, of his less prominent publications, including essays and lectures series. From the very earliest date, we find Durkheim keenly interested in the nature of the whole and in the whole/part relationship. Indeed, it becomes a central rhetorical figure thoughout his writings. He relies on it at crucial points in his arguments and, as often as not, he advances it as an ultimate rationale in proof of his main theses. As we examine his work, we discover a shift in emphasis and see him become increasingly interested in this problem from the standpoint of the category of totality, and from the perspective of the sociology of religion and the categories generally. Throughout his work is found the sociologistic strand of thinking, woven as a complex skein into his treatment of all these issues. My chronological treatment of his work is meant primarily to examine the varied ways and settings in which he develops the problems of the whole, whole/part, totality, the categories, and their relationships to his analysis of religion and society. Only through such a chronological commentary can we capture the various nuances in Durkheim's shifting use of these ideas and images.

Readers should be forewarned about the limits of the present study. There are some things it does not accomplish. The following analysis is more focused than many treatments of Durkheim's work, which attempt a global assessment of his theory, including its political implications and its relevance to contemporary debates in sociology today. This study cuts into the corpus of Durkheim's work at what I consider to be a vital point, one which reveals a great deal about the rest of his thought. I would immediately add that I do not therefore think that my analysis of Durkheim is entirely irrelevant to the dilemmas of the modern world (unless, of course, one is prepared to discount the importance of metaphysics and the related philosophical tradition). However, Durkheim's relevance appears at a different level from that claimed by treatments of him which aim

more explicitly at the political, ideological, social, and purely contemporaneous aspects of his work. As a result, little or no attention
will be given to the many issues which currently exercise
Durkheim's commentators, for example, the possible relationship of
his work to capitalism, socialism, liberalism, communtarianism,
structuralism, deconstructionism, modernism or postmodernism,
feminism, and a variety of others (e.g. Giddens 1971; Filloux 1977;
LaCroix 1981; Challenger 1994; Cladis 1992; Lehman 1993, 1994;
Meštrović 1991). Moreover, even the seemingly relevant notions of
rationalism, empiricism, nominalism, realism, and other terms are
largely circumvented as central reference points of the arguement.
While I also gesture at times (as infrequently as possible) toward
such omnibus terms (e.g. monism), I do so only to summarize my
detailed discussions of Durkheim's ideas. The more global characterizations serve only as punctuation marks, so to speak, in the
analysis. Indeed, one of my primary hopes is to avoid featuring such
"isms" in the treatment of Durkheim's work. These abstractions too
readily take on a life of their own in intellectual history and, as
tools of analysis, yield a pitifully small harvest for our labors. While
they have some value as intellectual shorthand, and as summary
characterizations of an author's position, they are too often used as
sorting devices to quickly locate Durkheim's arguments in relationship to other allegedly established standpoints. They short circuit
the detailed analysis of particular problems and usually lock us
into a set of intellectual party positions which are entirely destruc-
tive of thought. More importantly, they hardly do justice to any
important and complex thinker's ideas. In some recent treatments
of Durkheim, they have been orchestrated into a whirl of unilllu-
minating abstractions (e.g. Lehman 1993; Meštrović 1991; also
Nielsen 1996d). It is difficult to avoid them entirely, since they form
the staple of much of Durkheimian exegesis, and are sometimes
employed by Durkheim himself. However, I do intend to avoid them
as much as possible.

Similar remarks might be made about the short term, practical dimensions of his thought. They are of little concern to me.
Durkheim's view of modern industrial society, his political orientation (and that of his school), his interest in professional groupings
or educational reform, his relationship to current events like the
Dreyfus affair, and a large number of other questions are all important and interesting (e.g. Clark 1973; Pearce 1989; Cladis 1992;
Besnard 1983; Pickering and Martins 1994). I will argue that they
are much less relevant to the understanding of his main philosoph-

ical rationales than other "influences" operating across longer historical, civilizational spans. Indeed, one of my primary methodological tools in this work is a civilizational perspective, a view from the
longue durée. It is adapted ultimately from Durkheim and Mauss's
own thinking on this subject (Durkheim and Mauss 1971; also
Braudel 1980, 25–52; Nelson 1981, 83–84).

My approach is generally that of an "internalist," but of the
long view, interested in the fundamental philosophical rationales
and rhetorical tropes which go into the making of Durkheim's major
texts. I want to trace Durkheim's use of key foundational rationales
in his argument, ones which turn out to have a long philosophical
lineage. Insofar as I do address the practical implications of his
work, I am interested less in the short-term ones than in the long-
term vision of the possible future implied in his theories, in, so to
speak, Durkheim's "utopian" strand.

While this work covers a good deal of the ground around
Durkheim, it does not pretend to offer a general survey of his work
or an overview of his life (Lukes 1973; Jones 1986). It is a specialized treatise on a particular dimension—albeit, a central one—in
his writings. I want to examine the texts themselves and the way
in which Durkheim treats the problems of the whole and others of
concern to me. Any progress in the understanding of Durkheim (or
the ultimate advance of sociological theory, for that matter) is only
possible on the basis of such focused analyses of particular problems. These questions need not and should not be trivial ones; I do
not think the ones treated in this work are trivial. But they must
be specialized investigations, carried through as exhaustively as
possible, even at the risk of a certain repetition in the chronological
analysis. Only if we stick closely to our theme, and trace its development throughout his writings, can we hope to fully understand
its role in his thought or offer a convincing proof, rather than a
mere assertion, of our interpretation.

My treatment is argued at the level of Durkheim's deepest
philosophical assumptions about reality. Indeed, I will treat
Durkheim primarily as a philosopher, albeit a sociologically oriented one. He confronted the full range of inherited philosophical
questions. However, he is especially a religious and social philosopher. It is the religious element which increasingly predominates
and provides the basis for resolving the other philosophical and
metaphysical dilemmas in his work. Of course, behind religion lies
society. There is certainly nothing unusual about such a treatment
of Durkheim. His philosophical training and interests are well

known. There are already several works devoted to him as philosopher, in general, or to various particular aspects of his philosophy (LaCapra 1972; Schmaus 1994). Most of the literature on him necessarily says something about these philosophical themes. However, in keeping with my emphasis on the longer historical duration, I will be focusing on Durkheim's relationship to several thinkers who have not been examined very closely in conjunction with his work, in particular, Aristotle, Bacon, Spinoza, Kant, and the neo-Kantian Renouvier. In the conclusion to this work, as well as at several points along the way, I will suggest that Durkheim's philosophy bares a striking resemblance to Spinoza's system and, indeed, that the two thinkers emerge from similar historical conjunctures.

The empirical and theoretical validity of his sociology will also need to be put aside in these pages. This is not because I am uninterested in his research sociology and particular theories or that I think him a bad sociologist. On the contrary, I think there is much of value in his substantive empirical and theoretical work and, indeed, feel drawn to aspects of his sociological style of explanation (especially his sociology of religion and knowledge). However, these are not my main concerns. Any discussion of his ideas at the level of substantive theory must be left for another occasion. In any case, there is no lack of good, strictly sociological and anthropological, commentary on his major works (Douglas 1967; Pope 1976; Lester 1994; Pickering 1984; Needham's introduction to Durkheim and Mauss 1963; Stanner's essay in Durkheim 1994a, chap. 16). Durkheim may be judged empirically mistaken (as he undoubtedly often is) and his theories poorly conceived (which they sometimes are), but none of this in any way effects my analysis of his philosophical system.

I will have much more to say about the coherence of his formulations and his mode of argument. While there are several persistent themes in his work, his style of thought remains very complex. His developing theory is much more ambiguous than is usually realized and manifests a variety of theoretical and rhetorical tensions. These ambiguities probably emerge from several sources. I will emphasize those emerging from the tensions between the dualistic and monistic elements in his thinking. This book attempts to reassess these neglected monistic elements, bring to light these ambiguities, and offer a version of Durkheim which points toward a resolution of these dilemmas.

2

DURKHEIM'S INTELLECTUAL DEVELOPMENT AND THE DURKHEIMIAN THEORETICAL PROGRAM

Durkheim's Social Philosophy and the Revelation of 1895

It is widely agreed that Durkheim had a keen interest in religion. We are going to demonstrate in the following pages that he also had an abiding interest in the problem of the whole, the whole/part relationship, and the problem of totality. He used these metaphors (i.e. whole/part) and related modes of expression to capture his theoretical ideas throughout his career. In his mature work, we also find him systematically integrating his interests in the problems of society, religion, and the categories, including the notion of totality, or the whole, into a unified theory (Durkheim 1995b). Disagreement arises over the shifts in Durkheim's intellectual itinerary, when they took place, and their effect on his thought. This issue is particularly important for our work, since Durkheim's view of the problem of the whole appears to have been modified under the influence of his emerging interest in religion.

A key text in this connection is Durkheim's letter of 1907 disputing certain allegations of Simon Deploige (1938) about the allegedly German origins of his ideas. Durkheim argued that it was only in 1895 that he gained a clear sense of religion's central role in social life and also discovered the means for treating religion sociologically. He experienced this as a "revelation" and viewed his lecture course of 1895 on religion as a "line of demarcation" in his intellectual development, indeed, to such an extent that "all my previous researches had to be started all over again in order to be harmonized with these new views" (Durkheim 1982, 259; 1975

I:404). He goes on to remark that Wilhelm Wundt's ideas had no role in this change and that it was, instead, due to his reading in religious history, especially the work of William Robertson Smith and the British historians of religion.

This vexing passage can be interpreted in different ways, depending on whether the focus is on Durkheim's relationship to Robertson Smith, and the British historians, his evolving view of religion, or a variety of other possible questions, including his opposition to Marxism, his attitude towards socialism, the effects of the Dreyfus affair on his thought, or the influence of German thinkers on his work (Jones 1986; Meštrović 1991; Wallwork 1985; Alexander 1982; Pickering 1984; Hall's Introduction to Durkheim 1993). I want to remain close to Durkheim's own interpretive emphasis and examine his claim to have found the means of dealing sociologically with the problem of religion and, especially, the significance of his remark that his work needed to be "started all over again" to be made congruent with his new standpoint. Later, I will also argue that Durkheim and Mauss were concerned with other philosophers (notably Spinoza) and philosophical issues at this time; these also fed into their choice of the new means used to reanimate Durkheim's investigations.

The new means, in part, seem to have been the recent literature on primitive society and, especially, on totemism. Durkheim not only used the evidence of primitive religion and society, especially the Australian materials, as his crucial "test case," but also found even more important benefits for his emerging theory in the phenomena of totemism. It needs to be asked why Durkheim found totemism so intriguing. Apart from its allegedly "primitive" character and its relationship to his already established notion that "clan" organization was the earliest form of organized society (Durkheim 1984, 126–31), it was totemism's fascinating cultural content, in particular, its identifications of humanity with nature, that drew Durkheim to it as the most suitable means for his theorizing. Totemism was the best vehicle to develop his remarkable theory linking together nature, humanity, religion, and knowledge.

Less clear, but equally important, are the implications of Durkheim's remark about his work having to be "started all over again." This new start resulted in a decade and a half of research and writing and culminated in *The Elementary Forms of Religious Life* (hereafter abbreviated as *Forms*). It is particularly important to ask: in what ways does the major treatise of 1912 on religion, knowledge, and society (as well as other important work of this period by him and his school) recapitulate, in a new theoretical form, any of the ground covered in his earlier works, especially, but not by any means exclusively, *The Division of Labor in Society* (hereafter abbreviated as *Division*) of 1893? My argument is that the later work recasts central dimensions of the earlier one, despite their seemingly different topics. It needs to be recognized that the later treatise on religion is an examination of the category of "the whole," or "totality," its sociological substance as well as its symbolic representation, while the earlier work on the division of labor is also a study, from a very different standpoint, of the changing social forms and modes of legal representation of the whole. One key fact here is that Durkheim substitutes religion for law (or, more accurately, types of moral and legal sanctions) as the visible index or symbolic representation of society and its changes. In the process, he (perhaps inadvertently) shifts his emphasis from morality to religion. Thus, the later phase of Durkheim's work, one culminating in the treatise of 1912, is focused on a new conceptualization of "the whole" (and also, by implication, of the "parts" composing it) and its forms of symbolic representation. As we examine Durkheim's work from this standpoint, we discover that the problem of totality, or the whole/part relationship, is central not only to *Division*, but to much of his work between 1893 and 1912. From the beginning, a vast number, if not all of his writings, from his first publication on Albert Schäffle in 1885 to his important essay on the dualism of human nature in 1914, touch in one or another significant way on the problem of the whole, the whole/part relationship, and, increasingly, the category of totality. Evidence for this interpretation, and its importance for the understanding of Durkheim's work, is found not only in Durkheim's own writings, but also in a neglected passage from a later essay by Marcel Mauss. This passage sheds a good deal of light on the problems of concern to us in these pages.

The Durkheimian Program of Theory and Research

The key passage by Mauss occurs in the opening paragraphs of his 1938 essay on the category of the person. Mauss writes that the French school of sociology has devoted itself "*above all* [my emphasis] to the social history of the categories of the human spirit." They examine each of them in turn, starting with the Aristotelian list of categories. He notes that they study comparatively the forms taken by them in particular civilizations, their changing nature, and the reason for them being as they are. He observes that he and Hubert studied the notion of *mana*, in the hope of finding the archaic basis of magic and also the general and primitive notion of cause. In addition, Hubert studied the notion of time and Stefan Czarnowski began a study of aspects of the notion of space. Finally, Mauss writes, Durkheim examined "the notion of *the whole* [Mauss' emphasis], after having treated with me the notion of kind" (Mauss 1966, 333–34).

I can think of few more important documents for the understanding of Durkheim and his school than this Maussian text.

While it is well known, it has seldom been used as a central starting point for an understanding of Durkheim or his school. Although it was written twenty years after Durkheim's death, I would immediately point out the basic accuracy of Mauss's characterization. His description of the research program of the Durkheimians clearly refers back to the earlier period, when Durkheim himself headed the school. If these remarks are taken as an overview of their efforts and read beside Durkheim's comments on his intellectual itinerary and his work on religion, they require that we modify our image of his aims and the philosophical dimensions of Durkheim's project. Durkheim was concerned with the problem of the whole or totality.

Mauss was the leading figure in the Durkheim school after the master's death, his successor as editor of *L'Année Sociologique*, and editor of the posthumous writings of other members of the school, including Robert Hertz, one of several younger scholars killed during World War I. His intimate connection with the school might alone lend credence to his remarks. Moreover, Mauss's comments are clearly on the mark. Durkheim's writings confirm the preliminary emphasis on Aristotle as an important reference point for this part of their work (Durkheim 1995b, 8; Durkheim and Mauss 1963, 4–5). In addition to space, time, causality, genre, totality, and so forth, they also wrote on many other categories not directly linked to any list found in Aristotle, for example, the person, sacrifice, sin, expiation, death, and many others. A long list of references could be brought forth to support the view that the Durkheim school was interested—indeed, "above all"—in the sociological study of the categories of the human spirit. Durkheimian studies focused especially on items found in one of the Aristotelian lists (about which more is said below). These include the following: Hubert and Mauss on force and causality and, generally, on magic (Mauss and Hubert 1972);

Hertz on right and left (Hertz 1973), a study meant to contribute to the understanding of the notion of space (Hertz 1970, ix); Hubert on time (Hubert and Mauss 1929); Maurice Halbwachs and Czarnowski on aspects of the notion of space (Halbwachs 1941; on Czarnowski, see Mauss 1968, II:146); Mauss on the notion of substance (Mauss 1968, II:161–66) and, with Henri Beuchat, on further aspects of the notions of time and space in Eskimo society (Mauss 1979b); Durkheim and Mauss on the notion of genre (Durkheim and Mauss 1963); Bouglé (1969) on the notion of the whole in Hindu civilization. An expanded list of works within the Durkheim school would lead to studies of such categories as sacrifice by Hubert and Mauss (1964), death, and sin and expiation, by Hertz (1922; Nielsen 1986), memory by Halbwachs (1980; 1992), responsibility by Paul Fauconnet (1928), contract by Georges Davy (1922), and Mauss's (1990) reflections on totality in his study of gift exchange. These studies often develop ideas related to the issues of space, time, causality, and so forth. Later thinkers influenced by Durkheim, Mauss, and Hertz and working within their orbit (i.e. studying the categories) include Marcel Granet (1934) on the whole and other major categories in China, Jacques Soustelle (1940) on the notions of time and space in ancient Mexican thought, and Louis Dumont (1980) on the whole in Indian society and the West. The list could be expanded (Gurvitch 1971). Mauss himself never ceased to advance this type of study. In addition to the comments of 1938, noted above, in an essay of 1924, Mauss had already called for the development of a comprehensive "catalogue of categories" (Mauss 1966, 309).

Mauss's statement is also fully congruent with Durkheim's major work on religion, where the program of study of the categories is coupled with a new sociological theory of religion, knowledge and, I would argue, a new sociological metaphysic, a new view of "reality," in a larger sense. I would once again call attention to Mauss's otherwise puzzling emphasis on "the whole" as Durkheim's central domain within this program of theory and research, and to his remark that Durkheim's work on the whole was written after he had written with Mauss on the problem of kind, or genre. The references are obviously to Durkheim's work on the *Forms* and to the earlier essay on primitive classification written jointly by Durkheim and Mauss. Indeed, Durkheim's *Forms* represents the high point of his conceptualization of totality, one which includes not only a theory of religion and the categories, but also an entirely new vision of the relationships among nature, society, religion, and the other main categories.

Durkheim's interest in the whole is by no means limited to the ideas developed in the book on religion. I would argue that *Division*, of 1893, and much of his other work, also focuses on this problem. In the end, even Durkheim's most "empirical" and "scientific" work, *Suicide*, is informed, although less openly, by this problematic and will be interpreted later in these pages as a study of the problem of whole via its central "modes." No one would claim that the Durkheimians did nothing else, or that Durkheim, Mauss, and the others always pursued these topics with precisely the same methods and approaches. There are already differences between Durkheim and Mauss on these problems, ones which became even greater after Durkheim's death. However, the evidence does point to the centrality of such studies of the categories in their corpus. This is particularly true in the case of Durkheim himself.

When we unite Durkheim's remarks on his intellectual development around 1895, Mauss's comments on the overall Durkheimian program and Durkheim's special domain of work, and a summary review of the Durkheimian efforts, we can better appreciate Durkheim's emerging theory. The preliminary conclusions resulting from such a collation of evidence include the following: (1) that the Durkheimians did focus sharply, perhaps "above all," on the sociology of the categories of the human spirit; (2) that Durkheim focused first and foremost on "the whole" ; (3) that his final work, the *Forms*, was about the category of "the whole" or "totality" in relation to the other categories; (4) this later work on "the whole" or "totality" was a partial culmination of the need after 1895 for his work to be started all over again from the new standpoint of religion; (5) finally, the *Forms* needs to be read, in part, as a rethinking of his earlier effort to comprehend "the whole" in *Divison* as well as in his other early writings, where the problem of the whole/part relationship appears repeatedly as a major philosophical reference point.

Previous commentators have had to take a stand on the question of continuity and discontinuity in Durkheim's intellectual development, in particular, the meaning of a possible break in his work around 1895. Indeed, their answers to the question of Durkheim's intellectual evolution have usually been an integral part of their interpretation of him as well as their own theoretical perspectives. Where they have seen Durkheim going has often been related to where they wanted sociology to go. This was already true of Talcott Parsons (1937), whose view that Durkheim moved from sociologistic "positivism" to a more "idealist" standpoint, set the stage for later, alternative interpretations of Durkheim's development. Durkheim's more recent interpreters have all needed to face this issue, either accounting for a perceived discontinuity, or treating his writings as the expression of a uniform approach (e.g. for discontinuity see Alexander 1982; for continuity see Schmaus 1994). In either case, Durkheim has most often been read from one or another "presentist" standpoint, rather than from the viewpoint of the key ideas found in his own texts. As such, he has been made into the harbinger of every manner of contemporary perspective (Schmaus 1994, 12–17). Indeed, it is not clear that we have progressed very far beyond Parsons's way of posing the problem.

The problem of continuity is not my central concern. Of course, I have already implied a discontinuity in Durkheim's thinking, or at least, his way of approaching his central problem. I would immediately add that there is an enormous amount of continuity in Durkheim's theorizing. Much of it comes precisely from his commitment to the understanding of the problem of the whole or totality, rather than from any persistent allegiance to the idea of "collective representations" (as Schmaus 1994 argues). More important is the fact that the continuities and discontinuities in Durkheim's work frequently fit together in previously unsuspected ways. Without anticipating the following analysis, I would give only one main example. The whole/part problem is one which provides a steady, consistent skein in Durkheim's work. Here we find continuity. Yet his treatment of totality as a category after the turn of the century reflects a new way of conceptualizing this perennial interest. As a result, there is discontinuity within his main interests. In fact, from the very outset of his career, Durkheim wrote implicitly, and often quite explicitly, with the notion of the whole and the whole/part problem in mind. What changed in Durkheim was his approach to this problem and the new approach via religion and the categories was a major theoretical innovation. In response to the perennial question of continuity and discontinuity in Durkheim's theorizing, I would suggest from my present standpoint that Durkheim's work is continuous with respect to the whole/part problem and rather more discontinuous regarding the explanation of this problem via the category of totality. Indeed, some of the tensions in Durkheim's work emerge from his retention of the inherited philosophical assumptions about the whole/part relation in the midst of his later theorizing about the categories.

I also find a good deal of continuity around the problem of totality in Durkheim's work in another respect. While his manner of dealing with the problem changes as he moves towards a greater interest in religion and the categories, his later work retains much of the sociologistic method of explanation usually thought to be part of his earlier positivistic approach, including its emphasis on social morphology, moral density, social concentration, and related social dynamics. From my standpoint, the Durkheim who emerges from an examination of these continuities and discontinuities appears to be a different amalgam than previous interpreters have imagined.

I have suggested that Durkheim's thinking was deeply embedded in the religious and philosophical traditions of Western European civilization and represents an attempt to resolve a set of perennial issues through the use of a sociological method. It is necessary, before moving to the chronological treatment of Durkheim's writings, to discuss several important links in the chain of Durkheim's philosophical predecessors. I will do so in the next section. In particular, I will focus on the work of Aristotle, Bacon, Spinoza, Kant, and Renouvier. Other names could easily be added (e.g. J. S. Mill). Pascal's religious ideas on the dualism of human nature will emerge at several critical points in the discussion. I will also discuss those authors analyzed by Durkheim himself, including Montesquieu, Rousseau, Saint-Simon, the Pragmatists, and so forth. This is not an exhaustive list, nor is it meant to be. I do not mean to supply a complete philosophical prehistory of Durkheim's thought (however interesting such a study might be), but to lay the foundation for my analysis of Durkheim's ideas. With the exception of Spinoza, whose name has hardly ever been linked with Durkheim, this list contains few surprises, even when the relationships among these thinkers remain poorly explored.

3

DURKHEIM'S CONCEPT OF TOTALITY AND THE PHILOSOPHICAL TRADITION: SELECTED PREDECESSORS

Durkheim's focus on the category of totality and the whole/part problem requires that we approach his relationship to the intellectual tradition from a particular angle of vision. From this standpoint, a new list of intellectual antecedents, and different aspects of their work, become important for understanding Durkheim. I want to examine the doctrine of categories and the problem of totality in the work of Aristotle, Bacon, Spinoza, Kant, and Renouvier. Kant, Renouvier, and neo-Kantianism are generally agreed to have played an important role in Durkheim's development, but the links among them have not been very closely explored. Behind them lie other equally important thinkers. Aristotle's list of categories is mentioned by both Durkheim and Mauss. We will discover many echoes of Aristotle in Durkheim's discussion of the whole/part problem (an alternative view of Durkheim and Aristotle is Challenger 1994). The connection between Bacon and Durkheim needs to be explored afresh, especially their respective efforts to establish a "new organon" (Berthelot 1995; his introduction to Durkheim 1988). Finally, one of my major contentions is that Durkheim's sociology bears a striking architechtonic resemblance to Spinoza's philosophy. The latter thinker almost certainly exerted a strong formative influence on Durkheim, especially during his shift of emphasis around 1895. It is Spinoza's overall conception of totality which has most in common with Durkheim and it will be necessary to pursue the comparison of the two authors again at various points later in these pages.

Before moving to a discussion of these thinkers, we need to first ask: What precisely are the categories in Durkheim, Mauss, and their school? Since this is one of the main questions explored in the present work, I do not want to forestall the fuller discussion with a simple definition. The entire program of research concerning the full range of categories is hardly developed at all in Durkheim's early work or that of his school. As we will see, there are notable differences between the treatments of the problem of the whole/part relation in Durkheim's early work versus his more mature treatment of the category of totality. I would contend that Durkheim starts with the whole/part relation, in his earlier writings, and only later moves to a self-conscious consideration of the fuller range of categories, including a reconceptualization of the earlier whole/part problem.

Durkheim's notion of the categories is sometimes seen as primarily Kantian, that is, with an emphasis their role as constitutive forms of possible experience or as forms of representation. Durkheim does sometimes conceive of them in this "cognitive" fashion, and, as we will see, the Durkheimians (especially Hubert and Mauss) also employ Kantian modes of expression in their discussion of the categories in their essays on magic, time, and so forth. Especially when Durkheim wants to contrast the difference between individual experience and the collective categories as socially derived molds of thought, he sounds a good deal like someone trying to solve sociologically the Kantian problem of the categories. However, Durkheim's entire analysis goes far beyond the Kantian or neo-Kantian conception of the categories, or of the view of them as forms of representation. Durkheim distinguishes clearly between himself and the neo-Kantians, even while he remarks on their similar interests, when he writes: "For these philosophers categories shape reality beforehand, while for us they summarize it" (Durkheim 1982, 240; 1975, I:187). This "summarizing" of reality gives Durkheim's doctrine of the categories an ontological and sociological character, indeed, the first by virtue of his conception of the second. In this respect, it is closer to the ambiguous role ascribed by Aristotle to the categories as both forms of representation as well as facets of things or realities. As we will see, it is closer yet to Spinoza's analysis of these problems, especially his idea of God or nature as substance with infinite attributes (although Spinoza does not have a doctrine of the categories, as such, like Aristotle or even Kant). For the moment, I would emphasize that Durkheim sees the categories not only, or even primarily as "collective representations," but as modes of social being itself.

Durkheim and Aristotle

From an early date, Durkheim connects Aristotle's work with his own central problems. In a critical review of 1889 about Wincenty Lutoslawski's work on the political philosophy of Plato, Aristotle, and Machiavelli, Durkheim notes that Lutoslawski exaggerates Aristotle's scientific spirit. He argues that Aristotle's writings in the moral and social sciences rest on his metaphysics. He also is not an a priorist, despite his declaration that society is antecedent to the individual and his "lively sentiment for the reality of the social being (*d'être social*)," including its individual and sui generis reality (Durkheim 1975, III:158; 1986, 84). Durkheim goes on to note Aristotle's recognition that social facts were not merely a transformation of psychic life or sociology only an application of psychology. These sorts of remarks already place Aristotle and Durkheim firmly within the orbit of problems discussed in these pages. Durkheim refers frequently to Aristotle throughout his work. As Donald Levine (1995) has noted, Durkheim was one of the only classical sociologists to explicitly align himself with Aristotle. I want to turn from these general concerns to focus on the relationship of the Durkheim's work to the problem of the categories in Aristotle. There we can begin to explore the ways in which Durkheim does drawn upon Aristotle's ideas.

I have emphasized the importance of Marcel Mauss's remark that the Durkheimians took their preliminary starting point from Aristotle's list of categories and his assertion that Durkheim focused on totality. Elsewhere, Durkheim and Mauss (1963, 5) also associate the study of the categories with Aristotle. It is helpful to ask several questions at the outset. First, what is the list of categories in Aristotle to which Mauss refers? Second, how does the Durkheimian research effort relate to that list? Finally, where does the category of the whole or totality appear and how is it treated by Aristotle (and Durkheim)?

It is sometimes assumed, probably because of the word itself, that Mauss refers to the list of categories found in his treatise on *Categories* (Schmaus 1994, 190–91). In that work, Aristotle lists ten categories: substance, quantity, quality, when, where, relation, state, acted, acted upon. In the *Topics* there is a similar list of ten categories and these categories appear, in one or another form, in most of Aristotle's work (Ross 1995, 22). It is worth adding immediately that neither of these lists contains the category of whole (or whole/part). It is necessary to turn elsewhere for references to this category. In Book V of his *Metaphysics* (and elsewhere in that text), Aristotle presents what his editors call a "Philosophical Lexicon," not exactly a set of categories, but a list of key terms of philosophical analysis. Here, we do find a discussion of the whole and whole/part problem. Also, if we turn to Aristotle's *Politics*, we discover some particularly crucial references to the whole/part problem, this time in the more relevant context of a treatment of the relationship of the individual to the *polis*.

There is little doubt that Durkheim was thoroughly familiar with Aristotle's writings, including the *Nicomachian Ethics*, *Metaphysics*, and *Politics*. There is clear evidence from his lectures on the evolution of educational thought that Durkheim was quite familiar with the *Organon*, that is, Aristotle's logical writings, which included *Categories*, *Topics*, and so forth. Indeed, in that series of lectures, Durkheim refers not only to the *Organon*, but also to works such as *Parts of Animals*, where Aristotle discussed some of the issues relevant to this work, for example, the whole/part problem (Durkheim 1977, 133–38). He also discusses a variety of problems connected with the use of Aristotle's work in the Medieval world, including the problem of universals, the role of categories in thought, and some particular issues connected with Aristotle's logic (Durkheim 1977, 51, 57–60; Spade 1994). I will discuss this text of Durkheim later. I now want merely to reaffirm Durkheim's familiarity with the full range of Aristotle's writings, something already probable from his classical education. One likely conclusion is that the Durkheimians drew their list from a variety of Aristotelian works and seem to have been drawn especially to the *Politics* and *Metaphysics*, although we cannot rule out his other writings as a possible source of inspiration. Durkheim himself states that his teacher, Émile Boutroux had alerted him to Aristotle's notion that each science had to have its own special object of investigation (Durkheim 1982, 259). Moreover, Georges Davy tells us that, early in his career, Durkheim had intended to do psychological studies of quantity and quality (Davy 1911, 8). It is not entirely fanciful to find in this early concern a germ of Durkheim's later interest in the categories. As we will see below, the problem of quantity and quality emerges at crucial points even in some of his later writings and those of his school.

If we compare the Durkheimian list of categories, as it appears in both Durkheim and in Mauss, with any of Aristotle's lists, there are some interesting results. Durkheim (1995b, 8) refers to time, space, causality, substance, number, and personality, and elsewhere in his work to the whole, or totality (Durkheim and Mauss 1963, 88). Mauss provides a similar list, with only a few nuances of difference. The Durkheimian list overlaps with those found in Aristotle, but there are also some differences. One or another variant of time, space, causality, and substance appear in both the Durkheimian and Aristotelian lists, but personality has no obvious counterpart in Aristotle. However, if we examine the whole/part problem in Aristotle we discover that he addresses this issue, in connection with the citizen, without explicitly developing the abstract category of the person. As we will see, the Durkheimian interest in the category of the person may well have been derived more from Kant or from Renouvier.

Another problem which emerges in any comparison of the two sets of categories concerns the precise conception of "category" in each case. What are the categories in Aristotle? There is considerable disagreement about how Aristotle's categories, in his work by that name, ought to be conceived. Some etymological considerations are relevant. The Greek term *kategorein* has been translated as "category," that is, the Greek word has been simply transliterated into the English. The Greek term actually means "predicates," but can also mean "assertion" and other related things. The categories in Aristotle have an ambiguous character. They seem to be both forms of representation as well as predicates of being itself, that is, they have an ontological as well as a cognitive or linguistic dimension (Kneale and Kneale 1962, 25). However, if we turn to Aristotle's discussion of words (as distinct from categories) in the *Metaphysics*, the terms have a rather more indeterminate quality. Aristotle seems to be examining characteristics of language, how we speak of things. For example, the whole/part problem is treated as a problem of how we go about speaking of a certain sort of abstract relationship, regardless of the concrete subject matter. I have noted that Durkheim thought of them as somehow "summarizing" reality. This phrase is ambiguous. In particular, it leaves unclear their logical versus their ontological dimensions (S. Collins 1985). As I will later demonstrate, this is a crucial, if fruitful ambiguity in Durkheim's work.

Durkheim's connection with Aristotle's conception of the whole/part problem is complicated by the fact that Aristotle is not entirely consistent about the subject. At least, his perspective is complex. As we have already mentioned, neither the *Categories* nor *Topics* has anything much to say about the question (although they do say a good deal about substance). The two texts in which there are significant discussions of this problem are the *Metaphysics* and the *Politics*. Let us discuss each of these in turn, beginning with the latter work, since it is there that we find discussions which seem to most closely parallel Durkheim's sociological concerns.

Aristotle insists that the *polis* exists by nature and that humanity is naturally a political animal (*polites* or citizen), bound for life in a community. Aristotle's view is well-known and hardly requires much comment. I would emphasize the greater ambiguity in his conception of the whole/part problem, especially regarding the question of priority of whole or part. When Aristotle says something is "prior" to something else, this word can mean several different things. Seen in a temporal perpective, the *polis* is the outcome of the prior associations of household or family and village, which is an assemblage of households, just as the *polis* emerges from an assemblage of villages. However, although the family and village are prior to the *polis* in the order of time, ". . . the city is naturally prior to the household and to the individual, since the whole is necessarily prior to the part" (Aristotle 1995, 453; Aristotle 1955, 5–6). Here, the priority is related to the nature of the whole, the *polis*, its end. The individual is not self-sufficient, cannot exist without the city and the city is by nature prior to the individual.

From the standpoint of virtues, the household and the relationships among its members (husband and wife, parent and child) are also subordinate to that of the city, since "The goodness of every part must be considered with reference to the goodness of the whole" (Aristotle 1955, 37). Therefore, such matters as the education of children must be dealt with after a consideration of the *polis*. Indeed, Aristotle seems to go further than modern thinkers would like in his subordination of the individual to the community, for example, when he writes: "We must not regard a citizen as belonging just to himself; we must rather regard every citizen as belonging to the state. Each is a part of the state; and the provision made for each part will naturally be adjusted to the provision made for the Whole" (Aristotle 1955, 333). This view is tempered considerably by the fact that Aristotle also sees the *polis* as the appropriate locale for the fullest development of the human being's own nature.

Aristotle's conception of the whole/part relation is further complicated by his extension of the notion of part to a variety of other groups within the *polis*. At different times, he refers to the individual, the family, and the social classes as parts of the whole and, at times, breaks down these classifications even further by referring to the various classes (farmers, craftsmen, merchants, etc.) as parts of the whole (Aristotle 1955, 93, 160–66, 180–81).

Finally, Aristotle also distinguishes between (1) parts of wholes and conditions for the existence of wholes as well as between, (2) wholes and compounds in relation to their respective parts. Some groups (e.g. slaves, mechanics, freedmen) are "conditions" for the life of the *polis*, but are not true parts of it as are citizens. Also, a "compound" (*syntheton*) needs to be distinguished from a "whole" (*holon*). Here, added complexities emerge. "Compound" is used as the generic, inclusive term for all wholes. However, compounds can be either mechanical aggregates or true, organic wholes. Whereas the latter have form, organic unity among their parts, and serve an end, the mechanical compound is not a true unity, but merely a collection of units. The *polis* is an instance of a true whole (Aristotle 1955, 95–96, 108). For Aristotle, it is a whole not only through the necessary "association" among its members, but because of its nature as a true whole, that is, a certain kind of compound. Beyond a mere "association," a *polis* is also an organically unified compound. It is enormously interesting to see the appearance of the Durkheimian notion of "synthesis," one usually thought to derive from modern chemical analogies, in Aristotle's Greek general term *syntheton* (i.e. compound). It is also fascinating to see Aristotle argue that association is not itself sufficient to form a *polis*, but that wholistic unity—"synthesis"—so to speak—is also required (Barker 1959, 231–37). I strongly suspect this to be one source of Durkheim's central images of "association," "synthesis," and the "whole/part" metaphorology. This places Durkheim's emphasis on association in a new light. It suggests its subordination to the more comprehensive notion of a "synthesized" whole. As we will see, Durkheim's notion of association has a complex relationship with his idea of the whole.

These various usages of the whole/part distinction by Aristotle in the *Politics* are not easily separated from his conception of that which exists by nature (or *physis*) and, therefore, from the normative elements of his philosophy, nor did Aristotle emphasize such a modern, largely post-Kantian distinction between the theoretical/factual and the normative. In general, it would appear that the whole is naturally, if not always chronologically prior to its parts and that the whole and parts are truly characterized as such by their ability to embody that which exists by nature. In other words, only that which exists by nature and has an end can be a true whole. Only those parts which can legitimately contribute to, sustain, and, in turn, be nurtured by the whole can be true parts. Everything else is either a "compound" (i.e. a mechanical aggregate without a unity or end, therefore, not a whole), or exists as a "condition" of the whole (an element which operates functionally within the whole, but can never be a true part of it).

Some of Aristotle's distinctions in the *Politics* are more relevant than others. I would emphasize the importance of the following: (1) Aristotle's various applications of the whole/part distinction
to the *polis* and its components as the "natural" type of society; (2)
his general analogy of whole/part: *polis*/citizen; (3) his extension of
the whole/part problem to the relationship between the *polis* (i.e.
the whole), and its various component subgroupings (i.e. the family,
the village, social classes, etc. as parts). As we will see below, there
are some strong similarities between Durkheim's analysis of the
whole/part relations, especially in his early writings (e.g. *Division*),
and these facets of Aristotle' work. They are worth keeping in mind
as we proceed.

If we turn to Aristotle's *Metaphysics*, especially Book V, we
find two things of interest: (1) a list of words, a "philosophical lexicon," which does explicitly include the category of the whole and the
whole/part problem; and (2) a highly abstract treatment of the
whole/part problem, divorced from any particular substantive
applications, as found in the *Politics*. It would appear that the list
of categories with which the Durkheimians began must have been
one drawn from the "philosophical lexicon" of the *Metaphysics* as
well as from the *Categories*. The list in the *Metaphysics* V contains
all the categories which appear in the logical works, and others
besides, notably the whole, a category conspicuously absent from
the logical writings. What is odd is that Aristotle does not in *Metaphysics* V refer to the list as "categories." While this may be occasion for pause in our understanding of Aristotle, it should not trou-
ble us too much in our study of Durkheim. Even in Aristotle's case,
we should remember that the titles of his works, and the arrange-
ment of their materials, were the result of later editorial decisions,
and that the titles themselves are not always unambiguously
related to the subjects discussed. Even the meaning of the term
"metaphysics" is open to question. The term categories had a sufficiently general meaning to allow the Durkheimians to draw widely
on both of Aristotle's lists. Durkheim himself refers loosely to Aristotle, but in terms of Kant's idea of "categories of understanding,"
as if the two were somehow identical (Durkheim 1995b, 8).

The very abstract discussion in *Metaphysics* V actually contains several ideas relevant to Durkheim's work. First, there is the
emphasis on the whole as the form or unity of the material which
composes it. While Aristotle was not unambiguous, his philosophy
seems clearly to support a priority of a whole, as the form or principle of unity of a thing which is composed of other things, over its

parts. In Aristotle, we also get a clear sense of the whole having features or a character which cannot be derived from its parts. Here, we find another fascinating parallel with Durkheim, who repeatedly and consistently refers to the priority of whole over part. There are also some other minor correspondences. In his treatment of the whole/part problem, Aristotle uses as an example the form of a certain shape of bronze as a whole made of parts. In one of his definitions of "part," he writes: "The elements into which a whole is divided, or of which it consists—the 'whole' meaning either the form or that which has the form; e.g. of the bronze sphere or of the bronze cube both the bronze—i.e. the matter in which the form is— and the characteristic angle are parts" (Aristotle 1941, 774). It is perhaps not accidental that this example of bronze is put to the very same use by Durkheim. In the *The Rules of Sociological Method* (hereafter abbreviated as *Rules*), Durkheim argues for the unity of life, that it is one and is found in "the living substance in its totality. It is in the whole and not in the parts . . ." (Durkheim 1982, 39; 1988, 82). He thinks this is true of all syntheses and immediately illustrates the argument with the example of bronze's hardness resulting from the mixture of cooper, tin, and lead. I will reserve fuller comment on this passage until later in this study. This same example is found elsewhere in Durkheim (Durkheim 1961, 61, 256). There is little reason to think that Durkheim would have taken the nature of bronze as an illustration because of its contemporary resonance in his own time. It had a great deal more for Aristotle's, where the image of Homer's "brazen shields and swords" were still part of the popular imagination. While this is a minor point, it does add credence to the idea that Durkheim not only knew the *Metaphysics*, a fact clear from other sources, but drew on its concrete examples as well as, in all probability, its admittedly abstract way of phrasing the issue which interested him.

There is one final aspect of Aristotle's treatment of the whole/part problem which needs to be mentioned. He distinguishes between uniform and non-uniform parts. Those entities with uniform parts have parts similar to the whole. For example, water has uniform parts, since it is divisible into more water, but arms are nonuniform parts of a larger whole (i.e. the body), which is not itself similar to the parts composing it, and arms cannot be divided into more arms (Aristotle 1995, 602, especially the note by T. Irwin and G. Fine on "Part," from which my discussion and examples are drawn). This distinction has a parallel in Durkheim's conception of the whole/part relation in societies with mechanical versus organic solidarity. With mechanical solidarity, the parts are "uniform" (to use Aristotle's terminology) and they therefore can be subdivided into new wholes which are identical to the old ones. Clans can break off from the society and form whole societies which are the same as the old one. In similar fashion, foreign elements can be added more easily to societies with mechanical solidarity (Durkheim 1984, 104). There is a strong implication in Durkheim that it is the weakness of the bond in mechanical solidarity which leads to this fragility and permeability. Both outcomes result from a weak relationship among the parts, which are also, in some sense, "uniform." The more uniform the parts, the greater the fragility of the bond.

The distinction between uniform and nonuniform parts also seems related to the further distinction made by Aristotle between parts and conditions. The examples of conditions given in the *Politics* (e.g. slaves, mechanics, freedmen) refer to groups of non-citizens, those whose place in the society is least intimately related to the nature of the whole (i.e. the *polis* as the whole within which the citizen, but not the outsider, finds his nature developed). Of course, the correspondence of ideas is not perfect. Conditions of a whole are not thereby the same as uniform parts.

If we consider the parts in societies with Durkheim's organic solidarity to be the various components of the division of labor, then these parts cannot be subdivided into identical units, although they may be further specialized. Of course, the parallel in this latter case is far from exact, since the nonuniform quality of the aspects of the division of labor can, indeed, be reproduced in identical form in another place (e.g. there could be more than one bronze foundry). Also, Durkheim does not use Aristotle's precise terms to express his ideas. Despite these warnings, the similarities in the formulation of this aspect of the whole/part problem are suggestive, especially the general links among the notions of uniform parts, conditions, and the whole/part problem under mechanical solidarity.

In conclusion to this selective review of Aristotle's ideas, we are led back to Mauss's remark that the Durkheimians began their list of categories provisionally with those found in Aristotle. Aristotle seems to have been an important reference point. My sense is that he not only provided a starting point, with his various lists of categories, but that more importantly his many and varied discussions of the whole/part problem also provided a variety of valuable perspectives helpful to Durkheim in his attempt to develop his sociological conception of this issue. Like ancient and medieval thinkers, who found in Aristotle's philosophy a tool kit of ideas and concepts valuable for the creation of their own theories, Durkheim also could use Aristotle's writings for his own constructive purposes. He also preserved much of Aristotle's uncertainty about the precise status of the categories, whether they were logical symbols or had a more ontological bearing.

Durkheim and Bacon

The name of Sir Francis Bacon seems only tangentially linked to that of Durkheim. By comparison with other predecessors, he would seem relatively less central to an understanding of Durkheim's project. However, Durkheim does refer to him favorably on several occasions (Jones 1986, 62–63, 68, who notes the Bacon-Durkheim connection). As Jean-Michel Berthelot has argued, the spirit of Durkheim's scientific program may owe a good deal to the Baconian model (Berthelot 1995). I want to emphasize that the examination of his work also yields some helpful leads about Durkheim's understanding of the categories.

Durkheim refers to Bacon's *New Organon* in the *Rules* and elsewhere (Durkheim 1982, 62, 72, 110). It is worth recalling that Bacon's (uncompleted) attempt to forge a "new organon" echoes Aristotle's logical writings, which have come to be known as his *Organon*. Bacon had little use for Aristotle and his new starting point was, in part, directed against the late medieval or scholastic adaptations of Aristotle. I would suggest that Durkheim is attempting yet another "new organon" of his own, one sociologically rooted, yet addressing the same sorts of issues posed by Aristotle and Bacon.

Once again, an etymological insight is helpful. The title *Organon* has come to be used as the overall designation of Aristotle's logical writings. This word comes from the Greek, *organon*, which means "instrument." The English word has come to have the more general meaning of methods used in philosophy or the acquisition of knowledge. This is clearly the sense in which Bacon uses the term. His new organon would comprise a new logic appropriate to the advancement of learning. The first part involved his critical reflections on the barriers to knowledge, in particular, the "four idols" which stood in the way of the advancement of learning. This philosophical housecleaning was to preface the construction of a

new logical foundation for the sciences. Bacon completed only part
of this larger, constructive project. However, the critical introduction has remained a source of inspiration for several modern
thinkers, including Friedrich Nietzsche and, I would add,
Durkheim (e.g. Nietzsche's discussion of the "four great errors,"
focusing on causality, in Nietzsche 1968, 492–501; Nielsen 1986,
16–17, 35–36).

It is perhaps more to the point that Durkheim takes over the
meaning of the Greek word *organon* into his own philosophy. In his
later writings, he mentions that the categories of thought are
"instruments" for the collective mental processes of society. At one
point, he even suggests that the notions of institution, instrument,
and category are facets of the same notion, much as he identified
divinity, totality, and society (Durkheim 1995b, 18, fn.24; 1982,
240). We will explore these claims below. The parallel between
them is striking. For the moment, I will simply suggest that
Durkheim's conception of the categories has many echoes of both
Aristotle's original notion of logic as an "organon" or "instrument"
of thought as well as Bacon's effort to recast this instrument in a
new form. Durkheim is attempting a similarly radical recasting. In
my view, to be substantiated further as we proceed, it is this perennial historical problem, and not any immediate response to (e.g.)
pragmatism's "instrumentalist" view of logic or the categories of
thought, that provoked Durkheim to pursue his project of a sociological doctrine of the categories.

The relationship of Durkheim's idea to Bacon's treatment of
the "Four Idols" seems particularly relevant to our present discussion. Durkheim already refers to this part of Bacon's work favorably in 1895 in *The Rules* (Durkheim 1982, 62, 72, 110), and, in a
brief statement of 1908, reiterates this interest (Durkheim 1982,
246). He is equally concerned to exorcise those *idola* (Durkheim's
own usage) which inhibit the growth of sociology. Durkheim's opposition to "metaphysical dualism," which placed humankind outside
the universe of scientific understanding, as well as his attack on
"anthropomorphism," as a barrier to knowledge, might easily be
placed within the orbit of Bacon's critique of the idols of the tribe,
those idols which emerge from human nature and its self-concep-
tion. Durkheim's opposition to the tendency of prior analysts to rely
on one or a few abstract theoretical notions or ideas rather than
examine facts also allies him with Bacon's critique of the idols of the
marketplace as well as the idols of the theatre, those previous
philosophical systems which both Bacon and Durkheim took to

task. In general, Durkheim's claim to be studying facts, including social facts, especially well chosen and closely studied cases, places him close to the Baconian approach (although it is equally clear that Durkheim's work was driven strongly by philosophical and theoretical conceptions).

How is this affinity between Bacon and Durkheim related to the issues of the categories and the whole, or totality in particular? Bacon was a great enemy of the existing schema of abstractions, definitions, scholastic analyses, and logic. He speaks critically of Aristotle at many places in *The New Organon*, which itself was intended to forge new "instruments," a new logic. For example, in discussing the three types of "false philosophy," the first class of which was the "Sophistical," he writes that: "The most conspicuous example of the first class was Aristotle, who corrupted natural philosophy by his logic: fashioning the world out of categories . . ." (Bacon 1955, 481). Elsewhere, he argues in a related vein: "There is no soundness in our notions whether logical or physical. Substance, Quality, Action, Passions, Essence itself, are not sound notions; much less are Heavy, Light, Dense, Rare, Moist, Dry, Generation, Corruption, Attraction, Repulsion, Element, Matter, Form and the like; but all are fantastical and ill defined" (Bacon 1955, 464). If we find links between Aristotle and Durkheim on the problem of the categories, must we not exclude Bacon from this part of our discussion?

I think there is a neglected clue in Bacon's criticism of what he thought was Aristotle's (or the late medieval Aristotelian) penchant for abstraction. It is precisely in this area that the links are to be forged. Durkheim wanted to advance knowledge by moving it away from the analysis of concepts or ideas and towards the study of things, of realites. He repeatedly criticized other authors for being purely "dialectical" in their studies (e.g. his reviews in Nandan 1980). It is one of his favorite terms when he wishes to attack his opponents. In this he concurred with Bacon, who also called his contemporaries to move away from essentialism, the debate over abstractions, and the quest for definitions and move toward the study of facts, nature itself. On the other hand, Durkheim suggests, in effect, that we pursue those questions of definition and the study even of those categorial abstractions in a more scientific, empirical, and factual manner, that is, that we treat the abstractions themselves as facts to be investigated sociologically. Also, Durkheim continues the essentialistic method of definition, (derived from Aristotle as well as from Spinoza) in his study of religion. In doing so, he saw no contradiction between Bacon and Aristotle. Indeed, this is precisely the Durkheimian research agenda: the sociological study of the categories. Durkheim's audacity in relation to the inherited tradition of thought finds clear expression in his sociological synthesis of these two conflicting predecessors.

Durkheim and Spinoza

The names of Durkheim and Spinoza have not often been joined even though Spinoza has been linked to a dizzying variety of modern thinkers (Yovel 1992, vol. II). At the risk of adding yet another pair to the already long list, I do think this is a major oversight. Durkheim knew Spinoza's work. He mentions him as early as 1887, in his survey of the positive sciences of morality in Germany, where Spinoza is hailed as a pioneer of the notion of the "unconscious" (Durkheim 1993, 81). He always refers to Spinoza's ideas positively and sees him as an originator of theories he himself accepted. He frequently makes more indirect reference to some of Spinoza's central perspectives, without necessarily citing him (Durkheim 1983, 82; 1984, 40). Moreover, members of the Durkheim school testify to the links among Durkheim, themselves and Spinoza. Georges Davy (1911, 49) suggests that Durkheim's conception of the relationship between consciousness and society is similar to Spinoza's notion that the mind is the idea of the body. Both adopt a species of parallelism, although Durkheim does not focus on the individual mind and body, but on collective representations and consciousness in relation to society, or the "social body." As I will demonstrate later in these pages, this idea places the entire problem of "collective representations" in a new light and has enormous consequences for his analysis in his book on religion and the categories. There is also evidence for Spinoza's presence in the Durkheimian orbit at the particularly crucial period of the mid-1890s.

Marcel Mauss states (Besnard 1983, 144) that, early in his own career, he was undecided about his intellectual focus, dividing his studies among social morphology and other quantitative work, law, and, finally, religion. He adds that Durkheim suggested to him that he focus on religion, and that afterwards he did little else. He also notes that Durkheim's course on religion in 1894–95 was done largely for his own and Mauss's benefit. In a particularly revealing and somewhat cryptic comment, Mauss writes: "At that time, I had already decided the topics of my theses. One was on the close relationship between Spinoza and Léon L'Hébrew which I *discovered* (Mauss's emphasis) in 1893, but which was a subject I wearied of in 1897 as a result of an act of indiscretion that enabled M. Couchoud to spoil and sabotage this topic" (Besnard 1983, 145). Mauss apparently refers—with considerable pride at his discovery, but chagrin over the outcome—to Paul-Louis Couchoud, who did indeed publish a thesis on Spinoza which contains some discussion of his links to Léon L'Hébrew (Couchoud 1902, 302ff). More importantly, this comment by Mauss points to their familiarity with and interest in Spinoza's work. Mauss's investigations of Spinoza covered the years 1893–97, that fertile and complex period of transition in Durkheim's own thinking toward a greater interest in religion, primitive societies, and the categories. It is illuminating that these important shifts in emphasis came in a context also informed by an interest in Spinoza's ideas. Mauss never entirely lost his interest in Spinoza. His essay on the category of the person, mentioned above, contains a brief analysis of aspects of Spinoza's idea of the individual (Mauss 1966, 360). Equally telling in this connection is his correspondence with Madeleine Frances, who completed a dissertation on Spinoza in 1937 which employed methods and ideas drawn from Mauss's own work (Frances 1937; Fournier 1994, 649, fn.2, also 65, 71 for other references to Mauss and Spinoza).

Durkheim's own repeated gestures, at crucial points in his work on religion and the categories as well as on the dualism of human nature, to the Spinozist phrase, *sub specie aeternitatis*, to conceive of something under the aspect of eternity, are also suggestive in this respect (Durkheim 1995b, 437; 1970, 318). It is of great interest that this phrase, intimately associated with Spinoza's name, should appear in Durkheim's mature theory of religion, society, and the categories. Durkheim always argued that the categories operated in society as impersonal and universal elements of thought, that is, allowed things to be conceived *sub specie aeternitatis*. Others have noted Durkheim's links to Spinoza. The historian of modern philosophy, J. Benrubi (1933, I:152), some years later referred provocatively to Durkheim's work as a philosophy *sub specie societatis* and Léon Brunschvicg (1927, II:569–70) places Durkheim's work on religion, especially his conception of the sacred and his idea of the relation of the ideal to society, in the context of Spinoza's *Tractatus Theologico-Politicus* (Spinoza 1991). As I have noted elsewhere, Durkheim offers a resolution to the problem of the relationships among society, religion, and the categories which is reminiscent of Spinoza's philosophy (Nielsen 1987a, 290–91).

The above remarks and the following analysis of Durkheim's work lend credence to the idea that Spinoza was an important reference point for Durkheim. They both begin their work from similiar cultural locations and pursue it with similar intellectual strategies. Both are caught experientially between their traditional Jewish origins and a variety of forms of modern learning. Both break loose from their original moorings to create highly distinctive theories which attempt to retain the traditional horizons of religion and metaphysical philosophy, yet present them in uniquely "modern" scientific idioms. Spinoza's thought is difficult and subject to varied interpretations (Wolfson 1934; Bennett 1984; Garrett 1996). I can offer no complete analysis of his writings, but discuss only those dimensions of his thinking which are particularly relevant to an understanding of Durkheim's work.

Spinoza's overall philosophy is a study of the whole, or totality. This fact is clear to any reader of his *Ethics*. This notion of totality is best captured in Spinoza's conception of a single substance with infinite attributes, two of which are known by humanity, namely, extension and thought. He opposes Descartes' identification of thought and extension as two separate substances. Spinoza proposes a monistic, even a pantheistic system which preserves, yet transcends this dualism. He also indentifies his infinite substance with the traditional notion of God, now stripped of its anthropomorphic characteristics (a divestiture also familiar to Durkheim's readers). His formula is *Deus sive Natura*, God or Nature. In effect, God, Nature, and his single substance are all mutually identified and are expressions of one and the same reality. I would immediately call attention to the astonishing similarity between this view and the central summary idea of Durkheim's last book, that is, the identification of society, deity, and totality. Also, it is worth adding that in his essay on the determination of moral facts of 1906, he had also already stated the vitual equivalence between God and society in terms reminiscent of Spinoza's *Deus sive Natura* (Durkheim 1974a, 52; Spinoza 1985, 206, 417ff., 439ff.). This identification becomes important when we examine Durkheim's conception of the connections among nature, society, and the categories.

Spinoza pursues the analysis of substance in a particularly interesting way in his letters (especially the eighth and nineth letters, exchanged with Simon J. de Vries). This substance extends itself into the world through its various modes, or affections. Spinoza emphasizes that they are not precisely "parts" of the totality, since his substance is one and indivisible (Spinoza 1995, 18–19). The whole or substance cannot be grasped directly by the intellect, but understood only through its modes. These can be known through experience and the operations of imagination, which thinks (quite imprecisely) of totality in terms of divided parts and conceives of them from the standpoint of its basic categories of time, space, number, cause and so forth. Spinoza does not actually develop a "system" of the categories like Kant or even Aristotle, who he critizes on this score. He embeds them as implicit terms of analysis into his philosophy. As a result, one does find in Spinoza a treatment of time, space, substance, cause and others.

This distinction between substance and its modes is also expressed in terms of the ideas of *natura naturata* (nature natured) and *natura naturans* (nature naturing). The latter is the infinite whole of nature, or substance seen as an active and continuously creative force (Spinoza 1985, 434). The former is this same whole expressed in its modes, as a sum of individual "parts," so to speak, taken together. While Spinoza explicitly rejects the idea that substance and its modes can be thought of in terms of the distinction between a whole and its parts, in effect, it has that character. At least, infinite substance (or God or nature) is an indivisible totality, therefore a whole exists, even if there are no actual "parts" separate from it (although a "whole" without parts is a linguistic oddity, and clearly something different from a whole composed of parts). Spinoza's conception departs from the motifs surrounding Aristotle's treatment of the whole/part problem, without entirely rejecting, indeed embracing even more powerfully, the notion of a totality composed of one infinite substance. Only our imperfect forms of understanding rooted in the imagination and our inferences from cause and effect lead us to speak in this inadequate fashion about "parts" and the "whole." True knowledge is found in the correct definition of essenses of things, including substance, and is knowledge *sub specie aeternitatis*, knowledge under the aspect or form of eternity (Spinoza 1985, 607ff.). It is just such a system of definitions *more geometrico* (with corrolated discussions) which is provided by Spinoza.

Spinoza also argued that the notion of a single infinite substance necessitated parallelism between the attributes of thought and extension. In this respect, he also rejected Descartes' dualistic division between extended and unextended substance. This is expressed by him in the notion that the order and connection of ideas is the same as the order and connection of things (Spinoza

1985, 451). Put differently, the soul is the idea of the body, a Spinozist thesis which Durkheim cited in his lectures on pragmatism and which Davy attributed to Durkheim himself (Durkheim 1955, 170; Davy 1911, 49). Not only are their theories of individuation highly congruent, but Durkheim's notion of society as a "social body" (an organic analogy also found in Spinoza), which is paralleled by collective representations, adds news dimensions to this basic parallelistic approach. This type of linkage between collective representations and society is crucial and is a mark of Durkheim's emerging monism. It is precisely what Durkheim attempts in different ways all along in his analysis of consciousness and society and his study of the whole/part relation. In this respect, he departs from Descartes' dualism of extended and unextended substances as well as that of dualistic thinkers like Pascal. However, only in his final work did he fully implement this strategy.

One of the central arguments in my later interpretation of the *Forms* will be that Durkheim, like Spinoza, identifies God, Nature, and substance as equivalent expressions of the whole, but that Durkheim's analysis operates at the level of an explicit identification of God, Totality, and Society, with society now taking on the role of the notion of substance. Spinoza's analysis of substance and its modes as well as his theory of individuation is also reflected in Durkheim's entire way of treating society as a whole and of analysizing its "parts" (or modes) in relationship (and always in subordination) to that whole. This is particularly true of his understanding of the connection between society and the individual, as one key aspect of the whole/part problematic, but also of his analysis of the categories generally. In effect, the categories become ontological modes of the societal totality, ones expressed symbolically in the categories seen as abstract concepts. Durkheim's reasons for addressing these sorts of issues in the form of foundational social theory, rather than in the form of a traditional metaphysical philosophy like Spinoza's, will need to be explored briefly toward the end of this work. For the moment, I would add only that his dissatisfaction with the recent, major philosophical solutions (e.g. that of Renouvier) and his commitment to a variant of a "humanistic," scientific view of the world led him to create such a sociological formulation. It is noteworthy that Spinoza's metaphysical treatise is entitled *Ethics* and that Durkheim's social metaphysics emerges through a study of morality and increasingly religion. Practical interests in social and moral reform undoubtedly entered into his belief in the need for a sociological solution. In the following pages,

I want also to suggest the possibility, unanimously rejected by sociologists today, that Durkheim did conceive of society as a substance, perhaps the most important one. As a result, the notion of society had to be at the center of his conception of religion and totality.

Durkheim, Kant, and Renouvier

Durkheim's relationship to Kant and to the neo-Kantianism of his time seems to be one of the least problematic features of his intellectual background. He affirmed his kinship with the neo-Kantians on more than one occasion (Durkheim 1982, 239–40; 1983, 102). Durkheim has often been assumed to be a sort of Kantian, one who wanted to resolve Kant's questions sociologically. There is a certain narrowness in this view. As we have noted above, Durkheim absorbed and synthesized a wide ranging philosophical literature and it seems arbitrary to suggest that the Kantian strands of thought are notably stronger in his work that those derived from other sources (e.g. Aristotle, Descartes, Pascal, Rousseau, Comte, or others). In general, I would prefer to speak not of "influences," but of intellectual "strategies" emerging from philosophical problems and commitments which are, in turn, rooted in basic experiences and responses. From this standpoint, there is no need to deny Kant's influence on Durkheim (or that of a number of other thinkers), since he clearly absorbed many currents of thought. It is better to ask what intellectual and existential problems he was trying to solve and what strategy he had adopted to solve them. As suggested above, Durkheim's whole/part problematic owed as much to Aristotle (among others), despite the mediation of its central idea through Renouvier, and his strategy or resolving it as much to Spinoza (among others), as it did to Kant or neo-Kantianism. However, despite this, the work of Kant and, among the neo-Kantians, Renouvier, remains important. Their writings contain a more systematic philosophical analysis of the categories than any thinkers considered thus far. As such, they are an important reference point for Durkheim's own efforts, even if he departed frequently from their emphases.

The Kantian standpoint is prominent in several aspects of Durkheim's work. First, there is the distinction between judgments of fact and of value. Durkheim's way of posing this problem, perhaps even his solution, echoes Kant (Durkheim 1967). However, this issue is less central to the present work and I will omit discussion of it. A second echo of Kant is found in Durkheim's conception of the moral life. He frequently expresses the idea that Kant had captured at least part of the essense of morality in his notions of duty, the categorial imperative, and the sanctity of the human personality as an end. However, Durkheim always corrects Kant's emphasis on duty with an equally strong emphasis on the good. These issues, although important, are also less central to my conception of Durkheim's work. The whole/part orientation, especially as it works itself out in the concrete relationship between "individual" and "society," takes precedence over the particular Kantian moral, philosophical materials which are set within its frames.

A third point of contact between the analyses of Kant and Durkheim can be found in their emphasis on "synthesis." In Kant's philosophy of the transcendental ego, the categories function to provide a synthesis a priori of the manifold of sense impressions already made possible by the unifying media of the notions of time and space. At first glance, the categories seem to play much the same role in Durkheim's theory of representation. However, Durkheim argues that this synthesis is not accomplished primarily at a intellectual level through the catgories of the transcendental ego, but at a religious, and, ultimately, social level by society, whose processes provide the real basis of the categories. It is not clear that the synthetic a priori function of the Kantian categories is at all closely parallelled in Durkheim's notion of synthesis. As we have seen, Aristotle's notion of the synthetic quality of a whole and Spinoza's conception of totality were as important. Durkheim provides less an account of the cognitive workings of the categories, than an explanation of the relationships of the categories to other phenomena (i.e. religion and society). He distinguished himself from the neo-Kantians of his day by saying that with them the categories constituted experience and were *a priori*, while for him they summed up experience and were products of human artifice (Durkheim 1982, 232–40). Indeed, it is precisely Durkheim's emphasis on the problem of totality which gives his theory of the categories its peculiar slant.

It might be thought that the central legacy of Kant to Durkheim is Kant's actual doctrine of categories itself. However, even here the correspondence between Durkheim and Kant is anything but complete. Durkheim seems to speak in a Kantian voice when he refers in the *Forms* to the "categories of the understanding," yet his reference to Aristotle in the same sentence creates ambiguity (Durkheim 1995b, 8). Kant's treatment of the categories is much more analytical and systematic than Aristotle's (or Durkheim's). Kant separates out time and space as part of what he calls the "transcendental aesthetic." These are not categories, strictly speaking, but conditions of the synthesis of the manifold of sense impressions (Kant 1968, 65–78). The categories themselves form part of the transcendental logic, that part entitled the transcendental analytic. Kant identifies twelve categories divided into four groups of three each. Among them are quantity (unity, plurality, totality); quality (reality, negation, limitation); relation (substance/accident, cause/effect, reciprocity of active/passive); and modality (possibility/impossibility, existence/nonexistence, necessity/contingence). The sum of items in this list corresponds closely to Aristotle's, although Kant has systematially grouped them and uses them for a very different purpose. He also thinks he has discovered just those categories, and no others, which are necessary for the philosophical understanding of human reason. He criticizes Aristotle for having produced little more than a disorganized collection of categories, with no principles of unification (Kant 1968, 114). Kant thought that he had provided a architechtonic of the categories as well as an adequate philosophical account of them.

Kant includes the category of totality in his list. His first general heading (i.e. quantity) includes totality, along with unity and plurality and is seemingly a variant of the whole/part problem raised by Aristotle. The fact that Kant locates these ideas under the notion of quantity should immediately alert us to some differences between him and Aristotle. In Kant, totality seems related to the general problem of number, a relationship which is greatly strengthened by Renouvier. With the exception of a few highly suggestive remarks, Durkheim is largely silent on the issue of number and its relation to quantity (and quality). Indeed, this neglect of the category of number is something of a paradox in his work. Quite apart from correspondences between individual items, Kant's organization of twelve categories in four groups of three each has no counterpart in Durkheim. As we will see, Durkheim's doctrine of the categories does offer a systematic sociological account of them, but takes him in a different direction from Kant's own systematic philosophy.

The most important difference between Kant and Durkheim, one placing the latter much closer to Aristotle and Spinoza, is the fact that Durkheim does not limit the categories to a representative or a cognitive function. While they are a type of collective representation, they also have an ontological grounding in society and, thereby, are ultimately related to the whole of nature. In this respect, the double Aristotelian function of the categories as forms of representation as well as dimensions of being is more clearly preserved in Durkheim. Kant's purely transcendental use of them is too limiting for Durkheim's purposes. His agenda is much larger. Kant separates the cognitive function of the categories in the constitution of phenomena, as an aspect of his critique of pure reason, from the question of the existence of noumena, things in themselves, as well as from questions of practical reason and teleological judgment. He did this quite explicitly, to safeguard faith and human freedom by limiting the claims of reason (Kant 1968, 29). Durkheim does not want to separate the problems of knowledge, morality, and metaphysics and, in effect, reintegrates into a single social theory the questions treated by Kant in separate critiques. We will have more to say about this totalizing strategy as we proceed, but note only that Renouvier had already moved in this direction.

It has been argued that the neo-Kantians had a greater importance for Durkheim than Kant himself (Lukes 1973, 54–58). Durkheim might very well have agreed. He cites as decisive for his sociology the idea of Aristotle, which he learned through Émile Boutroux, that each science requires its own separate objects of study and needs to establish its own distinctive laws (Durkheim 1982, 259; Boutroux 1949). He also credits Renouvier as the proximate source of his central "axiom" (also of Aristotelian origin) that the whole is not equal to the sum of its parts (Durkheim 1975, I:405). Both were instrumental in conveying to him the full range of historical, philosophical systems. Durkheim made good use of them. It is worth recalling that Renouvier's ideas were still very much alive in France around the beginning of the twentieth century. Durkheim referred to him as late as 1913–14, in the lectures on pragmatism, as "the greatest contemporary rationalist" (Durkheim 1983, 30). Gabriel Séailles had published a valuable systematic account of Renouvier's work in 1905 (Séailles 1905). Octave Hamelin presented an important lecture series on him at the Sorbonne in 1906–7, published in 1907 (Hamelin 1927). Hamelin's philosophy of representation was strongly influenced by Renouvier's work (Hamelin 1925; also Picard 1908; Parodi 1930, chap. 5; Hester 1947; Scott 1951).

Renouvier is of particular importance. It is unfortunate that his and Durkheim's work have seldom been the subject of a systematic comparison. Steven Lukes (1973, 56–57) notes that his approach to the analysis of the categories departed from Kant's emphasis on pure reason, and implied that their source was in practical reason and, therefore, that they changed with social changes. This general suggestion, while helpful, is incomplete as an account of the parallels between them. We find in Renouvier's work an extensive discussion of many of the topics which later interested Durkheim. For my purposes, Renouvier's main work is his *Essais de Critique Générale, Premier Essai*, a sprawling multivolume study which first began to appear in 1854 and was subsequently revised and reissued in 1875 as well as in later years. The volumes consist of separate essays (really full length volumes) on logic (much of which is devoted to the categories), rational psychology, principles of nature, and the philosophy of history. This latter volume was republished separately under the title, *Introduction à la Philosophie Analytique de l'Histoire* (1896) and contains Renouvier's fullest treatment of religion.

Renouvier's work is heavily influenced by Kant's critical philosophy. In fact, it goes under the general name of "neo-criticism," although it is sometimes also entitled "phenomenalism" or even "personalism," because of the distinctive emphasis on the individual in Renouvier's later work. However, Renouvier engages the full range of thinkers in the philosophical tradition, including Aristotle, Descartes, Spinoza, Gottfried Leibniz, Immanuel Kant, G. W. F. Hegel, Arthur Schopenhauer, and Herbert Spencer. Renouvier is hardly a Kantian epigone. His system represents a genuine philosophical synthesis of its own, despite its partially Kantian lineage. The first volumes of his *Essais*, which deal with the categories, are especially important, and help set the agenda for Durkheim's later work in this area, despite the latter thinker's thorough departure from Renouvier's principles.

When we examine Renouvier's writings, we also find some interesting identifications. Renouvier already brings Spinoza into the discussion of totality in a way which allows us to treat his work as relevant to our problem. For example, in his discussion of Spinoza's ideas on the unity of substance, he remarks that in Spinoza, "pantheism and determinism find their Bible," one containing a conception of totality (*du Tout*), which was dominant until evolutionism radically modified our view of the whole (Renouvier 1912b, 373). Renouvier also considers the question of the "site of consciousness" and the possibility of a "common sensorium" in a way comparable to Durkheim's own later remarks on these subjects, suggesting the late-nineteenth-century currency of such questions

(Renouvier 1912a, 51–52). Apart from these fragments, Renouvier's full relationship to Durkheim is more difficult to summarize. I will focus on Renouvier's doctrine of the categories. However, in general, I will add that Durkheim's frequently noted remark (Lukes 1973, 54), that one should attach oneself to a great master and study his system, laying bare its innermost secrets, and that his master was Renouvier, needs to be taken seriously.

It is decisive that Renouvier does develop a doctrine of the categories. He is the main figure in nineteenth-century France who engaged Kant so thoroughly about this question. His neo-criticism extends Kant's critical method by rejecting Kant's distinction between the phenomenal and the noumenal realms. The resolution of the difficulties left by Kant's idea of the thing-in-itself had been a major point of departure for German metaphysics in the work of Johann Fichte, Friedrich Schelling, Arthur Schopenhauer, and others. Fichte's Ego, Schelling's Absolute, and Schopenhauer's Will were all attempts to locate and philosophically analyse the reality which Kant thought to be inaccessible to reason. Renouvier rejects the entire notion of a noumenal realm and, therefore, sees these approaches as fruitless (Renouvier 1875, I:40). He takes another direction and insists that only phenomena exist. Everything is to be understood in relation to representation (Renouvier 1875, I:33; Séailles 1905, 30–40). This "phenomenalism," when properly modified in a sociological direction, probably provided one starting point for the later Durkheimian conception of society as made up of and possible only through representations (now collectively conceived). Indeed, one of the reasons why the notion of representation was so common in French thought in Durkheim's time is the prominence of this theme in Renouvier's philosophy (Lalande 1962). Durkheim's clear shift in the focus of this problem from the individual to society is worth emphasizing. It parallels a seemingly opposite movement in Renouvier toward the notion of personality as the central reference point for philosophical understanding, one leading to his "philosophy of liberty" (Logue 1993).

Renouvier places the categories in a position of centrality as great, if not greater than they occupy in Kant's work. Indeed, his first series of the *Essais*, on logic, contains a discussion of the categories which occupies almost two volumes (Renouvier 1875, vols. I–II). His list contains nine categories, which for him are actually logical laws governing the world. The list of nine basic categories includes relation, number, position, succession, quality, becoming, causality, finality, and personality (Renouvier 1875,

I:181ff.; Séailles 1905, chap. 3). These categories are not grouped together in more inclusive sets, as with Kant. However, each category does contain three subdivisions or "moments" (derived seemingly from Hegel's method of thesis, antithesis and synthesis), which allows the elaboration of the nine basic ones into a twenty-seven-fold set of terms (see the chart in Séailles 1905, 93).

Renouvier sees the problem of reason and the categories as strongly "practical," in a Kantian sense. He places the categories in subordination to practical, moral conduct. Indeed, for Renouvier, the analysis of the categories begins with the central category of relation, but ends with the category of personality. For Renouvier, one must begin with the category of relation. It is of critical importance and implicated in everything. Nothing about existence can be discussed without it. All experience and understanding imply relations among ideas and things. In a similar way, at the end of the analysis of the categories, all other categories are dependent upon and, in a sense, summed up by the decisive category of personality. His famous system of "personalism" emerges from this emphasis, and, once again, begs comparison and contrast with Durkheim's collective understanding of the categories, including the category of the person itself. Durkheim's early insistence that society was, in some sense, an "individual" or "being"—quite a different idea, I might add, than the notion of the whole itself—might be thought of in this context, rather than as an importation from German thought or as merely an "organismic" analogy. Durkheim shows a strong tendency to collectivize many of Renouvier's main categories.

Renouvier rejects Kant's claim that space and time are forms of perception and not true categories. He places them within the alternation of thesis, antithesis and synthesis which he employs as the dynamic method for expanding his list of main categories. As a result, time and space become complex notions, with subdivisions corresponding to different aspects of these ideas. For example, he distinguishes within the category of position among points as a limit, as interval (*espace*), and as extension (*étendue*). He deals similarly with succession, with the instant as a limit, with *temps* as interval, and with duration (*durée*). In general, these as well as all the other categories are to be understood synthetically through that of relation.

Renouvier is also critical of Kant on another score. He claims that Kant's first *Critique* neglected to add finality, in terms of teleological goals, and personality to the list of categories. While true, the remark overlooks the fact that these ideas (purpose and personality) play a central role in Kant's other two critques. As Octave Hamelin has noted, Renouvier was not entirely fair to Kant on this score (Hamelin 1927, 154–62). However, Renouvier offers this critique because his phenomenalism requires that he reintegrate personality and finality into a single philosophical system, rather than dividing the world into a realm of necessity and a realm of freedom.

The notion of number plays an inordinately large role in Renouvier's system. It provides the basis for his critique of infinity and his claims about the impossiblity of an infinite time or infinite number of entities in the world. Renouvier argues that an infinite number is unimaginable, indeed, absurd (Renouvier 1875, I:54ff.). Here, Renouvier's system seems innocent of developments in mathematical thought, then already in progress, which were to establish the coherence of the notion of an infinite number (Kneale and Kneale 1962). As noted already, it is difficult to judge Durkheim's relationship to this central part of Renouvier's work. On the one hand, he lists, but says little in any direct way about the category of number, yet the category of totality implies a concern for number and had itself been included by Kant as one of three categories grouped under the notion of quantity. As we will see, the categories of quantity and quality do not appear as frequently in Durkheim's work as the notions of whole and part. However, he and members of his school do bring them into play often enough and at sufficiently significant points in their arguments for us to consider them as part of his categorial interests.

The centrality of the notion of relation in Renouvier (1875, I:231ff.) raises interesting questions when paired with Durkheim's own later emphasis on dynamic density, concentration, association, and so forth. It could be argued that Durkheim derived his notion of relation from Renouvier. This would seem to fit the dominant image of Durkheim as a "relational realist" (or "associational realist"). I hasten to add that the precise nature of Durkheim's so-called realism remains to be established. As I have already suggested, the meaning of the very characterization of "relational realism," usually opposed to so-called substantive realism (Alpert 1939; Wallwork 1972), needs greater clarification, especially in comparison with the whole/part concept, one which Durkheim himself says was derived from Renouvier and central to his work. It will occupy some of our time later in these pages. Morever, as we will see, the category of relation plays another role in Durkheim's thought, that of sociologically combining the categories, and thus reality itself, into a more synthetic whole around the notion of totality. This is largely its synthesizing role in Renouvier's own work. Therefore, it is plausible to think that Renouvier's key notion of relation is connected to some of Durkheim's central perspectives, even if we wish to hold open the precise nature of its influence.

The notion of force also plays a role in Renouvier's work as the synthesis term under the category of causality, combining the notions of act and power (*puissance*). Kant had already drawn attention to the problem of the possible existence of a fundamental force in the world. In general, he dealt with the notion of force without thereby bringing it within his discussion of the categories, or even within the discussion of causality (Kant 1968). In this respect, Renouvier's emphases are also new and rather closer to Durkheim's later way of talking about causality in terms of action, power, and force. Once again, Durkheim's shift of emphasis toward the social explanation of these ideas separates him from Renouvier, despite the overlapping interests. It seems likely that Renouvier must have provided some of the items on Durkheim's agenda for the study of the categories. While Durkheim learned a good deal from (and through) Renouvier, he modified his ideas at every point.

Much more could be said about Durkheim's relationships to these authors (as well as others). Indeed, we will take up the connection between Durkheim and Spinoza at various points later in these pages. However, this review lays a sufficient foundation for our central task: the analysis of his writings.

4

DURKHEIM'S EARLY WRITINGS AND THE DISSERTATION ON MONTESQUIEU

When we begin the examination of Durkheim's writings, especially those where he discusses other thinkers and offers lengthy paraphrases of their ideas (e.g. his reviews, his treatments of Montesquieu, Rousseau, and others), several things need to be kept in mind. First, we must be careful to distinguish Durkheim's summary of other authors' ideas from his own theoretical claims. Failure to observe this rule has led recent interpreters astray (for example, about his Schäffle review or his early survey of German thought). At the same time, we should pay close attention to those problems found in his predecessors which Durkheim thought worthy of emphasis and discussion. Even where he disgrees with them (e.g. in his lectures on Saint-Simon and socialism), his selection of topics often provides clues to his own aims and interests, if not his precise theories. With these caveats in mind, we are in a better position to interpret Durkheim's work.

Durkheim's earliest writings already betray an interest in our central questions. They also pose some of the interpretive problems just mentioned. The review of Albert Schäffle's *Bau und Leben des Sozialen Körpers* is one of Durkheim's first published writings and has become something of a focal point in the search for the sources of his ideas. In my view, it is a rather overrated "source." Schäffle played far less of a role in the development of Durkheim's ideas than is often sugggested. The review is primarily a summary of Schäffle's book. It reveals little with certainly about Durkheim's own thinking at this point. Schäffle is thought to be a major source of Durkheim's "organicism" and "social realism." Durkheim hardly needed Schäffle as a model for such organicist metaphors. As we have seen, they could as easily have been found in Aristotle, or in Comte, and several other earlier writers (Nisbet 1969). In his lecture course of 1888, Durkheim himself mentions Auguste Comte's

use of this metaphor (Durkheim 1978, 54). Perhaps more important, his so-called social realism required neither Schäffle nor
organicism itself to develop. The key fact is that the philosophical
notions of whole and part take priority in Durkheim's work over
organicism or even realism. They are themselves a main source of
these related usages, which are largely variants of this more central motif. The general rule employed by many interpreters seems
to be that the closer the writer to Durkheim in time, the greater the
likely influence on Durkheim. The short-term is made to predomi-
nate over the long-term. Indeed, this consideration tends to over-
shadow the distinction between "externalist" and "internalist"
approaches to intellectual history. Both frequently take the short-
term as their focus. By contrast, I am emphasizing the long-term
historical, philosophical, and religious roots of Durkheim's thought.

If we turn to Durkheim's review of Schäffle, we discover several points in the discussion where Durkheim touches on issues
central to our present work. At the essay's very outset, he poses the
problem of Schäffle's social realism and his use of the organicist
metaphor. While Schäffle "is clearly a realist" (Durkheim 1978, 93;
1975, I:355), he does not unambiguously accept the idea that society is, in some sense, an organism, but explicitly distances himself
from others who have argued such an idea. Indeed, it is unclear
whether Durkheim thinks Schäffle is an unqualified "organicist" at
all. It is even less clear, in any precise way, what Durkheim himself
thinks about these issues. However, he is keenly interested,
throughout the review, in the role of metaphors in social theory and
seems to want to move beyond them, if possible, into a more analytical treatment of particular questions of sociological research
and theory. Even at this early date, Durkheim seems to accept the
notion that society has a reality of its own and this reality is connected with the "collective consciousness." His very interest in
Schäffle implies this. In passing, Durkheim also uses a fascinating
phrase which he will repeat in *Division* and elsewhere. In summarizing a part of Schäffle's argument, he writes that "The substance
(*matière*) of which society is made comprises a double element: one
passive, the other active, persons and things" (Durkheim 1978, 96;
1975, I:358). Here, Mark Traugott translates the key term, *matière*,
quite appropriately as "substance." Both George Simpson and W. D.
Halls also translate *matière* as substance in a similarly important
passage in their respective versions of *Division* (Durkheim 1933,
256; 1984, 200; 1994b, 237.) How seriously should we take this reference to the "substance" of society? Does it point toward a real

problem emerging at an early date in his theorizing?

Most commentators have denied that Durkheim ever conceived of society as a substance in any sense of that complex idea (Alpert 1939; Wallwork 1972; Schmaus 1994). Ernest Wallwork suggests that Durkheim was a "relational realist" who frequently garbled his message with the unfortunate use of metaphors, ones hardly worth pursuing in a serious discussion of Durkheim's theories (Wallwork 1972). While I would agree that Durkheim's message is sometimes ambiguous, I think it a great error to overlook the enormous influence in his work of the central metaphor of whole and part, and, by implication, the less frequently featured notion of social substance. He sometimes uses this latter expression (society as substance) in his early writings, and implies it in other places. He later notes (and criticizes) the Saint-Simonian usage of an alternative idea of social substance. It is hardly irrelevant to his mode of thought. Its implications need to be given serious attention. When seen in the light of his overall theory, especially his later writings, where the problem of substance as a category is confronted more directly, these random usages take on a larger meaning.

When we turn to a point later in the same review where he again discusses these issues, we find him writing that a social consciousness exists and that individual consciousnesses are, in some sense, an "emanation" of it (Durkheim 1978, 102; 1975, I:364). However, he states that there is nothing metaphysical in it. There is no "stuff" composing social reality, only interactions and symbolic exchanges among individuals, who "interpenetrate one another" (Durkheim 1978, 103; 1975, I:365). Durkheim seems to present an anti-metaphysical, even "nominalist," interactionist view of social consciousness. At the conclusion of this discussion, he notes the strongly factual character of Schäffle's ideas and discusses Schäffle's division of states of consciousness into intelligence, sensitivity, and will (Durkheim 1978, 105; 1975, I:367). However, toward the end of the review, he remarks, in a manner congruent with the interpretive warnings lodged above, that he did not want to interrupt "the continuity of this exposition with discussions or remarks," but wished only "to reproduce the general movement of this beautiful analysis" (Durkheim 1978, 109; 1975, I:372).

What are we to conclude from this brief summary? It seems clear that Durkheim is primarily reconstructing Schäffle's ideas and not presenting his own views. He may (or may not) agree with them (it is difficult to tell), but I do think it clear that we are reading an exegetical summary. We might even question whether in 1885 Durkheim has any theory of his own. It seems obvious, given what we know about Durkheim's intellectual development, that these ideas have a "family resemblance" to some of Durkheim's own later formulations. But even if we assume some congruity between the views of Schäffle and Durkheim, sufficient ambiguities exist for us to remain uncertain whether Durkheim did or did not think of society in terms of a "social substance." What do we make of Durkheim's reference to the "substance" of society or his remark about the "emanation" of individual from collective consciousness? I am reluctant to draw any firm conclusions from this review. It is suggestive, but fundamentally inconclusive. I would much prefer to judge Durkheim by those essays which express his own theories more directly, or even by his less ambiguous treatments of others' ideas. For similar reasons, I am also skeptical of the "Germanist" thesis, which argues that Durkheim's year in Germany was the decisive influence on him and that his two long reviews of German philosophy and social sciences need to be seen as major statements of his own developing position (Durkheim 1975, vol. I; Hall 1987; Hall's remarks in Durkheim 1993; Meštrović 1991). These essays are even more summary in character (and therefore as ambiguous) as the Schäffle review. If any tentative conclusions can be drawn, it is that Durkheim's language was highly ambiguous and by no means ruled out the sort of interpretation we will be offering in this work. This essay also reveals one of Durkheim's characteristic rhetorical usages: to give with one hand and take with the other. He claims there are no "metaphysical" implications to the view of society he is discussing, yet simultaneously uses language which is highly provocative of such suspicions. One can only conclude that he does so either because he is tied to inherited philosophical categories from which he is unable or unwilling to extricate himself, or because he is, in fact, attracted however tentatively to some metaphysical position. These two possibilities do not necessarily exclude one another. Together they account for some of the ambiguity in his writing and help explain the strongly metaphysical undercurrent in his thinking.

In another early review (1885) of a book by Ludwig Gumplowicz, we find Durkheim characteristically preoccupied with the widest philosophical issues and linking his sociological concerns to them. The world exhibits both "unity and multiplicity," a contradiction analyzed and resolved repeatedly by philosophers (Durkheim 1975, I:345). One popular theory places unity at the beginning and derives multiplicity from it. Gumplowicz takes the opposite approach, placing multiplicity at the origin of things. Durkheim rapidly focuses these wider issues onto the problem of unity and multiplicity in social existence. After a discussion of Gumplowicz's main theses, Durkheim declares them (despite the logical rigor of the demonstrations) to be neither convincing nor helpful (Durkheim 1975, I:350). Durkheim grants that "society is a being (*un être*), a person," but not a metaphysical one. Nor is it a "substance (*substance*) more or less transcendent; it is a whole composed of parts (*un tout composé de parties*)" (Durkheim 1975, I:351). This requires that sociologists analyze the whole, identify the parts, describe and classify them, and examine the principles governing their combination. Finally, he suggests that we are both "agents and patients," with each individual adding to the current which inexorably engulfs them all (Durkheim 1975, I:352).

Durkheim's review of Gumplowicz contains a good deal of philosophical language, the repetition of which serves to reassert his main argument. I am interested less in the concrete thesis enunciated by Durkheim, which seems to place an unusual amount of emphasis on the individual's role in the social process, than the fact that Durkheim introduces the whole/part distinction as a way of defending his thesis and, in the process, again addresses the notion of substance. He resolves the problem of the relationship between individual and society, the possible priority of one over the other, by reducing it to the whole/part distinction. He denies that society is a "substance," while simultaneously asserting that it is a whole with considerable powers. As we proceed, we will see Durkheim using this method of argumentation again and again. It is also interesting in this particular context to witness Durkheim's use of the Aristotelian distinction, popular during the medieval period, of the individual as "agent" and "patient." While this distinction is entirely congruent with his emphasis on the whole/part notion, its usage here is unique in his work, and it is entirely supplanted by the latter distinction. Durkheim's reference to society as a "being," even more, as a "person," is certainly provocative. As suggested above, it may reflect his "collectivization" of Renouvier's "personalist" philosophy. Finally, the explicit denial that society is any kind of substance is fascinating. If nothing else, it indicates that Durkheim was acutely sensitive to this question, even at this early date in his career, before he had become well known or published a single major work. It is remarkable that he is able to imagine that anyone else might have considered treating society as a substance or suspected him of doing so.

When we turn to Durkheim's now famous review of Ferdinand Tönnies' *Gemeinschaft und Gesellschaft*, we are on ground familiar to most sociologists. This review has attracted a good deal of attention, because of the subsequent stature of the two protagonists as well as the later estimation of Durkheim's work by Tonnies himself (Cahnmann 1973, 239–56). However, I would recall that, at the time of writing (1889), Durkheim was still an unknown figure.

Since the theories of both Tönnies and Durkheim are familiar, we can move quickly to an examination of the key elements of interest to us in Durkheim's review. Durkheim briefly describes the empirical content of Tönnies' two concepts, *Gemeinschaft* and *Gesellschaft*. His evaluation involves a broad agreement with Tönnies' characterization of *Gemeinschaft*, but a fundamental disagreement over the nature of *Gesellschaft*. This disagreement goes to the heart of Durkheim's basic view of reality. In describing the historical differences between Tönnies' conceptualizations of the two types of social order, he explains:

> . . . while previously the whole was given before the parts, it is now the parts which are given before the whole. The latter is formed only by their juxtaposition. That is why, while the composition of *Gemeinschaft* was organic, that of *Gesellschaft* is mechanical. (Durkheim 1975, I:387)

He then proceeds to argue that *Gesellschaft* has its own internal type of unity, and is not a mass of atomized individuals held together only by fleeting individual contracts and the coercive power of the state. However, in his view, it is implausible that society could begin as an "organic" formation and become transformed into a purely "mechanical" one. Society is a fact of nature in its origin and remains one throughout its history (Durkheim 1975, I:390).

Durkheim's reading of Tönnies is remarkable in several respects. He associates Tönnies' characterization of *Gesellschaft* with Jeremy Bentham, Herbert Spencer, Sir Henry Maine, Karl Marx and the socialists generally. However, he seems unaware of Tönnies' heavy reliance on the work of Thomas Hobbes for his basic characterization of *Gesellschaft*. As a result, he also misses the way in which Tönnies juxtaposes the "rationalistic" natural law theory of society of Hobbes with a "natural law" oriented conception of *Gemeinschaft*. For Tönnies also, society is always a "natural" phenomenon, in some sense, but one resting on a dual natural law foundation (Nielsen 1988).

More important is the way in which Durkheim links the mechanical/organic distinction to the whole/part problem. It is a fine piece of intellectual *légère de main*. First, he assimilates Tönnies' discussion to his own emerging whole/part distinction. For him, Tönnies is saying that once (in *Gemeinschaft*) the whole preceeded the parts; now (in *Gesellschaft*) the parts preceed the whole and the whole is no longer a true whole, but only a juxtaposition of unrelated elements. Durkheim's wording is crucial to an understanding of his strategy. It is precisely because the part preceeds the whole in *Gesellschaft* that it is a "mechanical" formation. Durkheim thinks Tönnies' image of modern "mechanical" society is dependent on his having placed the part before the whole, and, in effect, having made impossible any unity except a fleeting and mechanical juxtaposition of parts (e.g. in contracts) or a coercive integration of them through the state. For Durkheim's emerging theory, the whole always preceeds the parts in all societies regardless of their form of organization. If he later chooses to reverse Tönnies' imagery, it is because he wants to oppose two forms of unity to one another, one characterized by unity through likeness, the other by unity through differences. But in both of Durkheim's later types (organic and mechanical solidarity), the whole preceeds the part. It is interesting that Durkheim criticizes what he sees as Tönnies' misguided effort to thus join Bentham and Aristotle into one theory. Durkheim entirely eschews Bentham and the utilitarians, and is decidedly in favor of Aristotle.

Another difference between the two authors involves Tönnies' use of a Kantian means/ends schema in the discussion of moral life in the two formations. He sees the "essential" or "natural will" associated with *Gemeinschaft* as the equivalent of Kant's moral imperative to treat others as an end and not only as a means. On the other hand, the "rational will" connected with *Gesellschaft* involves the widespread violation of this maxim, and the regular use of the other as a means to one's own ends in a system of mutual, if sometimes cooperative exploitation. This means/ends schema complements Tönnies' own metaphorology of "organic" and "mechanical" formations.

Although he does not mention it, Durkheim would certainly find this formulation objectionable. For him, even modern society depends on ties between individuals which logically predate and underpin mutual, rational exploitation. Moreover, the modern division of labor creates a new moral imperative of its own. It is interesting in this connection that Durkheim goes out of his way in some of his later writings to avoid the means/ends schema when discussing moral and social issues, since it would push him toward the sort of intellectual position adopted by Tönnies. His avoidance of it is also a measure of his attempt to distance himself from Kant, whose moral philosophy brings the means/ends schema strongly into play. As we will see, Durkheim often substitutes the image of a circle as a more compelling metaphor for social and moral processes. Although the source of this image is not entirely clear, it is certainly more congruent with Durkheim's whole/part metaphor.

In conclusion, it is striking how thoroughly Durkheim assimilates Tönnies' entire approach to his own guiding whole/part metaphor. In the process, he misconstrues the actual intellectual foundations of Tönnies' theory. We learn less here about Tönnies than about Durkheim's emerging perspective.

Durkheim's 1887 review of Jean-Marie Guyau's *L'Irréligion de L'Avenir*, raises particularly interesting questions for our purposes. It not only focuses on the topic of religion, but touches on many of the issues of concern in the present work. Durkheim also distinguishes more clearly between his summary of Guyau's views, his opinion of them, and his own ideas. He is less guarded than in the earlier review of Schäffle. Several points are particularly worth noting.

In his discussion of Guyau's review of those metaphysical systems which have been historically prominent, he notes that Guyau divides them into several groups, among which is monism. He notes that Alfred Fouillée's "idealistic evolutionism" is similar to monism and claims that such doctrines are increasingly influential. Monistic theories reduce "neither thought to matter, nor matter to thought," but combine both in a living synthesis, which spontaneously concentrates and then diffuses itself in action. He adds that monistic systems have the "great advantage" of allowing for "the great metaphysical and moral hopes which humanity has so far been unable to do without" (Durkheim 1994a, 31–32; 1975, II:157)

These remarks about Guyau's theory clearly represent Durkheim's summary of that writer's ideas. However, we are struck by the resemblance between this summary and Durkheim's own later comments in the 1901 preface to the second edition of the *Rules*. There he defends his notion of society and argues for the unity of life, adding that life is located in "the living substance (*substance*) in its totality," and is "in the whole, not in the parts"

(Durkheim 1982, 39; 1988, 82). Also, I would note his reference to how life concentrates itself and then diffuses itself in action, a seeming harbinger of his major images of religion and social processes in the *Forms*. Durkheim was hardly averse to drawing on monistic and substantialist language when it suited his needs. However, I would dispute P. Q. Hirst's (1975) contention that such phrases indicate a full-blown "vitalistic" philosophy. Rather, it is the whole/part metaphor which predominates. The monistic implication accompanies it. It is not "life" which is the key idea here, but that of the whole. I would also note Durkheim's usage, once again in 1901, of the notion of substance, this time in connection with the notion of totality. Here we see all of Durkheim's usages drawn together: the whole/part metaphor, the notion of totality, and the notion of substance (although now it is not social substance, but the whole of substance).

When we continue with his review of Guyau, we note that Durkheim views Guyau's doctrine as an advance in the scientific study of religions because of its sociological perspective (Durkheim 1994a, 33–34; 1975, II:159). Although Guyau (like Herbert Spencer) overemphasizes the speculative side of religion, his theory does provide a partial explanation of religious phenomena, if the factors are reversed and "sociability be made the determining cause of religious sentiment" (Durkheim 1994a, 35; 1975, II:162). Religion results from social sentiments which can be divided into two types. The "inter-individual" type links individuals to one another through respect, fear, and so forth. The second or "inter-social" type links the individual to "the social being (*être*) in its totality" and is found especially in the relationships between societies. The first leaves the autonomy of the individual intact, while with the second, the individual is merely "part of a whole of which I am the movements and of which I feel the force" (Durkheim 1994a, 35–36; 1975, II:162–63). By contrast with Guyau, Durkheim thinks that only the second type of sentiment can give rise to obligation and, consequently, to religion. In primitive societies, religion is a matter of the group, not the sentiments of the individual and the exhibitions of power from natural forces are of more interest to the group than to the individual. It is only those cosmic forces of interest to the group which will be deified. In this context, Durkheim remarks that "Religious society is not human society ideally projected beyond the stars; and the gods are not conceived as members of the tribe . . ." Instead, they form one or more other societies with an overall "international character" between which humans and gods maintain relationships (Durkheim 1994a, 36–37; 1975, II:163).

These latter remarks have a mixed quality when we think of them in light of Durkheim's mature views. On the one hand, we see him emphasizing the importance of rites and sentiments which tie the individual to the whole, to society itself, as productive of religion, rather than those more "individualistic" sentiments which are social, but which fail to create obligations. Religion is a product of social sentiments in the former sense. These form the basis for our cosmological ideas in which nature is seen in the light of collective sentiments. The "sociocentrism," which marks Durkheim's later sociology of religion and knowledge, is already quite in evidence. At the same time, it is odd to find him, at this early date, denying what came to be a central tenet of his sociology of religion: that religious society is, indeed, in some sense, a projection of human society and that the "gods" (at least in "totemism") are, in some sense, members of the tribe.

Of greatest interest in these passages is Durkheim's early concern, despite variations in the precise theory, about the links between religion, society, and nature. While we cannot say that he himself unambiguously adopts a monistic position, we can conclude that the problems which are resolved by a monistic philosophy are already critical to his work. He is seeking a theory which deals with these issues, that is, a theory which will systematically link society, religion, and nature. I would emphasize that Durkheim's own characterization of the monist position, as a philosophy which is not reductionistic, but unites matter and thought together into a coherent whole, looks suspiciously like Durkheim's own emerging goal. I would argue that Durkheim moves toward such a monist solution and that the many tensions and alternating emphases in his work between the so-called materialistic and the idealistic strains are the result of his effort to combine them into a more inclusive system.

When we turn to Durkheim's opening lecture on social science delivered at Bordeaux and published in 1888, we find him touching more directly on the whole/part problem. He notes that Auguste Comte revived the idea that social laws were natural laws and that sociology should seek to study a new reality, society. This reality is as real as a living organism. It is a real thing, although it exists only through the individuals who compose its "substratum." As a proof of this idea, he adds: "A whole [*tout*] is not identical to the sum of its parts [*la somme de ses parties*], even though without them it would be nothing." When they unite under a definite form, human beings create a "new being [*un être nouveau*] which has its own nature and its own laws. This is the social being [*l'être social*]" (Durkheim 1978, 50; Durkheim 1970, 86). It is interesting that we see Durkheim combine the organismic analogy and whole/part perspectives in these comments. He associates both with Comte. It is the organism metaphor which is favored by Comte, even though Comte thinks it a "metaphor of mediocre value" (see Durkheim 1978, 54; Durkheim 1970, 90–91).

The whole/part analogy serves as the basis for the demonstration that society is a reality different from the individuals who compose it. As we proceed in our discussion, we will see Durkheim repeatedly using this rationale. It is one of his favorite ways of asserting his central idea. Finally, we once again see Durkheim flirting with "substantivist" language in his references to the "social being" (a translation which I have substituted for Traugott's less determinate "social entity"). All such remarks in the early essays and reviews fit well with his later emphasis on social facts as "things." This language about society as a being has been taken as an indication of Durkheim's underlying "positivism," one which is alleged to "reify" society. On the contrary, it is precisely through such language that Durkheim commits himself to philosophical and ontological assumptions which repeatedly take him well beyond "positivism." It is not because he is a "positivist" that he sees society as a "being," but because he is an implicit "substantialist," that is, a certain type of sociological metaphysician. What type will become clearer as our discussion proceeds.

Durkheim's Latin Dissertation of 1892 on Montesquieu contains several helpful leads in understanding his emerging conception of totality, although the problem does not occupy center stage in that work. Durkheim always saw Montesquieu as a pioneer of his own brand of sociological thought, even though he was also critical of certain limitations he found in that author's work. There are two interrelated aspects of his work which earned him Durkheim's admiration as a pioneer of sociology. They are both relevant to our discussion.

The first is the question of the relationships among the different aspects of social life and among the sciences which examine them. Durkheim was critical of any social science which too readily treated the various elements of social life as unrelated. To treat morality, trade, religion, law, and other elements of social life as essentially separate from one another and to constitute sciences on this basis was to overlook a vital "methodological rule." Montesquieu recognized this rule. He saw that the various departments of social life "form a whole, of such a sort that, if taken separately and apart from the others, cannot be understood" (Durkheim 1965, 56; 1966a, 103). Moreover, he does not consider morality, trade, religion, and so forth apart from the "form of society, which extends its influence to all social things," since they are "the diverse elements or organs of the same social organism" (Durkheim 1965, 56; 1966a, 103). Although his formulation remained vague, Montesquieu saw the unity of the social sciences, since he realized that all aspects of society were "bound together by strict necessity and were members of a single body" (Durkheim 1965, 57; 1966a, 104).

In these passages, Durkheim freely mixes the whole/part and the organismic metaphors, but the focus is clear. The most important fact is that he sees Montesquieu as a pioneer precisely because he identified the unity of society, or the whole (and by implication, the whole/part relation). Durkheim only secondarily expresses this idea with an organismic metaphor and places primary emphasis on the category of the whole or totality. He adds to this that Montesquieu also recognized the importance of understanding types of societies. For an adequate classification, the mere identification of various similarities was insufficient. One must be able to compare "their structure and life . . . in their totality (*totalité*)" (Durkheim 1965, 62; 1966a, 111). Despite his inadequate classification of societal types in terms of forms of sovereignty, and his excessive emphasis on the sovereign's ability to mold the laws, Montesquieu had recognized that society, its laws and institutions, emerged from the real conditions of a country, including its population size, topography, and so forth. Durkheim distinguishes between a sociological conception of law and one which emphasizes the will of the sovereign. The former emphasizes efficient causes and the latter final causes. This Aristotelian distinction between types of causality appears as a criterion for the demarcation of sociology as a science. It will become clearer later in these pages that this emphasis on "efficient causes" rests uncomfortably with Durkheim's equal commitment to the trope of whole/part. He also suggests that Montesquieu went beyond the purely dialectical discussion of these problems, and recognized that "what is rational is precisely what exists most often in reality" (Durkheim 1965, 63; 1966a, 112). Durkheim uses a rather Hegelian sounding phrase, but one which could equally be attached to Spinoza's determinism. In any case, he finds that Montesquieu was the first to establish the fundamental principles of social science (Durkheim 1965, 61), a claim which he generally reserves for French writers (Durkheim 1973), but tempers the remark by observing that no one person, after all, is ever the sole originator of a new science. In sum, Durkheim finds Montesqueiu's significance as a pioneer precisely in his realization of the importance of the issue that is our main focus: the sociological problem of totality, or the whole/part relation.

5

THE FIRST APPROACH TO TOTALITY: WHOLES, PARTS AND THE TRANSFORMATION OF SOCIAL SUBSTANCE IN *THE DIVISION OF LABOR IN SOCIETY*

Durkheim's first sustained treatment of the problem of totality occurs in *Division*. The book is so well-known by sociologists, it is hardly necessary to summarize its main theses, nor will I do so in any detail. From the present standpoint, it is worth mentioning only a few particularly relevant facts: (1) the book is linked to Durkheim's contemporaneous treatment of Montesquieu, a fact evident both in his renewed emphasis on social types, or whole societies, and in his focus on the role of law in society; (2) the book deals directly with the relationship between the individual and society, indeed, this is announced near the very beginning as its primary focus; (3) it examines the changing forms of social solidarity in whole societies and is, therefore, quite evidently concerned with the sociological problem of totality; (4) it uses a classification of the types of legal sanctions as an index to the changing forms of social solidarity; (5) the book also offers a discussion of some "pathological" circumstances in which social solidarity does not result from the division of labor; (6) it contains a particularly important and debated theory of the social dynamics which bring about the change from one type of social whole to another. All of these themes are linked to Durkheim's fundamental interest in the problem of totality and the whole/part relationship.

I am proceeding on the assumption, made plausible by my earlier discussion, that this book was, indeed, an attempt to treat the problem of the whole or totality, but that it proved inadequate as a definitive resolution of the problem (although Durkheim continued to maintain many of the specific theses developed in the book). How does Durkheim envision totality, or the whole/part problem in this work? How does he develop his discussion? Indeed, is the book really about the problem of the whole or the whole/part relation?

This book has usually been seen as a contribution to Durkheim's interest in the sociological study of morality. It's first sentence states his desire to investigate moral life from the stand-point of the positive sciences and seems to place this aim at the forefront of his concern (Durkheim 1984, xxv; 1994b, xxxvii). Of course, this scientific aim is a central aspect of the book. However, in the book's preface, Durkheim also states another equally impor-tant objective: to understand the connection between individual personality and social solidarity and explain how increasing indi-vidual autonomy can emerge alongside increasing dependence on society. This is the book's "starting point" (Durkheim 1984, xxx; 1994b, xliii). Durkheim adds that this apparent "antinomy" is resolved by tracing the increasingly central role of the division of labor in society.

It is worth pausing immediately to ask if Durkheim's starting point—the connection between the individual personality and social solidarity—can, in fact, be identified with the whole/part problem. I think it can. Durkheim himself makes the equation at various points in his treatise. The evidence from Durkheim's essay on Montesquieu, as well as the fugitive references from some of his first essays, already points toward an early interest in the problem of the whole. In *Division*, this interest is moved to the more specific level of the whole/part relation. However, this relationship is also treated at several other different levels in this work. I want to begin by looking at the whole/part problem as an equivalent to the soci-ety/individual problem and then discuss the other conception of this issue, namely, whole/part as the question of the relationship between society and its subgroupings.

Early in the book's introduction, while discussing the scope of the problem of the division of labor as a moral issue, Durkheim begins to play with the whole/part metaphor. He asks if we are obliged to become a "rounded, completed being, a whole (*tout*) suffi-cient unto itself, or to be only a part of the whole, the organ of an organism (*la partie d'un tout, l'organe d'un organisme*)" (Durkheim 1984, 3; 1994b, 4). This remark already calls attention to both the mixture of metaphors as well as the complexity of the whole/part rhetoric in Durkheim. It also states one of Durkheim's central neg-ative reference points: the notion that the individual could ever be a "whole" sufficient in itself. In later comparing the strength of the

ties which create unity in societies bound by collective consciousness and by mechanical versus organic solidarity, Durkheim notes
the fragility of the more "primitive" type. Although mechanical solidarity absorbs the individual into the community, this binding link
can easily be forged or broken. "Despite the fact that the parts of
the whole (*les parties de l'agrégat*), when united, act only in concert,
it does not follow that they must either remain united or perish"
(Durkheim 1984, 104; 1994b, 123). The parts, especially subgroups,
do not truly need each other, and can therefore break off easily,
"since each one contains in itself the whole of what makes social
life" (Durkheim 1984, 104; 1994b, 123). In turn, since the individual is fully absorbed into the group, it can move only as a member
of the group. His place as a "part" in a larger "whole" is limited to
his participation in a homogeneously constituted group.

   In the same vein, while offering a critique of Fustel de
Coulanges' discussion of the primitive family and religion,
Durkheim remarks that such groups were "social masses" (*masses
sociales*) made up "homogeneous elements," where the collective is
highly developed, while the individual exists in a rudimentary state
(Durkheim 1984, 130; 1994b, 154). He immediately enters into a
brief discussion of why, therefore, communism can easily emerge
from this situation. Communism results from that form of cohesion
"that absorbs the individual into the group, the part into the whole
(*la partie dans le tout*)" (Durkheim 1984, 130; 1994b, 154). The
more advanced state of the Roman family, by comparison with
primitive societies, led it to link the individual, not directly to the
group, but to the person who is its image (i.e. the *paterfamilias*).
Here, ". . . the unity of the whole (*du tout*) is as before exclusive of
the individuality of the parts" (Durkheim 1984, 131; 1994b, 156).
Indeed, in a critical comment on Herbert Spencer's theory,
Durkheim remarks that "society is essentially a coherent whole"
(Durkheim 1984, 147). Although there is some ambiguity in
attributing this view to Spencer or Durkheim, it is clear from
Durkheim's other remarks that this was his basic view and the
starting point for a good deal of his work. In another later critical
remark on Spencer's view of altruism, Durkheim argues that the
individual in a complex society is not self-sufficient, receives everything necessary from society, and works for society in turn. This
results in a very strong feeling of dependence in the individual, who
thus "grows accustomed to estimating his true value, that is, to
regard himself only as a part of the whole, the organ of an organism" (*la partie d'un tout, l'organe d'un organisme*) (Durkheim 1984,

173; 1994b, 207). This final phrase repeats in almost identical terms the remark made in the book's introduction (Durkheim 1994b, 4). In a critique of Spencer's comparison of the sociologist with the mathematician, who attempts to understand the combinations formed by a set of individual balls, Durkheim makes one of his most unguarded comments concerning our topic. He argues that the comparison is imprecise and inapplicable to social facts. Instead, it is "the form of the whole that determines that of the parts. Society does not find ready-made in individual consciousnesses the bases on which it rests; it makes them for itself" (Durkheim 1984, 287; 1994b, 342; also 288, for a remark on "association" and the "substratum" that eluciates this quotation and makes the identifications at stake more precisely). Finally, in a passage disputing the proposed role of the state in curing the anomic division of labor, Durkheim comments: ". . . what causes the unity of organized societies, as it does of any organism, is the spontaneous consensus of its parts . . ." (Durkheim 1984, 297; 1994b, 351). Just as the brain expresses, but does not create unity in the organism, the regulatory action of the government finds as its "necessary condition" the internal solidarity of society. While it may be possible to discuss the "reaction of the whole (*l'ensemble*) upon the parts," it is necessary that "the whole also must exist" and that "the parts must already be solidary, one to another, so that the whole (*le tout*) becomes conscious of itself and reacts accordingly" (Durkheim 1984, 297; 1994b, 351).

Besides the various references to the whole/part problem, there is a extraordinary passage where Durkheim traces the general transformation from the segmentary structure of mechanical solidarity to the division of labor and organic solidarity. He remarks: "The increase in the division of labor is therefore due to the fact that the social segments lose their individuality, that the partitions dividing them become more permeable, in a word, that there occurs between them a coalescence that renders the social substance (*la matière sociale*) free to enter into new combinations" (Durkheim 1984, 200; 1994b, 237). This latter remark cries out for comment. We have already noted Durkheim's usage of this term (i.e. *matière sociale*) in a similar connection, as well as his references to the "social being." We will see him using it in other ways when we examine his subsequent writings and, in general, look at its implications later in this book. For the moment, before returning to this notion of "social substance," I would like to make a few other remarks on the above quotations from Durkheim. In particular, I want to link them more systematically to our central focus: the problem of totality, or the whole/part relationship.

The above passages show that Durkheim did, in fact, conceive of his work as a study of the whole. He refers to the whole/part problem repeatedly throughout the book in precisely these terms. They have the character of a "formula" for him. Perhaps as important, he frequently discusses the whole/part problem even when he does not use this precise terminology. However, the uses of this particular set of terms is common enough to make us think that they are vital to the analysis. The categories of totality and of whole/part are clearly central to the book's structure, even when the concrete analysis takes Durkheim into a number of different manifestations of these general categories.

Durkheim also identifies the changing society/individual relationship as a particular instance of the various balances struck between whole and part under different circumstances. The analogy is clear—whole/part:society/individual. It should also be noted that the book's "starting point" in the problem of the changing relationships between individual personality and social solidarity is just that: a starting point. Durkheim had a good deal more on his mind.

The above quotations also suggest that the whole/part relation is not exhausted by reference to the society/individual problem. Indeed, it is striking how the whole/part problematic reappears in different guises throughout the work, especially in the form of the relationship between society, seen as a "whole," and its subgroupings, seen as "parts." One receives the strong impression that Durkheim is operating with a set of abstract categories which are instantiated in a variety of ways. These categories control the analysis. He evidently has a broad set of philosophical problems in mind. They have a logical, and almost certainly a chronological priority over his sociological conceptions and analyses. Durkheim develops his sociology with this philosophical tool kit, drawn from Aristotle, Spinoza, and others, in hand. He hardly ever relinguishes it, although he adds some new instruments along the way. Indeed, we hear particularly strong echoes in Durkheim's analysis of clan society of Aristotle's notion of a whole with "uniform" parts.

I hasten to add that Durkheim's approach is distinctive, if not entirely unique, among classical social theorists. There is nothing inherently "natural" about such a metaphor for the society/individual relationship or even for the view that sociology is the study of society. For example, Max Weber argued strongly against the view that sociology was the study of whole societies and offered a critique of some contemporary German writers about this issue (Weber 1975, 87–90, 199–205). Similar contrasts might be made with George Herbert Mead's work (Mead 1934). The point is that the language of whole and part reflects a particular philosophical assumption about reality being carried over into sociological discourse. As such, it helps mark the philosophical lineaments of Durkheim's thought and separates him from other writers.

What is equally interesting at this juncture in Durkheim's intellectual development is the fact that he freely mixes the metaphors in his discussion. The whole/part rhetoric is combined, and at times seemingly interchangeable, with the organism/organ metaphor. In turn, this latter distinction sometimes refers to the society/individual relationship and at other times to the society/subgroup relations. This makes for some indeterminacy in Durkheim's metaphorology, and in his theoretical and philosophical categories. This ambiguity has led many of his commentators to view him primarily as a proponent of an "organismic" image of society. While this view is not entirely false, at least not in Durkheim's early work, it also misses the central point: it is the whole/part categories which are regulative and not the organism/organ metaphor. The latter is a subset of the former, not the reverse. It is important to recognize this fact, if we are to understand Durkheim's use of his philosophical inheritance, his early work, and his later intellectual evolution. In fact, the organism metaphor is considerably muted in his later writings. However, the categorial focus (i.e. whole/part and totality) remains the same, although it is modified in the direction of a more self-conscious sociological focus on totality.

We should also note in the above quotations the appearance of Durkheim's central idea of the dependence of the individual on society. This notion of dependence is modified, strengthened, and deepened in his later work on religion. It is developed in a specifically sociological form and used to combat other religious variants of this idea inherited from the theological tradition, ones especially current among Protestant writers of his day (Nielsen 1987a). However, it is already in evidence in his first book as a general conception.

The remark quoted above about the transformations of "social substance" gives pause. What is Durkheim saying? Is he arguing merely that individuals must be freed from existing social constraints in order to form new group allegiances? I think not. Durkheim's language is telling and requires close examination. The construction is passive. There is no reference to active human agency. On its face, the phrase seems to imply a conception of the social as a "substance" which can undergo various modifications. At times, this "social substance" is bound into fixed structures which, as circumstances change, break apart and free the "substance" for the formation of new social structures. In the example of the changing forms of social solidarity, Durkheim seems to be arguing that the breakdown of the walls separating the "social segments" (primarily clans, but also other "segmentary" groupings) brings them into contact and, more important, recasts them into new forms. These new forms can only emerge if the "social substance" is allowed to recombine in new ways.

Durkheim's remarks on the nature of the primordial social unit, the horde, are helpful in this connection. He writes that the horde, although only a hypothetical construct not seen in pure form in reality (an "ideal type" to use Durkheim's own phrase), would have to be seen as "the true social protoplasm, the germ from which all social types would have emerged" (Durkheim 1984, 126; 1994b, 149). I would add that it is their logical antecedent and foundation. This group is conceived of as an "absolutely homogeneous mass whose parts would not be distinguishable from one another" and which would lack any distinct form or organization. As a result, it contains no differentiations, neither of groups nor individuals. When set within a primitive social structure, it becomes the clan, or a set of clans, and a segmentary society emerges. This latter type of society is historically prior to the later, more complex form. It also undergoes modifications, while retaining its basic features as a segmentary structure, and remains crucial even at more advanced phases of development. This segmentary type can be modified in the direction of larger territorial units without necessarily losing its segmentary character and, thus, mechanical solidarity can persist in the organization of much more advanced societies (Durkheim 1984, 135–36; 1994b, 162–63). Indeed, at a later point in the argument, Durkheim goes out of his way to note that the more advanced type of society, with a developed division of labor, does not result from the cooperation of individuals at all, but can only emerge from the previous societal type. Individuals as such could not be harmonized by cooperation into such a "coherent whole" (Durkheim 1984, 218; 1994b, 261). Only because there is a "whole" already established as a cohesive unity prior to the division of labor can there emerge such a differentiated system. The whole not only must preceed the parts, in the sense of individuals, but also any subsequent, more differentiated system of parts. "For social unities to be able to differentiate themselves, they must first be attracted or grouped together through the similarities that they display" (Durkheim 1984, 219; 1994b, 262). Association preceeds cooperation (Durkheim 1984, 220; 1994b, 262–63). Society is always prior to the individuals and all later developments necessarily imply the primitive segmental type as their predecessor (Durkheim 1984, 220–21; 1994b, 264). The "social substance" can be released and undergo modifications to form the more advanced type of society, but it is not so much the individuals who are thus loosened to recombine voluntarily in new ways as individuals, but the social substance itself which undergoes modifications under the impress of strictly mechanical forces. There is never a time when there is an individualistically based "social contract" (see his later critique of Rousseau on this point, Durkheim 1965). Society can only be gestated by society, just as Durkheim is to argue later that one must see the cause of any social development in previous social states (Durkheim 1982). This has been interpreted as a purely methodological dictum about social causation, part of Durkheim's theory of science and epistemology. But it also forms part of his social metaphysic. The social substance, already united in the hypothetical horde, a homogeneous mass in which all the units are identical, is structured at the beginning of all organized society in the form of clan based society, and undergoes new combinations, while always remaining social throughout and never dissolving into its individual parts. As we will see in *Suicide*, when and if the individual parts do break loose from their moorings, there is no society, no whole, at all in any meaningful sense. There is only an atomized, egoistic mass, rather like the individual balls which he criticized in Spencer's image or the grains of sand in a pile to which Durkheim is to refer later in illustration of his conception of an entity which is no true whole.

At this point, Durkheim's theory of the causes of the societal transformation needs to be introduced. This remains a debated aspect of his work. Durkheim's own later writings have perhaps helped to create some of the confusion about his basic position. However, in this work, Durkheim makes the clearest possible statement of his theory. It is surprising that he could be misunderstood, or understood in such diverse ways by later interpreters. The issues center on his conception of dynamic density or "concentration of the social mass" (Durkheim 1994b, 250). This term seems to imply a greater or lesser degree of intensity of social association, including a strong component of physical comingling. However, Durkheim also implies (rather inconsistently) that the process could perhaps have something to do merely with enhanced communication. In any case, the societal transition takes place under the influence of an increasing dynamic density. This is its central "cause" and, in Durkheim's view, it operates quite "mechanically" and "necessitate[s]" this change. About this latter fact, he is unambiguous (Durkheim 1984, 205, 212; 1994b, 244, 253). This increased social density is itself the expression of an increased population density, which in turn results from several causes, including both shifts in social morphology, that is, in the distribution of populations, but also an increase in absolute "volume" or total population size (Durkheim 1984, 205; 1994b, 244).

In *Division*, Durkheim was already willing to grant some exceptions to this rule and was later to soften, but not entirely relinquish his claim that increased volume itself was decisive (Durkheim 1984, 204–5; Durkheim 1982, 136–37, 146). He never altered his view that social density or concentration was decisive in societal change. I think confusion has resulted from Durkheim's seeming "retraction" of the earlier claim that dynamic density is a function of population volume. It has led to the view that his theory envisions social morphology, including social density, as an outcome or mere "sign" of the operation of collective representations (Schmaus,1994). This view is mistaken. Even with his modified position, his concept of dynamic density still retains a highly physicalistic cast. Durkheim never abandons this central idea of dynamic, collective association, even in its most physical sense. As we will see, it plays a central role throughout his writings, including his final book on religion. It is featured prominently in the work of his school (Mauss 1979b). Durkheim was willing to yield ground on the place of absolute numbers in these processes. This is characteristic of his general ambiguity about the role of number in society and his failure to address the category of number in any direct way, even in his mature theory of the categories.

More to the point is the relationship between this conception of social density and Durkheim's latent "substantivist" philosophy. I would suggest that the former is an expression of the latter. When joined, the two ideas (i.e. the whole and the concentration of the social mass) reveal Durkheim's basic assumption that society is, in some sense, a substance with latent creative powers, an assumption revealed repeatedly in various, if sometimes guarded fashion, from his first book on the division of labor to his last one on religion. However, it is not necessarily identical with any particular type of stable social structure, nor, even less, with the merely "interacting" individuals who are its parts. It is related, as Durkheim later emphasized in various ways, to the transformations and "rhythms" of societal life, the systole and diastole between the whole as a "social substance" in its unbound state versus its institutionalized forms. As we will see, this latter distinction is already introduced in the *Rules* and *Suicide* as the division between unbound and bound, free-floating and institutionalized, forces of society. In the *Forms*, the distinction reaches its fullest expression in the examination of societal concentrations and dispersions. In sum, there is evidence that Durkheim does indeed imply a philosophical conception of social substance which emerges within the interstices of his particular sociological analyses. It is not easily equated with the relations among independent "parts," but is largely identified with the different manifestations of unbound social concentrations, seen as peculiar kinds of manifestations of the "whole," one which logically (and perhaps chronologically) preceeds the individuals composing it. It is increasingly seen as a "force" or "power," perhaps the most creative power in existence.

This entire argument will appear odd to modern sociologists, schooled in the distinctions inherited from the time of Harry Alpert (1939). He set the tone for the later discussion by denying that Durkheim was a "substantial realist," and asserting that he was an "associational realist" (or what others have called a "relational realist"), who could not possibly have believed that society was a "substance." Variants of this view have been widely adopted by later sociologists (Wallwork 1972; Meštrović 1988; Schmaus 1994). Talcott Parsons (1937) also shares this general assumption, if little else, with the above authors. But Alpert overlooks the many passages where Durkheim uses precisely such a phraseology. He also interprets other seemingly "substantialist" remarks to exclude this possibility. He glosses over the critical fact that the category of substance also figures prominently in Durkheim's last book (and in the writings of his school). He especially fails to connect these references to Durkheim's emerging notion of the whole, which I take to be the key regulative idea in the analysis. The situation is more complex, and different, than Alpert or his followers allow. I concur instead with George Simpson's earlier estimate, criticized by Alpert (Simpson 1933; Alpert 1939), that Durkheim is at least ambiguous. At many points, he uses language which clearly suggests the "substantialist," and not merely the "associationist" position, even though, at other times, he draws back from such implications. But every turn in his later argument implies that his notion of "association" is itself not to be identified with individually based social interactions as sociologists now understand this notion (e.g. as social exchange, transaction, action, symbolic, or other social interaction, etc.). Such perspectives give an inordinate place to the individuals whose interactions constitute society, while Durkheim starts always with a whole which undergoes modifications and instantiations.

It might be argued that Durkheim's central argument in the *Division* is already focused on the association of representations. From this standpoint, Durkheim would be arguing from the outset that society is defined only by reference to collective representations and that these emerge (by some unspecified process) through the association of individual representations (Schmaus 1994). Social density is then interpreted in terms of collective representation. Of course, Durkheim does emphasize the place of the collective consciousness in the composition of segmentary societies and he frequently states (especially after the latter 1890s) that social life is somehow identified with collective representations and, therefore, is in some sense "mental," a sort of collective psychology. The idea that his standpoint remained unchanged and was consistently expressed in this view of collective representations is tempting. I also think it is fundamentally flawed. It leads to an "idealist" conception of Durkheim's theory. It uncouples the representational from other social dynamics to an unwarranted degree. It requires its exponents to argue that Durkheim never claimed any importance for social morphological causes in his first book. This argument is untenable and badly misrepresents *Division*. Moreover, as we will see, throughout his mature work, Durkheim consistently binds, yet separates the idea of social concentration and the purely representational within the context of a larger whole. His images of association refer to the collective activity of bodily co-present actors and cannot be identified exclusively with or subordinated to the association of collective representations. This perspective also eliminates the central problem in Durkheim's "sociology of knowledge," that is, the relationship between social structure and dynamics and the categories. This would certainly have puzzled Durkheim, who repeatedly argued that the categories took society's organization as their model. I see no way of escaping the fact that the collective representations which did interest Durkheim must be linked to something else that is also social, even substantial.

I am not supporting a materialistic interpretation of Durkheim's thesis. My view argues for both the fundamental "parallelism" which Durkheim establishes between collective representations and society as well as the unification of these two parallel spheres implied in his persistent use of the notion of the whole, or totality. It is precisely this system of rationales and their related rhetorical thrust which lead Durkheim (not without ambiguity) into a highly substantive image of society. Indeed, a substantivist reading of Durkheim's work is the only route through which we can achieve a relatively consistent Durkheim. All other interpretations end in aporias. This issue and the usages connected with it reach an apogee in his final book. They play an important role in delineating his particular brand of philosophically informed sociology, what I am calling his "sociological monism."

Another conclusion can be drawn tentatively at this point. Durkheim's early and shifting use of the whole/part rationale, his flirtation with substantivist language, and his repeated reliance on physicalistic images of social concentration and social forces are supplemented in his later work by a more systematic analysis of these very images themselves. The system of categories, especially the category of totality, as well as the images of substance and power, become objects of investigation. Durkheim attempts to explain sociologically the origin of the categories of totality. While the earlier work is guided by the categories of whole/part, there is no attempt made to explain them sociologically. The notion of totality in the form of the whole/part relation operates from outside of the sociological analysis as an externally imposed philosophical concept. It is not yet grounded in society. Ironically, the early Durkheim is more naively philosophical than the later Durkheim, who remains philosophical, yet is also much more sociological in his attitude toward the categories which he applied in his earlier work. His agenda after 1895 or so now requires that he take on the problems of philosophy and its categories as sociological problems. The potential for all these changes was clearly there in his first book, a fact noted implicitly by others (e.g. Cornford 1912). The *Division* was already a study of the whole and its differentiations.

In conclusion, I do not want, at this point, to exaggerate my claims about the issue of social substance. However, I do think Durkheim's usage is not accidental or merely metaphorical window dressing. This phrase appears in his review of Schäffle, his first book, and later again in the *Rules*. Throughout his career he gestured towards it in varying ways. To be fully appreciated, the references to social substance need to be joined with other key ideas in his rhetoric such as social density, concentration, social forces, energy, and so forth. These latter terms are all logically subsidiary to and imply the central idea of social substance, even if Durkheim is loath to parade this assumption. Indeed, without the first idea, the others make little sense, and appear as fragments broken away from some more central, but unknown root metaphor.

6

THE PROBLEM OF TOTALITY IN
DURKHEIM'S TRANSITIONAL PERIOD

Social Facts and the Whole/Part Problem in
The Rules of Sociological Method

Durkheim's *Rules* appeared originally in 1894 as two essays in the *Revue de Métaphysique et Morale*. They were published, with some small revisions, in book form in 1895 and a second edition came out in 1901, with an important new preface (see Berthelot's variorum edition, Durkheim 1988; Gane 1988). I will treat the entire work, including the second preface, in this section. This methodological study contains important early discussions of the themes of the present work. There one discovers some of the most unguarded statements of his position on the place of society in nature, the problem of social facts, the whole/part question, the differences between unstructured social currents versus social institutions, the nature of the social "energy," "force," and so forth which go into social facts, especially collective enthusiasms, and a number of other related issues. Many of Durkheim's most telling images appear in this work, indeed, in a form which was to confirm the worst suspicions gathered by his contemporaries from a reading of his first book. Here, the most extravagant claims, in the abstract, seem to be made for the "reality" of society, with little of the substantive sociological content which made plausible the analyses of his first and third books. As we have seen, some of his most direct remarks about Sir Francis Bacon's work also appear in the *Rules*. As Jean-Michel Berthelot (1995) has noted, his discussion of the whole/part problem plays a particularly important role in this text. It occupies a central place in the first chapter and reappears in slightly modified form in chapter 5. I want to focus on the whole/part problem and its relationship to several other key images in his work, especially the problem of force or energy, the reality of social facts, and the problem of constraint.

We have already noted above that Durkheim regularly uses a set of analogies to establish the reality of society as a being in its own right. This is often done in conjunction with the whole/part metaphor. For example, he compares society with material substances such as bronze, water, and others which are composed of parts, but which manifest a visible reality of their own as wholes, distinct from the parts which compose them. We need to examine these usages more closely from the standpoint of their utility as analogies and in relation to our main themes.

Durkheim's analogies are especially fascinating in one respect. The new entities of water, bronze, and so forth, created when their parts combine, are all objects visible to common sense. Although we know from scientific analysis that their distinctive existence emerges from a combination and synthesis of other elements, they appear to us in sense awareness as unifed, real objects in their own right. Durkheim regularly argues that the case is similar with society. However, society or social facts more generally are not visible in the same way. We can observe the coacting individuals who make up the "parts" of society (the "whole"), just as we can perceive the material objects connected with social existence. As we have already noted, in his earlier writings Durkheim sees the "substance" (*matière*) of society as composed of both material objects and human actors. While we can see the material objects connected with social activity, we do not and cannot observe an entity, society, in the same way that we see water, bronze, and so forth as a material "whole" created from a combination of "parts." Only in certain very limited settings (e.g. small groups, crowds, etc.) can we actually observe society. Of course, Durkheim is willing to substitute a variety of objectively observable measures as tokens of society, its real existence, solidarity and dynamics (e.g. population density, legal sanctions, suicide rates). But this is quite another matter than seeing the existing "whole" itself. As they stand, the analogies hardly serve to demonstrate Durkheim's strong thesis. Such phenomena can be interpreted in other, less "wholistic" fashion, as sociologists generally do today. When applied to the combination of human beings, the analogy breaks down at the level of sensory observation. Durkheim's persistent use of such metaphors, despite their limitations, is an indication of his commitment to them as well as to the philosophical standpoints embodied in them. This commitment has been overlooked by many commentators. They have broken off their analyses when they encounter his metaphors

(Wallwork 1972, 72–73), avoided them by one-sidedly emphasizing the idea of collective representations as an unobservable theoretical entity in his system (Schmaus 1994, 4–5), or otherwise applied "presentist" perspectives such as "agency" and "structure" or "voluntarism" to his work. They have convinced themselves that Durkheim did not really mean what he plainly asserts throughout his work. None of these approaches takes Durkheim's own language seriously. They fail to appreciate either the implications of his mode of argumentation or the dilemmas he created for himself in so arguing. Let us return from this point to a consideration of Durkheim's discussion of the "reality" of society in the *Rules*.

Durkheim reaffirms an argument already noted from *Division*, that society is a part of nature. In line with his view of "social facts" as "things," Durkheim argues (in a passage critical of Comte) that nature is composed only of things (Durkheim 1982, 63; 1988, 112). If sociology is to be a science, it must, therefore, deal with a certain class of objects or things. In his view, other schools of thought (e.g. natural law theory, Hobbes, and others) see only the individual and do not conceive of society as a natural phenomenon. Durkheim argues that social life is natural, not because it originates in the individual's nature, but "because it derives directly from the collective being, which is, of itself, a nature sui generis . . ." (Durkheim 1982, 144; 1988, 216). Individual consciousnesses in association give rise to a "new form of existence." Society constrains the individual, but also is a spontaneous product of reality. ". . . [T]he reality from which it (i.e. social life) emanates goes beyond the individual" (Durkheim 1982, 144; 1988, 91; also Durkheim 1982, 177). For Durkheim, society is a manifestation of nature and its study is not possible unless we affirm the "unity of nature," against any "metaphysical dualism" or "anthropocentric postulate," which grants humankind a privileged position in or outside of the world (Durkheim 1982, 46, 177). The postulate of the unity of nature is necessary, but not sufficient to ground the new science.

Durkheim sees both "anthropocentrism" and the refusal to adopt a "naturalistic" view of society as barriers to the advance of sociology. I call attention to his emphasis on the limitations of anthropocentrism for two reasons. First, as noted above, it ties him to Bacon's critique of the "four idols." Second, and more important, his attack on anthropocentrism is in considerable tension with his later view of this problem, beginning with such texts as *Primitive Classification*, but articulatated most fully in *Forms*. In those writings, Durkheim forges a theory of the role of human society within the larger cosmos which brings into play "sociocentrism," a sort of "collective anthropocentrism" which he contrasts with traditional "anthropocentrism" (Durkheim and Mauss 1963, 86).

Durkheim's discussion of the whole/part problem echos his previous book and is a harbinger of later themes. In attempting to establish social facts as a proper object of study, Durkheim argues that since they do not have "the individual for a substratum, they can have none other than society . . ." (Durkheim 1982, 52; 1988, 97). These social facts "penetrate" and impose themselves on the individual. It is interesting that Durkheim immediately makes a distinction between two types of social facts, institutions (i.e. well established beliefs and practices) and facts which are not found in "crystallised form," but have the same objective character and influence over the individual. He refers to these as "social currents," such as those found in an "assembly." Such social currents involve "great movements of enthusiasm, indignation and pity" and these originate in "no particular individual consciousness" (Durkheim 1982, 52–53; 1988, 98). He goes on to refer to the common emotion produced by an assembly, such as a crowd, but also to currents of opinion of longer duration (Durkheim 1982, 53; 1988, 99).

Durkheim makes a distinction familiar from his later work, when he argues that social facts are not social by virtue of their generality, but by being taken collectively. These collective states are refracted through individuals, but are then things of a different kind. The double character of these two categories of facts is demonstrated by their frequent separate appearance from each other. Collective facts do not exist only in a state of immanence in individuals. They are immanent in society. Social facts are general because they are collective, that is obligatory, not the other way around. They are conditions of the group repeated in the individual. "It is in each part because it is in the whole (*tout*), far from being in the whole because it is in the parts (*parties*)" (Durkheim 1982, 56; 1988, 103). An outburst of collective emotion is echoed in each individual because of the "special energy derived precisely from its collective origin" (Durkheim 1982, 56; 1988, 103).

Durkheim develops these arguments in several different ways. The image of an energy behind social facts is repeated in slightly modified form later in the book. It is a staple of Durkheim's theory. For example, Durkheim argues that in society the individual finds himself in the presence of a force or power which is superior to him, dominates him, and on which he is dependent. However, this force is an entirely natural one and the state of dependence is also natural (Durkheim. 1982, 143; 1988, 215). He adds that religion is a sensory or symbolic representation of this state of dependence, whereas science provides a more adequate and precise notion of it (Durkheim 1982, 143; 1988, 215). The appearance of a theme which is developed to its fullest only in the *Forms* is not surprising. Religion represents the reality of society to the individual, but in a form which is purely symbolic and appeals only to the senses. It is true only within these limits. Science delves more deeply into the truth behind religious symbols and accounts for the actual social reality which is their source.

The distinction between unbound social currents and the institutionalized forms of social constraint is of considerable interest. Durkheim does not identify constraint only with the institutionalized forms of social force, although he does continue to see the sanctions behind social norms as a proof of the constraining power of social facts. This argument is congruent with his method of demonstration in *Division*, where changes in the balance of types of legal sanctions (repressive and restitutive) were used to identify the shift in the form of social solidarity. However, in the *Rules*, this image of institutionalized social forces is coupled with the idea of unbound social tendencies, social facts which are equally external to the individual and as constraining as established institutions. This type of social forces is sometimes identified empirically with crowd behavior or related collective enthusiasms (e.g. Lebon 1960), an idea for which there is some warrant in Durkheim's text (Durkheim 1982, 52–53). I think it is more useful to see it as a theoretical development of Durkheim's earlier sense that the "social substance" undergoes modifications when older social segments are broken down and brought into contact with one another and mixed, so to speak, resulting in an increased social concentration. Indeed, his discussions of social types and the explanation of social facts, strongly imply the idea that the development from one type to another involves modifications in the composition and concentration of the social substance. These latter images of "concentration" are found in the *Rules* at precisely the point where he also discusses "association" (Durkheim 1982, 136; 1988, 205–7). They also play an important role in Durkheim's later discussion of the evolution of educational thought. Durkheim's conception is by no means derived from crowd psychology, nor is it limited to such phenomena. Rather, it is a more explicit recognition of the independent significance of the problems already raised in his first book, a recognition that was to be further modified in his later work. Durkheim never relinquished his early idea that "association," even among "representations," depended ultimately on a "social concentration" in the most physical sense.

The central fact is that Durkheim now features the problem of "social substance" more directly by focusing on the unbound social tendencies which also constrain the individual and serve to demonstrate the reality of society. These two forms of social constraint provide him a more general way of introducing a dynamic element or a concern with sociocultural change into the discussion, a concern already present in *Division*. This element grows in importance as his work matures, until, in the *Forms*, it serves as the molten core of social substance and force which gestates institutions and ideas, indeed, the idea of divinity itself. Durkheim shys away from thematizing this notion of social substance, and even goes out of his way at times to deny that he ever implied that society was such a substance. No one would claim that Durkheim fully develops this notion. However, I would argue that his work implies such an idea and, at many points, is largely incomprehensible without it.

Why does Durkheim consistently utilize the images of power, force, energy, and constraint when he argues for the idea that society is a reality? The fact that he does so has been well established by his commentators and evident from our survey of even his early writings. Such assertions also appear in his later work. As we will see, the seemingly mechanistic images of force and energy are, if anything, featured even more prominently in his masterwork on religion. He is evidently unable to conceive of society (or anything else) as a reality without conceiving of it as a force or power. The two images are inextricably intertwined. Society is a reality, sui generis, precisely because, and only because it is a force. Moreover, it can be studied scientifically only if it is a force, a source of power or energy, a reality which generates such forces. One is reminded of Freud's contemporaneous (but abandoned) effort to create a general psychology based on a concept of libidinal energy, a comparison which I cannot pursue in these pages (Freud 1954).

The source of this idea is not entirely clear. It is sometimes thought to have been borrowed from contemporary physics, just as his use of the image of synthesis is thought to come from chemistry and that his theory is entirely physicalistic (Vialatoux 1939; Takla and Pope 1985). I would not minimize the physicalistic dimension of Durkheim's theory and, in a sense, it is a central aspect of my interpretation. However, I think the root image of power or force comes from elsewhere than the contemporary sciences. Durkheim's aquaintance with these fields was almost certainly very incomplete, better in the biological and medical fields than elsewhere (Hirst 1975). In any case, his use of these images hardly goes beyond the metaphorical. They serve as metaphors in the demonstration of his main theses and as markers pointing to wider philosophical issues. This use did not require detailed knowledge of the modern sciences. It could have just as easily been derived from philosophical and religious sources. The religious tradition was widely familiar with the images of Divine power. Aristotle has a well-developed conception of energy. Philosophers since the seventeenth century had also regularly used the idea of force in connection with their philosophical images of reality. Indeed, I would suggest that it is in the work of such philosophers as Spinoza that Durkheim finds the idea that the reality of a thing is to be defined in terms of force or power. For example, in his a posteriori proof of the existence of God, Spinoza writes: ". . . since the ability to exist is power, it follows that the more reality that belongs to the nature of a thing, the more powers it has, of itself, to exist" (Spinoza 1985, 418).

Spinoza's images are strikingly similar to Durkheim's, both in the general form of the proof as well as in its application to the specific subject matter of religion. Both assume that the very reality and existence of a thing is to be equated with its force or power. Moreover, the greater the reality, the more power it displays. The greatest existent (i.e. God) is therefore to be seen as that entity with the greatest power. This type of argument is very similar to Durkheim's view that society also has a greater energy at its disposal than the individual for the production of outcomes. Finally, as with Spinoza, the greatest power is symbolized popularly in religious form (i.e. as God). However, for both authors, the truth (philosophical or sociological) is that God is also nature (substance with infinite attributes, God or nature, for Spinoza, society for Durkheim).

There is no escaping the circle of ideas and images which inform Durkheim's theory. Society, force, energy, religion are all bound together in his conception of reality. They are all modes (among others) of the totality which he is attempting to define (and, of course, dissect) and which he ultimately comes to see in terms of the self-identical trinity of divinity, totality and society. In his early work, Durkheim has not yet arrived at a satisfactory answer about how to conceptualize the whole. He has identified most of the cen-

tral elements which go into the mix, but only after the turn of the
century does he develop an understanding of the categories and a
more adequate account of religion and its relationship to society
and knowledge. Only then do his concepts begin to assume a more
systematic form. At this point, he remains dominated by the
whole/part analogy, which he fleshes out in ad hoc fashion with references to social concentration, energy, force, and so forth. Indeed,
he continues to use this language until the end of his career, even
when he adds new concerns and forms of explanation. The
whole/part metaphor is one of those philosophical tropes which
Durkheim never relinquishes, for it defines the essense of his philosophical problematic, even when he has altered his understanding
of its sociological bearings.

Religion, Totality, and Society in
Durkheim's Lectures on Socialism

Durkheim's lectures on socialism provide important leads
about our central themes. They were published posthumously by
Marcel Mauss, who also wrote an introduction to them. There he
reiterates what is already evident from *Division*, that the relationship of society and the individual was Durkheim's main problem.
He also remarks that Durkheim's interest in socialism was connected with his practical interests in social reform, but that
Durkheim deeply opposed struggle between classes and nations
and wanted changes "only for the benefit of the whole of society (*la
société toute entière*) and not of one of its parts (*fractions*) . . ."
(Durkheim 1962, 34; 1992, 29). Mauss also makes a rather cryptic
reference to the fact that circles existed at that time (i.e. circa 1895)
which commented on Marx's work like others commented on Spinoza (Durkheim 1962, 34; 1992, 29). The precise meaning of this
remark and its bearing on our discussion is not transparent. Does
it refer to any activities of Durkheim or members of his school? As
I have noted above, Mauss at this time was also engaged in the
study of religion, at Durkheim's suggestion, and, in particular, in
the study of Spinoza's philosophy. In general, the context seems to
imply a disparaging comparison, that both authors' texts were the
object of "cults" by groups which studied their works closely to
unearth their secrets. However, little can be concluded from this
particular remark, except that Spinoza was very much in the air at
that time.

The lectures on socialism were delivered in 1895, the same year as the series of lectures (now lost) on religion to which Durkheim himself attributed so much importance. The fact that Durkheim was teaching about the history of socialist doctrine and the problem of religion at the same time suggests that we might look for hints in the socialism series concerning the problem of religion, totality, and society. They are not hard to find. However, we must be cautious in reading them. Since these lectures do discuss questions related to our present focus, it is especially important to determine when he is presenting his own ideas or those of Saint-Simon and his followers, and, in the latter instance, whether or not he agrees or disagrees with their ideas.

Durkheim's view of socialism is quite clear. He distinguishes between communist utopias and socialism, properly conceived. The former have been around since the time of Plato, and are largely the literary product of isolated intellectuals. Such doctrines include a strong element of asceticism and a general animus against property ownership. Only if the inherent human tendencies to greed and, consequently, vice are curbed can society be perfected. Such formulations are utopian, in the sense of having no principled connection with any existing social structure, and can be found at any point in history.

By contrast, socialism requires definite historical conditions, which have only emerged as a permanent feature of society in modern times. As a result, the first inklings of socialism only begin to appear in the eighteenth century, and only blossom in the nineteenth. Durkheim defines socialist theories as those which insist upon a close connection between economic functions and "the directing and knowing organs of society" (Durkheim 1962, 56; 1992, 51). He later adds that theories can be socialist even if they are not directly related to the economic order, but have a connection with it. While socialism is defined essentially by its economic concepts, it is capable of being extended beyond them (Durkheim 1962, 63; 1992, 57). It is not concerned with narrow questions, such as that of wages or any other such issue, but the relation of the economy to the rest of the community. Socialism aspires to a reorganization of "the social body, by relocating the industrial apparatus within the totality (*l'ensemble*) of the organism" (Durkheim 1962, 61; 1992, 55). Communist theories attempt to develop the moral life of the state's leaders and therefore isolate them from the economic arena. Socialist theories envision the state creating a "a union between the various industrial and commercial relations, for which it would be

like a *sensorium commune*" (Durkheim 1962, 72; 1992, 65–66). We
will need to return to the idea of a "common sensorium." It appears
already in Renouvier and will later concern Durkheim in connection with religion. For now, let us move ahead with Durkheim's
analysis. Communist theories separate the community, especially
its leaders, from the economy just as the sacred is separated from
the profane, thus giving all earlier communist utopias a religious
(perhaps even a primitive?) quality.

Socialist theories could emerge only with modern society.
Among modernity's central features is the increase in importance
and scale of economic activities and the fact that social activities
take on a more self-consciously human character (by which
Durkheim apparently means a secular character). Also, the state
must have become stronger so that its regulatory role does not seem
to exceed its capacities. Finally, it is crucial that the economic system expose itself to the influence of the state, if the state is to perform its unifying role (Durkheim 1962, 76–79; 1992, 69–71).

Durkheim reviews the early history of socialist thinking in the
eighteenth century, but his remarks on the socialism of Saint-
Simon and his followers, especially Saint-Armand Bazard, are of
the greatest interest. For Saint-Simon, society can be reformed only
if there is developed an encyclopedic compendium of the sciences as
the adequate basis for such changes. This task also requires the
development of a new science, "social physiology," or what Auguste
Comte later called "sociology." This new science, once created, takes
on this encyclopedic task. Its aim is to "synthesize all human
knowledge and embrace the whole universe, while remaining
homogeneous; in fact, no longer consisting of any but positive sciences, it would itself be positive, in its whole (*ensemble*) as in its
parts" (Durkheim 1962, 134; 1992, 125). This new human science
will be modeled on the existing natural sciences, since humanity is
merely part of nature. Since "the universe is one," the same method
can be used to investigate each of its "parts" (Durkheim 1962, 135;
1992, 125). Strongly organismic language is used by Durkheim to
describe the new science and its object. He credits Saint-Simon
with being one of those who discovered the notion that "the social
being . . . is not a simple aggregate of individuals, a simple sum, but
a reality sui generis, which has a distinct existence and a nature
which is peculiar to it." He quotes Saint-Simon's remark that society is an "organized machine (*machine organisée*), all of whose
parts contribute in a different way to the movement of the whole,"
and, in a quick gloss, adds that Saint-Simon is describing "the

social organism" (Durkheim 1962, 136–37; 1992, 127).

The odd juxtaposition of mechanical and organismic metaphors is worth noting. They are both used to capture the more general notion of a whole and its parts, each doing so in markedly different language. Durkheim clearly preferred organic to mechanical metaphors for modern society (as we have already seen from his review of Tönnies). A similar comment could be made about Saint-Simon's repeated reference to the notion of the social whole as a system of functions (Durkheim 1962, 189; 1992, 176). Durkheim notes that this analysis in terms of whole and part, and the emphasis on the need for a directing agency for the economy, reoccurs at other points in Saint-Simon's work. It distinguishes Saint-Simon's view from that of the classical economists, since the latter conceived the economy in individualistic terms, while for Saint-Simon, it represents "the whole substance (*toute la matière*) of politics" (Durkheim 1962, 178–79; 1992, 167; for other references to the Saint-Simonian notion of the economic life as a social substance see 1962, 188, 195, 238; 1992, 175).

Durkheim detects a movement in Saint-Simon's ideas from an earlier emphasis on the sole authority of the sciences and the reconstruction of society on a purely secular foundation, to a later phase where religion and moral sentiments play an increased role (Durkheim 1962, 222ff.; 227). Saint-Simon thought the new social organization and its ideas had to be international in scope if they were to be effective. National patriotism is merely another form of egoism. The international organization of scientists and professionals generally provide the basis for such a new wave of internationalism, and not the relations among national states. Cosmopolitanism and industrialism go hand in hand for Saint-Simon. Such professonal sentiments have a greater degree of universality and are a formidable antagonist to narrow national spirit. Ultimately, a European wide organization would be succeeded by a new social organization embracing the whole of humanity (Durkheim 1962, 217, chap. 9 generally).

The organization of international life will not be possible on the basis of industry and science alone, but will require a new morality and religion of a similarly international scope. The unity of the sciences, physical and moral, leads naturally to a unified religious view, since religion's true function is not to provide a super-terrestial object for man's devotion, but to provide for "the sentiment of the unity of reality" (Durkheim 1962, 225; 1992, 209). The unifying agency of the universal law of gravity, drawn from the sciences, finds its complement in the religious idea that this law is a divine one. In a particularly evocative passage, Durkheim explains;

> The idea of God and the idea of the fundamental law are therefore only two faces of the same idea, the idea of unity. Viewed from one side, this unity would appear under its more particularly abstract, scientific, metaphysical form; seen from the other, under its sensible and religious form. (Durkheim 1962, 226; 1992, 211)

Durkheim quickly emphasizes that this interpretation of Saint-Simon is not at all fanciful and goes on to quote some passages from that author confirming his reading. Indeed, it is precisely the sentiment of universal unity which best characterizes Saint-Simon's perspective (Durkheim 1962, 228; 1992, 212).

Durkheim thinks that Saint-Simon's religious view divorces religion from the specific idea of God, and is free of anthropomorphisms (Durkheim 1962, 231; also 151 for a similar remark about Comte; 1992, 215). The aim of his "new Christianity" is to create a religious system in which "everything in nature participates in the divine" (Durkheim 1962, 232; 1992, 216). The universe is one and divinity is immanent in the world, a thesis which is as far as possible from any notion of duality (Durkheim 1962, 232–33; 1992, 217).

Durkheim concludes by saying that the "Saint-Simonian religion can be nothing other than a pantheism asserting the fundamental identity of all beings and deifying extension as well as thought" (Durkheim 1962, 234; 1992, 218). This view is, on one side, scientific, on the other, religious, and both without contradiction, since ". . . pantheism, or at least a certain kind of pantheism, also has this double aspect. For as the God, whose existence it recognizes, can only be at one with Nature, it can be regarded sometimes as nature studied by the sciences, sometimes as the divinity adored by religion" (Durkheim 1962, 234; 1992, 218).

Durkheim proceeds to trace the later development of Saint-Simon's ideas in his follower Saint-Armand Bazard. Among these developments is the identification of religious ideas with thought in general and with the solidarity of society. In Bazard's variant of pantheism, everything emerges out of religion. Religion provides the sole basis of unity. It is the most effective curb on egoism, thus guaranteeing social solidarity.

Finally, Durkheim offers several interesting criticisms of both Saint-Simon and Bazard. Since they begin with economic interests as the substance of society and locate the material and the spiritual on the same plane, the only religion they can develop is a "materialist pantheism." He further suggests that "[T]he God of this pantheism was only another name for the Universe and could not constitute a moral power" of any use to humanity (Durkheim 1962, 279; 1992, 260). The result is a deification of matter and material needs and a "mystical sensualism," which is incapable of curbing the passions and, indeed, ends by encouraging comfort and ease.

We have not provided a full summary of all Durkheim's observations about socialism in these rich lectures, but have focused on those issues central to the present work. However, certain points emerge with great clarity. One is Saint-Simon's image of the state as the "universal sensorium." Durkheim could hardly have accepted the state in this role. He could and did accept some version of the idea of a universal sensorium. He cast religion in this role. In a letter of 1899 to Gaston Richard, published by Richard only in 1920, Durkheim notes that religion's role in the representative life of society is comparable to that of sensation in the individual.

> Just as we sense things under the forms of colors, etc., society represents its life and that of objects with which it is in contact under the form of sacred things. It colors them with religiosity. (Durkheim 1975, II:9)

Richard thought this letter proved that Durkheim already had the central ideas for his 1912 volume on religion worked out as early as 1899. While I think Richard exaggerates the value of the letter as a proof of his own claim, it does demonstrate that only a few years after his lectures on socialism and his turn toward the topic of religion, Durkheim saw its role as that of a sensorium of society and, in this respect, perhaps as an alternative to the Saint-Simonian state. We will need to examine the implications of this idea further when we look at his mature treatment of religion. For the moment, I would add only that the notion of religion as a "universal sensorium" strengthens Durkheim's image of society as a "being" and a "reality" beyond the individuals who compose it by establishing its added need for a "sensory" system. This image is also congruent with Durkheim's "parallelism." Not only do individual representations appear in parallel to the individual body, but society itself, as a "whole," contains collective representations, preeminently found in religious form, which parallel those of its social structure. Finally, as we have already seen, Renouvier had raised the question of a "universal sensorium." Durkheim's treatment allows him to begin resolving another philosophical problem inherited from Renouvier.

These lectures also address the question of pantheism. On the one hand, it is clear that Durkheim rejects Saint-Simonian pantheism, indeed, calls it a "materialistic pantheism" (where "materialistic" is certainly a term of criticism for Durkheim). In doing so, he evokes the dualistic distinction between the spirit and the senses. It would be easy to conclude that Durkheim was a dualistic, through and through, and simply rejected any solution to modern society's problems couched in pantheistic terms, even when the solution did rely heavily, in a fashion generally supported by Durkheim, on a renovation of religion and morality. However, our discussion has also brought to light the fact that Saint-Simon's doctrines, as reconstructed by Durkheim, bear a striking resemblance at several points to Durkheim's own later doctrine. At this point in our discussion, I do not wish to demonstrate all these similarities. They will become clearer from my later discussion of the *Forms*. I will mention only that Durkheim also attributes a great importance to the problem of unity or the whole, places sociology in the position of a unifying social science, gives sociology itself the role of both accounting for the true nature of religion as well as providing the foundation of adequate knowledge for a reformed social system, and has a similarly keen desire to gestate social solidarity on an international, cosmopolitan basis, and not only through the agency of professional groupings. Even when there is a disagreement, for example, between Saint-Simon's notion of the economy as the "social substance" and Durkheim's clearly more sociologistic conception of this idea, there is a similar focus of attention.

It is striking that Durkheim should bother to emphasize Saint-Simon's notion of social substance, just as he had raised the same issue in his review of Schäffle. Most important, when Durkheim offers his critique of their pantheism, his criticism is presented in terms which imply that this particular type of pantheism is inadequate, but that another version might not be. The central idea of this particular version of pantheism—the identification of the whole of nature with divinity—is rejected by Durkheim. However, his own later identification of totality, divinity, and society, reiterated at several points in his work, opens the door for a tempered pantheism, a "pantheism of society" (see Durkheim 1995a, 245), which initiates the unification of nature through the medium of society itself. When we note how much importance Durkheim later attributes to society in the gestation of religion and the categories, we will be in a better position to see just how far he goes in the direction of a modified pantheistic solution to his theoretical dilemmas.

Had Durkheim drawn more than he realized from Saint-Simon's spirit? My sense is that the Saint-Simonian legacy in Durkheim is, indeed, very strong, but that Durkheim's final standpoint ultimately owes as much to Spinoza. It is worth recalling that Saint-Simonian pantheism itself was developed under the partial influence of Spinoza's ideas (Bouglé and Halévy 1924). Durkheim's formulation of Saint-Simon's position is accomplished in a way which features Spinozistic images as well as ones found in his own later work. When he writes of Saint-Simon's theory that "the idea of God and the idea of the fundamental law are only two faces of the same idea, the idea of unity" and later adds that "a certain kind of pantheism" sees God as one with nature, he has, in effect, already identified and interrelated the three key elements in his own later perspective.

Totality and Its Modes in *Suicide*

The sociological analysis of suicide raises difficult, yet central issues for our present interpretation of Durkheim's work. Published in 1897, it was already completed by 1895 (see Pickering 1984, 51, 228). It is located in that banner year for Durkheim, an exceedingly complex one, in which he published the book version of the *Rules*, effectively completed the work on suicide, presented his first extensive lectures on socialism, underwent the self-described "revelation" connected with his first lectures on religion, and helped set Mauss on a clearer path for the study of both religion and the work of Spinoza. It is not surprising that Durkheim later saw this period as one of great transition in his thinking, in which his previous work had to be "started all over again." The mixture of topics and questions and the intense pace of work at this time have all the earmarks of a personal "effervescence," perhaps for the emerging Durkheim school, even a collective one. The book on suicide is part of this wider intellectual milieu.

It is a complex book, although it has frequently been taken in very straightforward fashion by later interpreters. On the one hand, as Robert Merton (1968) once suggested, it is perhaps the paradigmatic work of classical theory and research in sociology, establishing the model for the future (especially in America). There exist treatments of the book from this angle of vision (Douglas 1967; Pope 1976; Lester 1994). My aim is to link its theoretical argument to our main philosophical themes. From this standpoint, the book is not only a contribution to the mainstream of sociology, but also a work with deeper philosophical dimensions, indeed, with a complexity that is occasionally daunting. I will argue that there is no understanding this well-known classic of sociological "positivism" without seeing it as a study of the whole/part problem and the modes of totality.

It is not surprising that the book contains familiar references to Durkheim's central idea. It's preface states the characteristically Durkheimian theme in stark form: unless societies exist, there can be no sociology, and societies cannot exist if only individuals exist (Durkheim 1951, 38; Durkheim 1975, I:48). The rather "ontological" ring of this assertion is pure Durkheim. It is the sort of statement which alerted his contemporaries and made them immediately suspect that Durkheim was arguing more than a narrowly scientific case. It might easily be disregarded today as the expression of a strategic attack on individualistic, psychological explanations (which, of course, it also is) or the attempt to establish another emergent, nominal level of analysis. However, later in the book, Durkheim once again defends his sociological analysis of suicide, by remarking that "Collective tendencies have an existence of their own; they are forces as real as cosmic forces though of another nature . . ." (Durkheim 1951, 309; 1995a, 348–49). He argues for the reality of collective social forces by reference to the uniformity of their effects, ones demonstrated earlier in the book. Moral acts like suicide are reproduced with an equal uniformity and depend on forces external to individuals. These forces must be moral, but apart from individuals, society is the only "moral being" and, therefore, these forces must be social. Durkheim adds that the precise name for such forces is less important than our recognition of their reality. It is especially important that we "conceive of them as a totality (*ensemble*) of energies which cause us to act from without, like the physico-chemical forces to which we react." They are not verbal entities, but things sui generis, indeed, in Durkheim's view, ". . . they may be measured, their relative sizes compared, as is done with the intensity of electric currents or luminous foci." Social facts are objective, a proposition which defies common sense (Durkheim 1951, 309–10; 1995a, 349).

Durkheim defends his main thesis, especially against the criticisms of Gabriel Tarde, by arguing that collective tendencies are of a different nature than individual ones. When individuals combine, they form a new type of psychical being, with its own way of thinking and feeling. While individual minds contain "elementary properties" which make social facts possible, the latter arise only when these properties are "transformed by association." Association produces "special effects" and is "something new" (Durkheim 1951, 310; 1995a, 350).

This argument from "association" has become familiar to readers of Durkheim and is often taken as the key reference point in Durkheim's theses about the reality of society. But I want to emphasize that Durkheim's argument does not end there, nor is "association" his ultimate rationale. He immediately proceeds to prove his case by reference to the whole/part idea as well as to another fascinating set of categories. Durkheim writes that the only way to dispute his argument is "to admit that a whole (*tout*) is qualititively identical with the sum of its parts, that an effect is qualitatively reducible to the sum of the causes which engendered it . . ." (Durkheim 1951, 311; 1995a, 350). But such an approach makes all change inexplicable. As Durkheim mounts his counterattack against Tarde, he utilizes this motif in another interesting way, by arguing that it is superficial to criticize his theory as "scholasticism." Although he and his school refuse to find the substratum of social phenomena in individual consciousness, they instead locate it elsewhere, in "that (i.e. that substratum) which is formed by uniting and combining all the individual consciousnesses." He adds that this substratum is not "substantival or ontological," but instead is "nothing other than a whole composed of parts (*tout composé de parties*). But it is just as real, nevertheless, as the elements that make it up . . ." (Durkheim 1951, 319; 1995a, 361). It is worth dwelling for a moment on this remarkable and rather confusing defense, in the midst of what is taken as Durkheim's most "positivistic" treatise.

First, let us note the reappearance of the whole/part rationale at the decisive point in the proof. We have already seen the whole/part rationale serve a number of different purposes for Durkheim. It has an omnibus quality. It appears here very much like the "formula" found in his first book. It is one of his central modes of argumentation for his main theses, but it is not altogether unified or transparent. It is remarkable that Durkheim uses it here and elsewhere to defend his main contentions against Tarde (and others). In fact, it proves nothing at all with any certainty, except perhaps that Durkheim is willing to rely on metaphors in his analysis and finds such a philosophical category "satisfactory" (Hulme 1924). At minimum, it tells us how unquestioned a category it was in his thought. It is unlikely that Tarde would be convinced by such a "proof" or see in it anything but a confirmation of his view of Durkheim's theory.

In the above passage, Durkheim employs the additional distinction between quantity and quality in conjunction with the whole/part conception, and links both to his notion of cause and effect. We have noted Davy's comment (1911) that early in his student career Durkheim had planned to carry out psychological studies of the problems of quantity and quality, but gave up this plan in favor of his focus on morality and society. This distinction remained important for Durkheim. Its appears not only here, but as an organizing motif in his essay on the two laws of penal evolution (Durkheim 1978, 153–80). It also surfaces more briefly in the writings of Henri Hubert and Marcel Mauss (1929).

Here, he argues that wholes are qualititively different from the parts composing them; effects are qualitatively different from the sum of their individual causes. Durkheim seems to rest the whole/part distinction on an even more basic pair of notions, that is, quantity and quality. Wholes are qualitatively and not merely quantitatively different from their constituent parts. But how? What exact "quality" distinguishes them from their parts (other than the tautological fact that they are, by definition, wholes)? Moreover, if wholes are "effects," even if they are qualitatively different from the sum of their causes and parts, then they can hardly be prior—in any sense—to their parts, as Durkheim regularly asserts elswhere in his work. This is all very confusing. The logical and ontological seem to be thoroughly mixed up in this crossing of categories. Even if we are willing to grant Durkheim some analytical latitude, we must still maintain that he has hardly worked out the use of these terms with any consistency. My sense is that he cast off the quantity and quality distinction as a central one precisely because it rested uncomfortably with the whole and part problem. Its rather rare appearance here only serves to mark its secondary significance.

It is more difficult to understand Durkheim's emphasis on the problem of causality in the midst of his whole/part discussion. There is little question that the category of causality was central to his epistemology (Berthelot 1995). It appears in his three books of the 1890s. He insists upon casual analysis in the *Rules* and provides important illustrations of its operation in *Division* and *Suicide*. Yet the causal analysis, with its "linear" reasoning and temporal horizon, wreaks havoc with the "simultaneity" implied in the whole/part analogy. Durkheim elsewhere seems quite aware of this fact and, as we will see, goes out of his way to argue that cause and effect are less like means and ends than they are like a circle of forces which encompasses the elements within its field (Durkheim 1975, II:210; 1983, 67). He also uses a discourse of temporal simultaneity, as he did in his review of Jean-Marie Guyau, to account for the individual/society relationship and to evade the linear implications of his causal language. Indeed, his entire sense of the transformation from the undifferentiated, homogeneous horde to organized clan society implies less a causal process than the emergence of the whole/part relation itself. In these ways, he moves the causal sequences back into a whole/part or, often, a circular metaphor.

As we will see, the discussion of causality takes on an entirely new character in the later work of Durkheim (and Hubert and Mauss). The earlier use of cause and effect to account for social pheneomena is supplanted by a study of the sociocultural roots of causality as a category and, in so far as this takes place, it is no longer possible for Durkheim to utilize the notion of cause as he did in his early work. The entire structure of Durkheim's theorizing is effected when the category of causality itself becomes one of several categories which are to be accounted for sociologically. This move represents another instance of the overall shift in Durkheim's work toward a more self-conscious sociological understanding of the categories and, in the process, a more nuanced sense of their use. The category of cause (along with time, space, substance, the person, etc.) increasingly becomes one mode of the totality of society, one which is structured by and through society. This raises the most difficult problems for Durkheim. It places an even greater burden on his new science of sociology. Sociology now becomes not only a science of causes and consequences, but also a science of the modes of thought themselves, including causality. If the historical changes in the category of causality must be explained sociologically, each new historical form of the notion of cause must be correlated with the types of thinking available to members of the society at that moment and, ultimately, with the types of society themselves.

These references to the whole/part problem are not the only aspect of *Suicide* of interest for our present purposes. I want to return to the text and examine the central elements of Durkheim's theory of suicide, including his discussion of egoism, altruism, anomie, and fatalism. I want to show how they are related to the whole/ part question, the problem of totality, and to what I am calling Durkheim's emerging sociological monism. A careful examination of its theoretical logic reveals that this most "positivistic" of Durkheim's writings is deeply saturated with the sort of philosophical implications of interest to us.

It is useful to recall Marcel Mauss's comment, in his introduction to the posthumously published lectures on socialism, that Durkheim took for his main problem the relationship between individual and society (Durkheim 1962, 32; Tiryakian 1962). We have already seen that *Division* is also concerned with this question, and have attempted to show the ways in which this problem is merely a variant of the larger, more general, issue of whole/ part. When we examine *Suicide*, it quickly becomes clear that this book is also focused on the same problem (i.e. society and the individual), although it approaches it with different tools and, in fact, goes more deeply into the question.

The book maps out a set of categories of moral experience which, on inspection, turn out to be part of a more inclusive perspective. All sociologists know that Durkheim proposed an explanation of the social suicide rate by reference to four social causes of suicide. He entitled these four causes egoistic, altruistic, anomic, and fatalistic suicide. He devoted a good deal of attention to the first three types, but said little about the fourth (i.e. fatalistic), aside from some brief, if telling remarks consigned to a footnote at the end of the sixth chapter of his second book, comments which hardly tap the real suggestiveness and potential value of this concept. The anomic and egoistic types are given the most attention, since they are most integrally related to the situation of modernity. With several important exceptions, the altruistic type is most closely related by Durkheim to experience in "traditional" societies. Sociologists have generally paid the greatest attention to the concept of anomie, cherishing it as one of their profession's most important discoveries (Orru 1987).

My concern is less with any one of Durkheim's concepts, taken alone, than with the network of concepts taken together. When seen as a matrix of categories, which define the horizons of experience, they take on a very different quality than when they are treated separately as causes. Durkheim's analysis establishes a relationship of polar opposition among his four categories. There is a fourth type of suicide (i.e. the fatalistic) opposed to anomic suicide, "just as egoistic and altruistic suicides are opposed to each other . . ."

(Durkheim 1951, 276; 1995a, 311). The implications of this remark are considerable. It is odd that Durkheim does not develop them.

The sense in which these types of social causes are "opposed to each other" is certainly puzzling. At the most obvious level, they constitute opposites because they reflect extremes of the presence or absence of particular social forces. Egoism is the opposite of altruism because egoism represents the "insufficient presence" of society in the individual, especially the absence of "collective activity," while altruism is a state of "too rudimentary individuation," in which "the ego is not its own property" and one's goal is found entirely outside of oneself (Durkheim 1951, 221; 1995a, 238). The same relationship can be easily established between anomic and fatalistic suicide. In an anomic condition, human acitivity is released from all restraint, a "longing for infinity" establishes itself in the soul, and "reality seems valueless by comparison with the dreams of fevered imaginations" (Durkheim 1951, 257, 256; 1995a, 285, 287). By contrast, fatalistic suicide derives from excessive regulation, with "passions violently choked by oppressive discipline" (Durkheim 1951, 276; 1995a, 311).

From this rather conventional description of Durkheim's theoretical logic, it is easy to move toward the conceptualization of two continuous "variables," group integration and normative regulation, and then view the entirety of Durkheim's work as an effort to demonstrate the fit between this bivariate conceptual framework and the varieties of social suicide rates among different groups, seen as indices of the groups' varying social or moral states. There is nothing intrinsically wrong with such a "scientific" reading of Durkheim. Sociologists since his time have acquired considerable mileage out of this interpretation. Indeed, it calls valuable attention to Durkheim's keen interest in the possible measurement of social forces. However, it does not go very far toward unearthing the wider theoretical and philosophical problems haunting his book.

Durkheim makes the remark, early in his book, that "suicides are only the exaggerated form of common practices" (Durkheim 1951, 45; 1995a, 7), thus immediately linking "pathological" to "normal" social practices. As a result, he is extremely sensitive to the fact that acts of suicide emege out of, and thus, are an integral part of the commonly shared moral order of society. They are not monstrous growths which can be sheared from the social body by some act of moral vivisection—although he knows that this is precisely what is attempted by the preventative practices of society's "morally healthy" members. Rather, they are the expressions of the very moral values which constitute the social order itself.

Durkheim later extends this basic insight when he argues that suicides are merely "the exaggerated or deflected form of a virtue" (Durkheim 1951, 240; 1995a, 263). If virtues and vices are so intimately connected, it frequently becomes difficult to disentangle them. As Durkheim notes, the experience of anomie is really the twin brother of the notion of progress. Egoism, altruism, and anomie are combined in every moral idea, but in differing proportions in different societies. This is the case because social life simultaneously assumes that the individual possesses a personality, is ready to sacrifice it if the community demands, and is also open to change or "progress." In all societies, these three currents of opinion coexist. They each constrain the person, pulling in three different and even contradictory directions. When they offset one another, "the moral agent is in a state of equilibrium" and this shelters the person from the thought of suicide. But if one of these forces exceeds "a certain degree of intensity to the detriment of the others . . . it becomes suicidogenic, while individualizing itself" (Durkheim 1951, 321; 1995a, 363).

Let us note Durkheim's reiteration that each type of suicide—save the fatalistic, whose analogues he appears unable or unwilling to trace—corresponds to a central and recurrent mode of social organization. In his own language, suicide is a deflected form of a virtue. This "mirroring effect" in moral experience and expression is remarkable. It allows us to establish a set of correspondences between "pathological" forms of expression and commonly shared moral virtues. Durkheim has already begun this job. Anomie and progress are analogues. Anomie is the preeminent "disease of the infinite" (Durkheim 1951, 287; 1995a, 324; also 1951, 248; 1995a, 274), but this sense of infinite striving is attached to our central value of progress (perhaps our only real value, in which all others become increasingly submerged). Egoism as a pathology is similarly connected with the value of individual autonomy and moral personality. Of course, Durkheim is keenly aware that anomie and egoism are intimately associated experiences, which can be distinguished from one another only by the sort of careful theoretical analysis attempted in his book (Durkheim 1951, 258, 287; 1995a, 288, 324). Altruistic suicide is a type evidently connected with our highest moral values. When we sacrifice ourselves—the very word is laden with positive moral overtones—for the community or the group which has nurtured us, we give back the life it has given us and indeed are obligated to do so when requested. While fatalistic suicide seems less closely related to a value (or, at least, Durkheim does not link it to one), its negative emphasis on the idea of passions which are choked and horizons which are limited would lead us to associate it with the positive value of order and temperate rule.

It is of interest that Durkheim sees "moral health" in terms of a balance between opposing social forces which operate on the individual. When the four opposing forces are in balance or equilibrium, then society (and the individual) is in a state of moral health. When one force predominates in society and pulls more strongly on the individual, then pathologial manifestations are most likely to emerge. The harmony or balance of opposing forces is the best state. Here, Durkheim seems to recast a theory which is developed in a similar form in ancient Greek thought.

In both Thucydides and in Aristotle's *Ethics*, the notion emerges that virtue is a "balance" or "mean" between opposing values (Aristotle 1995; Nielsen 1996b). If we can conceive of Durkheim's fourfold sense of moral experience in terms of two axes which cross one another, the optimum state of moral health is achieved when the individual is at the crossroads of the two axes, the meeting point of the ordinate and abscissa, ground zero of moral life. From this standpoint, the extremes or pathologies of moral life are found in the circle defined by the orbit of the points at the furthest remove from this center. All other points within this circle represent the infinite variety of mixtures of the four defining forces of moral experience, with groups and individuals clustering in one or another of the four main quadrants defined by these coordinates. As we will see below, this circular or "field" metaphor is not entirely fanciful or even alien to Durkheim's analysis. In general, this image and the accompanying whole/part metaphor rest uncomfortably with those "formulae" of his which envision rates of suicide resulting in inverse variation from social causes (Durkheim 1951, 208; 1995a, 222).

This brief examination of Durkheim's central theoretical ideas is meant to demonstrate the complexity of his analysis. As he notes, the entire system of concepts is interpreted in terms of collective forces or tendencies. Anomie, egoism, altruism, and fatalism as causes are systems of social or moral forces which exercise constraint over the individual, are individualized in them. They appear especially related to the "freefloating" forces identified in the *Rules*. There is little doubt that in presenting such a sociological and causal analysis of suicide, Durkheim is once again taking up the question of society and the individual, the whole and the part. It therefore seems appropriate to link his fourfold conceptualization of suicide to this wider problem. Let us look first at the "society" and the "whole" side of the picture.

Society is a whole made up of collective forces or tendencies which distribute themselves according to a fourfold set of possibilities. This division establishes four modes of social force which occur throughout the social totality. These four modalities of force operate to either increase or decrease the constraint found in the four concrete types of causes. The drawing together of these fourfold forces to a point of fully balanced, optimum pressure on the individual would be a state of social equilibrium or health. By implication, any excessive pressure of one of these four competing social forces on the individual leads to a deformation of the individual consciousness and a potentially pathological response. While Durkheim focuses on social rates of suicide, which result from the operation of these collective forces, he also is keenly interested in the individual forms of the different types of suicide, and devotes an entire chapter to this problem (Durkheim 1951, chap. 6). If we look at that chapter, we discover that Durkheim examines the ways in which the social forces composing the types of suicide, can combine within individuals to yield mixed types of individual experience. This allows for a much greater degree of complexity in Durkheim's elaboration of the outcomes of the four causes. In fact, he ends with three "basic types" and three further "mixed types" (Durkheim 1951, 293). However, none of this modifies his basic emphasis, indeed, it actually confirms the way in which Durkheim wants to look at the whole and the part. It merely allows for a greater complexity in the working out of the four central modalities of moral force. In effect, the three modes of the whole (i.e. society), when they manifest themselves within the part (i.e. the individual) become six possible outcomes (only six since Durkheim omits reference to fatalism, whose addition would certainly create other logical and experiential possibilities).

It is imperative to recall that these four possible modes each also have two possible realizations, one in the form of a positive value, the other as a mode of pathology (e.g progress/anomie, community/altruism, autonomy/egoism, etc.). We know from his argument that if the social forces giving rise to one of the four modes operates to the exclusion of the others, it leads to one of the four types of suicide. However, by implication, it must at the same time be leading to a maximization of moral force placed on the positive value also associated with that mode. Is Durkheim saying that too great an emphasis on, for example, the positive value of progress will necessarily also lead to an increase in the pathology-creating social force of anomie? Is he saying that too great a development of those moral currents encouraging autonomy and cultural-moral personhood will lead to an increase in the forces of egoistic pathology? Indeed, this seems to be precisely his argument. Only a balanced, equilibrated system of social forces, one which gives an equal share, so to speak, to the four positive moral values corresponding to the four pathologies will generate a morally healthy society. Any other mixture of the social and moral forces will lead to an imbalanced, morally distorted society. The imbalanced type of society is a lesser whole, an incomplete totality, because it does not contain an equal measure of the four moral forces. It is a deformed totality, since the modes, the four moral forces of the system, are not equally represented, are not exerting equal force. One or another of them usurps its position as a part and tries to become the whole of the social moral tendency. This usurpation of a part trying to serve as the whole is a common critical theme in Durkheim (Durkheim 1961, 245; 1957).

I have difficulty reading Durkheim in any other way. Is he perhaps saying instead that the collective forces of society can, for example, create pressure for the value of progress and also simultaneously operate through other collective forces to minimize the anomic tendencies of individuals? Could the moral forces making for a, for example, solidary social community operate together with other moral forces which gestate egoism? If this were Durkheim's theory—that the social forces creating pressure for the vice, which reflects only a distorted form of a common virtue, could operate independently of the collective forces creating that very virtue itself—then society would be in a chronic state of collective self-contradiction, with one set of forces gestating, for example, values of progress and another gestating anomie. This seems entirely incongruent with the aims of Durkheim's theory. Moreover, if this were the case, it would hardly be necessary to carry out large scale collective reforms of the whole society, since it would then be possible merely to neutralize that portion of the collective forces leading to the pathological outcome. This would be too easy a solution for Durkheim and, in any case, entirely contradicts everything he says elsewhere in his book (as well as his other writings) about the moral condition of contemporary society.

There is another implication to Durkheim's analysis, one even more directly related to the whole/part problem. The fourfold set of moral forces which constitute egoism, altruism, anomie, and fatalism are collective tendencies, modes of the society seen as a total field of social forces. Within this whole, there operate the four "partial" forces already discussed. They are partial forces because they are, in fact, each only one positive value which operates within a larger, fourfold totality of moral forces made up of three other competing centers of moral force. We must recall that, for Durkheim, the types of social causes of suicide are collective forces. Egoistic suicide, for example, is the outcome of a collective moral tendency, a social force, just as are the other four types. From this standpoint, the individual is a "part" caught within the field of social forces defined by the "whole," by these four modes of morality or society (the two are identical for Durkheim). It is within the individual consciousness or the part that the battle is fought out among these competing forces. The microcosm reproduces the macrocosm, so to speak. More prosaically, the four modes of morality, or society, operate as forces competing to mold the individual's mental and moral structure. While Durkheim's method of statistical proof requires that he examine rates of suicide, as evidence of these social forces, this is not in fact the central aspect of his theory. The social forces denoted by the theoretical concepts operate directly on individuals who are parts of larger wholes, while the rates measure only how the various groups, also seen as parts of a yet larger whole, register the distribution of these forces.

I would emphasize that in *Suicide* the "duality" noted elsewhere in Durkheim's writings has a fascinating quality. He argues that the simultaneous double existence led by each person is actually the result of a double movement in which we are both "drawn in a social direction," while at the same moment:

> . . . we tend to follow the inclination of our own natures. The rest of society weights upon us to constrain our centrifugal tendencies, and we for our part share in this weight upon others for the purpose of neutralizing theirs. We ourselves undergo the pressure we help to exercise upon others. Two antagonistic forces confront each other. One comes from the collectivity and seeks to take possession of the individual; the other comes from the individual and repulses the former one.

Although he quickly adds that the social force is the stronger of the two, since it is composed of "a combination of all the particular forces . . ." (Durkheim 1951, 319; 1995a, 360–61). He then adds several interesting remarks about measuring these forces. He apparently thought they might be susceptible to measurement and his language of weights and centrifugal tendencies is captivating. This points again to the real character of these forces in his system.

I will leave these problems of measurement for discussion at another time and add only that *Suicide*, with its copious use of statistics, should not necessarily be taken to fully realize this effort at measurement. I instead call attention to the recurrence of the image of a center from which individuals tend to fly out under the "centrifugal" forces of their own "natures," ones which are entirely antisocial or nonsocial in their tendencies if not constrained by the forces of society. This sort of opposition is very common in Durkheim's work. However, the crucial fact is that this "duality" is hardly a sociologically meaningful one. All of the collective goods of society are on one side, and the "individual," the other pole of the duality, is nothing but a bundle of unregulated impulses. If it is meant as a real polar opposition, it is a highly asymmetric one. Indeed, its asymmetry is so great as to require a more adequate metaphor to capture this duality. Indeed, Durkheim frequently supplies one, usually the whole/part image, or, as often, that of a circle (e.g. the centrifugal force image above, but also others we will note below). Durkheim's basic mode of theorizing pits social forces against the individual in a way which leaves the individual with little except its untutored, animal nature. I would suggest that Durkheim's actual theory in *Suicide* is informed by the notion of society as a whole or totality of forces which are then distributed through a fourfold set of social modes which pressure and mold the parts (i.e.individuals) and also cause a typical distribution of outcomes. In this theory, society is everything. The individual is only a residual point of "force" whose natural role is to resist being molded by social forces or, at most, be employed by society in the molding of others.

The interjection of the term "modes" above is my choice, not Durkheim's. I have not been able to discover anywhere in *Suicide* where he uses this term (although, as we will see, it appears elsewhere). We could as well designate this fourfold division of forces as parts of an overall totality of societal forces, in keeping with Durkheim's already varied usage of the whole/part perspective. However, I think the term "modes" is in keeping with his general theory and imagery. It is quite calculated on my part and is meant to invoke the similarity between Durkheim and Spinoza. We will recall that, for Spinoza, God or nature is substance with infinite modes and attributes two of which are known (extension and thought). Indeed, as we have already noted, Spinoza himself had to frequently correct his correspondents' tendency to slip into thinking of his modes as parts of a whole. If I may create a parallel with Durkheim's theory, I would say that the whole of society is a social substance made up of collective forces with various modes, four of which he identifies in *Suicide* as two sets of polar opposites emerging from rule over the individual's passions and the integration of the individual into group life. While this analogy is only an analogy and may stretch Durkheim's theory a bit on the bed of Spinoza's terminology, I do think it to be congruent with Durkheim's actual procedure. As I will demonstrate later in this book, Durkheim's *Forms* gives a fuller, if rather different account of these ideas of society, divinity, social substance, and force, and the modes under which society appears (i.e. the categories).

7

BETWEEN REVELATION
AND REALIZATION:
THE DEVELOPING PROBLEM OF
TOTALITY IN DURKHEIM
FROM 1898 TO 1912

The Whole in Durkheim's Lectures on
State, Society, and Professional Ethics

According to Mauss, the lectures on professional ethics are the sole text of a draft, made between 1898 and 1900, of a course offered frequently by Durkheim. It was given several times at Bordeaux in the years between 1890 and 1900 and again in 1904 and 1912 at Paris. The topic was central to Durkheim's thinking and figures prominently in his preface to the second edition of *Division* (published in 1902). Indeed, some of the historical material in the lectures appears in almost identical form in that preface.

The second lecture opens with a discussion directly related to our theme. Durkheim claims that all social activity involves an element of moral discipline and notes that "every social group, whether it be extended or limited, is a whole made of parts (*tout forme de parties*); the ultimate element, whose repetition constitutes the whole is the individual." For the group to maintain itself, "each part" cannot operate as if it were independent, "as if it were itself the whole." Rather, each part must work in a way that allows "the whole to survive (*subsister*). But the conditions of existence of the whole are not those of the part," since they are two very different things. Individual interests and group interests are not identical. In fact, there is frequently a "real antagonism" between them (Durkheim 1957, 14; 1950, 20). The aim of moral discipline is to confront the individual precisely with aims which are not his own, but which are integral to the existence of the whole. These are often presented in terms which evoke divine sanction. Durkheim emphasizes that group size plays an important role. The larger the group, the more regulation is needed. In a small group, "the whole is little distinguished from the part." The interests of the whole are clear to all, as are the ties binding each to the group. As society becomes more "extended," individuals cannot easily comprehend the full "social horizon." Rules are needed, otherwise the individual's actions necessarily "become antisocial" (Durkheim 1957, 15; 1950, 21)

Later in the text Durkheim argues, in connection with a discussion of the early development of the kinship group and political society, that the "organization of partial groups, of clans, families and so on . . . did not precede the organization of the total aggregate (*l'agrégat total*) which came about from their combination." However, the former is also not developed from the latter. Instead, Durkheim argues that "they are interdependent (*solidaires*)" and "mutually condition" one another. "The parts are not organized first to form a whole which is subsequently organized in their image, but the whole and the parts are organized at the same time" (Durkheim 1957, 46; 1950, 57).

Durkheim adds that political societies imply the existence of authority above the segments which constitute them. The same society can be both politically unified and segmented in subsidiary groups in another sense. Federal states, castes, clans, and other such groups, which often form up political societies, become ordinary secondary groups if they are subordinated to a unifying authority. In that case, they ". . . cease to be a whole and no longer emerge[s] except as a part" (Durkheim 1957, 47; 1950, 58). In a similar vein, Durkheim remarks that, if the individual's sphere of action is to be fruitfully developed, the person must be freed from to much constraint by the secondary groups as well as the state. Therefore, there must exist above these secondary groups some more general power, which establishes law for them and reminds each that "it is not the whole, but a part of the whole, and that it should not keep for itself what rightly belongs to the whole" (Durkheim 1957, 62; 1950, 76). Such is the only way to avoid this "collective particularism." In turn, if the state is to be the liberator of the individual, then it requires "counter-balance." There must be other collective forces to limit its action, and these are found in the secondary groups (Durkheim 1957, 63; 1950, 77).

In a later discussion of the role of the state in the creation of individual rights, Durkheim criticizes the natural rights theory, which assumes the state to be disturbing to preexisting naturally endowed right. He argues instead that the state creates these rights, making a reality of them. Human beings are human only because they live in society. Without those features which are of social origin, the human being is nothing but an animal similar to other animals. Society lifts the individual above physical nature. It has been able to accomplish this "because association, by grouping the individual psychic forces, intensifies them, carries them to a degree of energy and productivity infinitely superior to what they could achieve if they remained isolated from one another." The result is a "psychic life of a new kind infinitely richer and more varied than that . . . of the solitary individual." This collective psychic life "penetrates" and "transforms" the individual. Since "the group is a moral force superior to this extent than that of its parts, the first tends necessarily to subordinate to itself the second. These latter (i.e. the parts) are unable not to fall under dependence on the latter (i.e. the group). Here there is a law of moral mechanics, just as inevitable as the laws of physical mechanics" (Durkheim 1957, 60; 1950, 74).

Finally, in a discussion of the early development of the right of contract, Durkheim notes that the bond of contract is not of an early date and could only have emerged if the sacred character attached to things and persons, and given to them by the group, were transferred to the individual's transactions. The individual acknowledges obligations to other individuals within the group because "something of the sanctity of the whole is communicated to its parts" (Durkheim 1957, 178; 1950, 209). The particle of divinity found in each member of the clan is employed to engage in individually binding transactions.

These lectures are strongly oriented toward the problem of whole/part relations. The above discussion demonstrates that Durkheim approached his material with these central perspectives in mind. It is interesting that Durkheim identifies the whole/part problem with the differing "interests" of each, ones which do not coincide. Here, the whole/part: society/individual analogy is made to operate at a less fundamental level than his other, more stark, opposition between society and the wholly untutored human being. Also, we would note the odd and contradictory reference in the same passage to the idea that the whole emerges from a "repetition" of the individual parts. This "additive" image is not at all congruent with Durkheim's usual image of the whole being more than the mere arithmetic sum of the parts. However, in this context, with its focus on the need for individual discipline, the additive emphasis seems appropriate. To emphasize the need of the whole for discipline, he must first emphasize the possible opposition and independence of the parts which compose it.

In other respects, the issues dealt with in these lectures lend themselves to our problematic. The whole/part problem appears simultaneously to have three dimensions: (1) state and secondary group relations, (2) secondary group and individual relations, and (3) state and individual relations. The relationships among the state and other secondary groups are a central concern and, as we see above, are readily cast into the whole/part rhetoric. The same is true for the individual and group relationships, especially as they are connected with the state. The secondary groups must not entirely dominate the individual and thus usurp the place of the true whole, when they are themselves only a part. We see much the same set of whole/part concerns and the same fear of the part usurping the whole as we saw in *Suicide* and *Division*.

The developmental theme of the earlier book is also reiterated, but with somewhat different emphases. Individuals are freed from the group constraint found in earlier forms of society only by the state, which purchases the rights of the individual from the groups which dominate them and simultaneously turns these once powerful groups into "secondary groups." Once accomplished, however, it is necessary to prevent the riot of individual egoism which is threatened when the part becomes disconnected from the whole. Therefore, the state must now help reinsert the part into the whole, or the individual into newly created secondary groupings, especially the so-called professional or occupational groups.

The stark reiteration of the characteristically Durkheimian idea that man without society is merely an animal is also worth noting. We have already seen that it is strongly implied in his theory in *Suicide*. It will be important to recall this idea when we turn to his essay on the duality of human nature. A close examination of this problem will later confirm what can already be guessed from this remark. Durkheim more than once suggests that the individual, unaided by society, can be little more than a processor of individual sensory inputs or an unruly seat of desires. If man is only an animal outside of society, with nothing more than his bundle of senses, and everything which we usually call "human" comes from association and then "pervades the individual" and "transforms him," we can only conclude that there is no true "duality," but only a whole with parts which are molded into their true (i.e. social) *telos* by their association with the whole. In Jean-Jacques Rousseau's language, humans are potentially perfectable, but in Durkheim's view, this potential perfection is only realized in and through society, that is, through the whole. Indeed, as we will see, at the time of these lectures, Rousseau is very much on Durkheim's agenda. At this point, we might also recall the earlier discussion of Durkheim and Aristotle. In these lectures, we see Durkheim's very Aristotelian approach to the whole/part problem applied to the relationships among the state, secondary groups, and the individual.

While there are a large number of other issues treated in these lectures, I will not now enter into a fuller discussion of them. It is sufficient to have shown the central ways in which Durkheim is still highly preoccupied with the problem of totality and with charting the vicissitudes of wholes and parts. Let us turn instead to a discussion of his various essays published during the interim period between 1898 and about 1906. During this period, Durkheim began to grapple in earnest the new evidence he had been gathering about primitive societies, especially totemism, kinship systems, and religious life. These essays, along with several others dealing with topics outside the orbit of primitive society (e.g. collective representations), show Durkheim moving toward a new and modified conception of totality, one which continues to be linked to an enhanced rhetoric of moral forces, emotion and sentiment, social dynamics and symbolic representation.

The Problem of the Whole in Durkheim's Essays I: 1898–1905

Collective Representations, Religion and the Individual

One of the most celebrated distinctions in Durkheim's work is between individual and collective representations. The essay by that title has found an honored place in Durkheim exegesis, although its relatively early date of publication (1898) might lead us to suspect that it was not necessarily his last word on the subject. The argument is well-known. I would like to suggest that it is also best understood from the standpoint of the problems raised in this work. After examining this essay, I will add a few briefer remarks on several other essays of this period, notably his essay on "Individualism and the Intellectuals" of 1898, his first systematic definition of religion in 1899, and a long essay of 1903 (with Paul Fauconnet) reviewing recent sociological literature. While these essays are less important for my purposes, they do contain several ideas which need to be included in the analysis.

It is particularly interesting that Durkheim's famous essay opens with an attempt to legitimate the uses of analogy in scientific proof. This should not be surprising. As we have seen, many of his central arguments for the new field of sociology have rested heavily on the method of proof by analogy, especially the whole/part notion. This analogy continues to play a key role in this essay. In his first sentence, Durkheim notes that analogy can be a useful method of "illustration" and "secondary verification," even though, strictly speaking, it is not a method of "demonstration." He thinks it helpful to compare laws established in different domains of investigation, since a law discovered in one area may be applicable elsewhere (Durkheim 1974a, 1; 1967, 1). He then notes that things can be made intelligible only through comparison and "analogy is a legitimate form of comparison" (Durkheim 1974a, 1; 1967, 1). Durkheim offers a critique of the biological sociologists, not for their use of analogy as such, but for having tried to infer the laws of society directly from their knowlege of biology. He adds that if specifically sociological methods have already begun to establish the true nature of social organization, it is then permissable to compare these findings with those established for animal organization (Durkheim 1974a, 1; 1967, 2). Durkheim quickly discards the analogical comparison between sociology and biology and suggests instead that it is more sensible to examine the analogies between sociology and psychology (Durkheim 1974a, 1–2; 1967, 2). Since both are concerned with representations, we may assume that the two realms of representation, individual and social, have something in common. In particular, he wants to demonstrate "that both maintain the same relation with their respective substrata" (Durkheim 1974a, 2; 1967, 2).

It is worth noting how many of his key ideas Durkheim brings into play in these introductory remarks on analogy. As he has already shown in the *Rules*, comparison is the only legitimate method for sociology, and is perhaps even identical with sociology itself (Durkheim 1982, 157). Comparisons also form a central part of his work on suicide. Here, he expands the notion of comparison to include comparisons through analogy. He asserts the need to first develop independently founded laws in the study of social phenomena as a prerequisite to the later use of analogy with other fields. I think we can assume that he is gesturing to the laws he believes he has established in his books, *Division* and *Suicide*. Durkheim does not remind us of what we already also know at this point—that he used comparison through analogy, especially the whole/part notion, to establish some fundamental features of his new science well before he had carried out any studies which might establish social laws. In effect, he violated his own strictures. Moreover, it is very likely that analogies formed the philosophical basis of the investigations which led to these very laws. In these remarks, Durkheim moves rather freely among the problems of comparison through analogy, comparison aimed at the establishment of laws, and comparison of laws, once established, from different investigatory domains, while assimilating this latter procedure to the use of analogy. It is in this final context that he raises the essay's central problem: the relationship of representations (individual and collective) to their respective substrata. This problem is, indeed, intimately connected with the problem of analogical comparison and we discover Durkheim once again resting his analysis heavily on the whole/part notion.

In his discussion of the problem of representation, Durkheim generally wants to reject physical epiphenomenalism and argues for the existence of a specifically mental memory. He does so in part by adopting the strategy of arguing for the reality of "unconscious" processes. He even suggests the possibility that thoughts can travel over distances and that there might exist "waves of thought" (Durkheim 1974a, 19; 1967, 21). A good deal has been made recently of Durkheim's references to "the unconscious," much more than is warranted by the actual importance of these references in his work. His ideas have been compared with those of Sigmund Freud and even Carl Jung, and forays have been made into the texts to see if there are any references to Freud in his work. These discussions have proven fruitless. They are certainly without value for my present purposes. Durkheim's discussions of "unconscious" processes are brief and, at best, are hardly comparable either in scope and detail to Freud's extensive mapping of this field (Simpson 1963, 3). For example, in this text, his argument for the existence of "unconscious" mental processes, as well as much of the rest of the essay, is meant primarily to offer a proof by analogy to aid in the demonstration of the relative autonomy of representations from their foundation in the individuals who bear them. The discussion of unconscious processes is entirely subordinate to his wider sociological aims (Durkheim 1974a, 1, 23ff.; 1967, 1, 25ff).

More relevant to my purposes is the direction taken by Durkheim in his complex discussion of collective representations.

Representations continue to exist in themselves, apart from the material substratum, and have the power to react directly upon one another and combine according to their own laws. These facts about representations are analogous to the relationship of individual and society. Collective representations result from the association of individuals in society, but surpass it. He sees a close analogy between the relationship of psychic life of individuals to its physiological substratum, and the relationship of social life to the social substratum (Durkheim 1974a, 25; 1967, 27). The externality of social facts from the individual is even more evident than the separation of psychic states from the physiological basis in the individual organism. Collective representations are external to individual minds and do not result from them, but from the association of individuals, quite a different thing for Durkheim. While each individual contributes to the process, "the private sentiments become social only by combination under the action of forces sui generis developed in association." Through combination, they are altered and "*they become something else* (Durkheim's emphasis). A chemical synthesis results which concentrates and unifies the synthesized elements. . . ." This also transforms them. Durkheim adds that this synthesis is "the work of the whole (*le tout*), it is the whole which it has for a setting. The resultant which disengages itself surpasses each individual mind (*esprit*) as the whole surpasses the part (*le tout déborde la partie*). It is in the whole (*dans l'ensemble*) as it is by the whole (*par l'ensemble*). This is the sense in which it is exterior to the individuals (*particuliers*)." For us to accurately understand this new reality, we must investigate "the aggregate in its totality (*totalité*)." In keeping with his sense that this reality is really a new kind of being, he insists that it thinks, feels, and wishes, although it can perform these actions only through "the intermediary of particular consciousnesses." Such social phenomena are not dependent on the characteristics of individuals. Instead, individual differences are "neutralized and effaced" through this process of "fusion" (Durkheim 1974a:26; 1967, 28–29).

This lengthy paragraph is remarkable. It not only combines two of Durkheim's most persistent metaphors—the whole/part idea and the creation of collective representations through synthesis—it also gives priority to the former over the latter. This fact requires special emphasis. In fact, Durkheim explains the process of creation of collective representations by reference to the whole/part analogy. The whole creates the synthesis of individual minds. This synthesis is "in" and "by" the whole. Indeed, this entire conception gives a particular slant to his familiar notion of association. The latter is not merely "social interaction," or even mental combination of individual representations into collective representations. It is not merely the mutual impact of social, or less, mental atoms, but something more, really a totalizing process in which the individuals become transformed into parts. The process is one of mutual interpenetration and is highly creative. In some respects, this is already familiar ground. It echoes his earlier arguments from the hypothetical notion of the horde concerning the formative quality of the movement to organized segmentary society, in which a social whole emerges and, along with it, the part. This is not surprising, although it does give pause to those who would see the notion of synthesis, like that of the organic analogy, as architechtonic in Durkheim's work or want to derive it primarily from a chemical analogy. Even Durkheim's close collaborator Célestin Bouglé, in his preface to this collection of essays, is highly ambiguous about the priority of the notions of synthesis or whole/part in the analysis (Durkheim 1974a, xxxviii–xxxix; 1967, ix). Durkheim always conceived his notion of synthesis along the lines of the whole/part problem and appears to have taken his lead ultimately from Aristotle. Both of them regularly employ the whole/part metaphor to examine the combination of elements in both organisms as well as chemical syntheses. There is also an echo at the end of Durkheim's discussion of his study of Rousseau, which was done around the same time this essay was published. Durkheim's insistence that the divergent individual elements are "neutralized" evokes the image of Rousseau's "general will." The "general will" differs from the "will of all" by virtue of the fact that it is not a mere sum, but a mathematically transfigured whole in which each individual's will is combined and transformed into a new entity.

Durkheim later discusses further ramifications of this problem. In doing so, he presents some arguments which I think have greatly misled his sociological interpreters into thinking that he is a sociological "idealist." As I have suggested above, it is best to avoid such formulae in reading Durkheim's work. Durkheim is not unambiguous in his discussion of how collective representations are related to their social substratum. They are born of the social substratum, but not absorbed in it. The basic matter of the social consciousness is in close relation with the number of social elements and the ways in which they are grouped and distributed. But once collective representations have been created, they have an autonomy and can attract, repel, and form various new syntheses with

one another. Thus, new representations can be caused by the interaction among existing ones, and not only by the social structure
(Durkheim 1974a, 30–31; 1967, 34). Durkheim then mentions a
new field which would investigate these "social products of the second degree" and determine their "laws of collective ideation"
(Durkheim 1974a, 43, fn. 1; 1967, 35, fn. 1). He is keen to combat
the label of "materialist" and goes out of his way to state that his
"sociological naturalism" argues not only that "the distinctive property of the individual representational life" is "spirituality," but
that social life "is defined by a hyperspirituality." He adds that the
word "hyperspirituality" might sound "metaphysical," but points
only to a "body of natural facts which can be explained by natural
causes" (Durkheim 1974a, 34; 1967, 37–38).

After reading such a succession of claims, joining such a variety of ideas and images, it is not surprising that Durkheim was
understood in varying ways in his own day and continues today to
provoke widely different responses. From my perspective, I would
emphasize several things. Durkheim makes a clear distinction
between the fundamental forms of social consciousness and the
later "social products of the second degree." The former seem
clearly to include what he later calls the fundamental categories of
any culture, which are linked (in both form and content, as
Durkheim also argued) to their social substratum. Indeed, without
this basic idea, there is no making sense of Durkheim's work,
including his mature sociology of religion and knowledge. In this
respect, Durkheim is consistently naturalistic and sociologistic and
places the emphasis on the determinate links between the categories and the social substratum. However, the products of the "second degree" can emerge from the combination of existing representations, which operate together in accordance with "laws" as yet
undiscovered. They can presumably be explained—how is
unclear—without direct reference to the social substratum. This
appears to be a strand of "internalist" or "intellectualist" thinking
in Durkheim, one which is clearly not itself grounded in his sociological theory, as is evident from his footnoted hopes for a future
theory of ideation. I would emphasize that this hope refers to the
phenomena of the "second degree" only, and not to the basic categories of thought.

Durkheim himself never developed this theory of "collective
ideation" dealing with the (presumably) nonsocially determined
processes of collective representations. In this essay, it is not clear
how one gets even from the individual to the collective representa-

tions, no less what the precise character of these secondary intellectual processes might be. The phenomena of the "second degree" are clearly also of secondary importance from the standpoint of Durkheim's fundamental philosophical and sociological concerns. They are to be studied historically (and perhaps somehow even sociologically); they represent all of the diversity of thought and ideation which always also interested Durkheim. However, I want to emphasize that nowhere in his work does Durkheim develop this "theory of ideation." Instead, he always focuses only on the sociologically determined dimensions of collective representations, what he might have called those phenomena of the "first degree," for example, the categories. When he did speak of this possible theory of ideation, he seemed uncertain whether such processes of the "second degree" were entirely divorced from social constraints or whether they were connected to society, perhaps in a different fashion than the categories. However, he gives no hint what the connections might be. I would add that, in his last book, Durkheim distinguishes, but in an entirely different fashion, between two degrees of relationship between the categories and society. The distinction now is between the dependence of the categories on religion and social processes for their general birth (the first degree), and the ways in which society provides the actual model for the categories (the second degree) (Durkheim 1995b, 441). In the *Forms*, both degrees are defined socially.

Durkheim's references to the "hyperspirituality" of collective representations should not mislead us into thinking that he was ever an idealist, or underwent a move from positivism to idealism (as Parsons 1937 thought). In using this term, he wanted to combat the accusation of "materialism," and to do so in a language which would highlight the anti-materialist implications of his work. He uses the term "hyperspirituality" quite conditionally: *if* we are to call individual mental life (in accordance with his foregoing argument) "spiritual," *then* we will by extension call collective mental life "hyperspiritual." I would note the highly rhetorical quality of this argument and also recall that he immediately follows with a reiteration of his "naturalistic" standpoint. Durkheim wants his "naturalism" in sociology to fall somewhere outside of the distinction between "idealism" and "materialism." In truth, Durkheim has no theory of these pheneomena of the second degree. He therefore has no complete theory of the "hyperspiritual" realm, only a theory of the categories, one which he never presented as anything but a naturalistic and sociologistic theory.

When we turn to Durkheim's essay on individualism and the intellectuals, published in 1898, we seem to find outselves on very different ground. The individual, individualism as an ideal, and the "part" seem to be the primary focus. Written in the wake of the Dreyfus affair as a defense of individualism as an ideal and of modern intellectuals as a group, it finds him developing his idea of the modern "cult of the individual" in terms which are strictly sociological. Modern individualism in its highest form does not evolve from egoistic sentiments or from the individual at all, but is a collective product. It is quite opposed to the egoistic individualism of the utilitarians. Rather, it glorifies the individual in the form of humanity in general. For Durkheim, this religion of the individual, like all religion, is a social institution (Durkheim 1994a, 70; 1970, 275). When the individualist defends the rights of the individual, he defends society, in so far as society itself has hallowed the individual for certain purposes (Durkheim 1994a, 69; 1970, 274). Not only is the individual a social product, developed admittedly in parallel to the development of society itself, the "cult of the individual" is a social creation. If we have individual rights, it is because society gives them to us. They are not given by "nature" or "natural right." This argument is highly congruent with the lectures on professional ethics. Durkheim generally sees the individualism of the Enlightenment Age as a crucial, but partial step on a longer road to an enlarged sense of individualism. It is necessary to "complete, extend and organize individualism" (Durkheim 1994a, 70–71; 1970, 277). We must use our modern liberties to improve society, not merely, as in the past, for purely egoistic purposes, a path which helped to discredit individualism as an ideal. Individual rights need to be employed to "elaborate the functioning of the social machine . . . ," which is still too hard on individuals, in order to fully develop the individual's possibilities (Durkheim 1994a, 71; 1970, 277).

Durkheim's image of a social machine, rather than a "social organism," is in keeping with the context of possible social reforms. It also fits his rhetorical usage, since a machine has something of an artifical quality and can be improved, while an organism is less susceptible to such changes. I cannot now pause to examine the possible meanings which might be attached to this "organized" individualism, or in what sense it would complete or extend the individualism inherited from the past. It seems clear that it would locate the person's "individual" actions much more thoroughly within social group life and put them in the service of social improvement. Even when society gestates greater individualism, it is society which accomplishes this change. Society can gestate individualism as a moral phenomenon (after having created earlier more purely collectivizing moral values). Also, under given circumstances, this individualism can degenerate into unbridled egoism. The individual alone can be only the latter, a physical center for egoism, but never by itself gestate moral individualism (or any other moral value, including the collectivizing ones). Individuals can only "personalize" collective values, adapt them to their own experiences, and, ideally, integrate their individual contributions into society and its reform. The individual is largely a fragment of society. As he argues later, in the lectures on education, the individual and society are not truly opposed to one another (Durkheim 1956:78). The best part of the individual is an "emanation" of the group (Durkheim 1961, 73; 1974b, 62), a remark which echoes his review of Schäffle (Durkheim 1978, 102). These remarks illustrate the varied uses to which Durkheim put the whole/part opposition, especially when it was developed alongside the society/individual distinction.

The essay on religion published in *L'Année* in 1897–98 contains at least one related sequence worthy of note. It once again concerns Durkheim's favorite theme: the relationship between individual and society. In this essay, he defines religious phenomena as obligatory beliefs and clearly defined practices related to the objects of the beliefs. Religion itself is an "organized and systematized whole (*ensemble*)" composed of such phenomena (Durkheim 1994a, 91; 1969b, 160). This definition is relatively unproblematic in itself. He goes on to define the obligatory, that which involves command and authority, as social in origin. In a familiar series of statements, he argues that only in society can we find a thinking being greater than the individual. Its superiority to each individual's force results from the fact that it is a "synthesis of individual forces" (Durkheim 1994a, 93; 1969b, 160). The powers before which individuals prostrate themselves are not physical powers, but social ones, products of collective sentiments. They are products of the collective mind (*l'esprit collectif*). This mind sees reality in a different way from the individual. Society has its own mode of existence and thought, its own needs, habits and passions, which do not correspond to those of individuals (*des particuliers*) (Durkheim 1994a, 95; 1969b, 162). Society itself has fashioned the representation of sacred things.

I want to draw attention to Durkheim's extension of his definition and analysis of religion to include certain individual beliefs and practices. He points to the existence of individual versus collective religious phenomena, but emphasizes the secondary quality of the individual ones. Durkheim thinks it obvious that "private belief" derives from "public belief" (Durkheim 1994a, 97; 1969b, 164). It is equally obvious to Durkheim that the individual only personalizes the public or collective religion. At this point, Durkheim enters a fascinating reference to the temporal dimensions of this relationship between collective and individual religious phenomena. Personal religion is the subjective dimension of the public religion, but it should not be thought that the two religions are "successive historical phases." Rather, they are "contemporaneous." The individual participates in the creation of social states while he is simultaneously effected by them. The internal life of the individual "grows parallel" to social life, at the very moment when the latter itself is developing. There is no question of "two distinct timescales." This is how all collective activity becomes personalized (Durkheim 1994a, 97; 1969b, 164–65). He concludes by modifying his definition to include reference to these individual or "optional" religious beliefs and practices.

This discussion is characteristically Durkheimian in its social determinism, or, if that word is too strong, in the priority it gives to society in the gestation of religion. When he wants to accommodate the individual to his analysis, he does so in a form which sees the individual's religiosity as an instantiation of the collective beliefs and practices and, of course, as a purely optional (rather than obligatory) variant of these collective forms. However, the temporal analysis introduces a fascinating modification and, in a few sentences, exposes one of Durkheim's hidden assumptions, one already noted in his discussions of the whole/part relationship in *Division*. The whole and its parts are inseparable from one another (almost by definition), but when seen in a temporal light, they are also parallel developments within a single time scale. Durkheim is not entirely unambiguous about this process. His emphasis on the mutual influence of individual and society, on the individual being formed, while also simultaneously forming society, gives room for the sort of "dialectical" sociological interpretations advanced by more recent writers, who merge Durkheim's distinctions with those of G. W. F. Hegel, Karl Marx, George Herbert Mead, and others (e.g. Berger 1967). Whatever the value of these latter accounts, they hardly capture Durkheim's own central line of thought. Instead, I would emphasize, as Durkheim himself does, the notions of temporal simultaneity and parallelism (also Durkheim 1975, I:57). When the emphasis falls on these elements in the argument, then the notion of the whole (i.e. society) reappears more clearly as the central idea, within which the individual develops his own variant of the collective life, by personalizing the collective. We see organized society coming into existence simultaneously with the birth of the individual as a human being. The whole and the part emerge together.

The essay on sociology and the social sciences published by Durkheim and Fauconnet in 1903 contains valuable material for our purposes. The dual authorship poses few problems, since Durkheim was its senior author. I think we can assume the essay's congruence with his overall thought. Moreover, many of the paper's themes are familiar ones and echo his own statements elsewhere.

In their brief review of the development of sociology, we find reiterated the earlier Durkheimian idea that religious or metaphysical dualism, which set humankind in a world apart, needed to be overcome for the social sciences to emerge and human phenomena be interpreted in terms of natural laws. This could be done only by insisting on "the unity of nature" (Durkheim 1982, 177; 1975, I:123). The authors immediately add that this alone was insufficient, since materialistic monism also locates humankind within nature. However, this philosophy obviates the need for sociology and psychology, since it makes both individual and collective existence only an "epiphenomenon of physical forces" (Durkheim 1982, 177; 1975, I:124). Instead, a philosophy was needed which also recognized the fundamental heterogeneity of things, a development credited to Auguste Comte (Durkheim 1982, 178; 1975, I:124). Each realm of nature had to have its own laws, irreducible to one another, and even Comte still saw these various realms unifed into a larger, homogeneous whole.

Durkheim and Fauconnet review the ideas of some major figures in the history of sociology, including Auguste Comte, Herbert Spencer, John Stuart Mill, Franklin Giddings, and Georg Simmel, especially their ideas about general sociology. They are particularly concerned to distinguish their view from that of Simmel. They think his separation of social "forms" and "contents" to be illegitimate, since it eliminates the actual stuff of social life, which can only very arbitrarily be seen as a nonsocial "content." Society is made up of such things as law, morality, and religion. They are its living and active reality (Durkheim 1982, 191; 1975, I:140). In an especially interesting characterization of Simmel's position, Durkheim and Fauconnet claim that he does not see society as a productive cause. He fails to understand this because, for him, society is merely the outcome of "actions and reactions exchanged between the parts, that is, between individuals." For Simmel, "it is the content which determines the container, it is the matter which produces the form." They then question the very possibility of understanding this form if one also abstracts from the matter composing it (Durkheim 1982, 191; 1975, I:141). Simmel should have admitted that society is a body with its own special mode of action, and this is "not to be confused with individual interactions." Then it would be possible to see the forms of association as the outcome sui generis of association (Durkheim 1982, 191; 1975, I:140). Their critique of Simmel's work continues, and they conclude their review with a guarded reassertion of the Comtean idea that the sociological method must be applied to "the totality" of social facts (Durkheim 1982, 194; 1975, I:144). However, I want to pause to examine especially the remarks about Simmel.

Although the Durkheimian critique of Simmel is far from complete, it is of considerable importance. Its general approach is similar to Durkheim's earlier attempt to undermine Ferdinand Tönnies' conceptions by critically filtering them through his own metaphors. Durkheim and Fauconnet discuss Simmel's emphasis on "forms of association." Given their own view of "association" as a critical feature of social life, indeed, as we have seen, one which creates all the distinctive features of society as a reality sui generis, this critique may seem surprising. But their criticism is entirely in line with our present sense of Durkheim's thought. They dispute Simmel's method precisely because he has identified society with the interaction between "parts," or individuals, when he should have seen it as a productive cause resulting from the whole, rather than the individual parts composing it. Durkheim reveals his basic assumptions quite openly: societal processes, including what he described in his first book as the "modifications of social substance," and, what he repeatedly designates as "association," are not to be identified with the interactions of individuals. They also call attention to the fact that Simmel's forms of association do not refer to the social morphology, or geographical distribution of populations and their dynamics. They clearly view this as a great shortcoming. It is interesting to see them distinguish their emphasis on studying the totality of social facts from Simmel's seemingly more fragmentary method. In their view, Simmel has no unified conception of the whole. They argue this thesis later in the essay, when they criticize Simmel for failing to examine clearly defined categories of facts. In their view, he executes only philosophical meditations on general themes, where each investigation provides a total view of society seen from a particular angle of vision (Durkheim 1982, 193; 1975, I:143). We will return to this remark and to Simmel's method later in this work and suggest that he does, in some of his writings, have his own conception of the "whole." For now, I would note that, coupled with the emphasis on the "contents" as the living, active stuff of society, we get a picture of Durkheim similar to the one which has already emerged from our earlier discussion. The emphasis is on reconstituting the whole, which, in turn, is seen as a living reality composed of the "matter" of which it constitutes the form. This entire language is much more "substantialist" than commentators have allowed, yet it is Durkheim's own language and reveals some central tendencies of his thought. In these passages, the distinction between matter and form is opposed to Simmel's more Kantian form and content duality. The two pairs are far from identical and the difference betrays Aristotle's influence on Durkheim.

In a further review of recent (largely German) work on various phenomena in the social sciences, they note a similar fragmentation in these efforts and sound a related note. They argue that all the phenomena treated in these investigations emerge from a single reality, namely, society. Specialists must escape from their self-imposed limitations and communicate their findings through the key idea of society. At the moment, each examines only a "portion of the whole" and mistakenly assumes it to be "the whole itself." As a result, the more "adequate notion of that whole—that is to say, society" evades their grasp (Durkheim 1982, 204; 1975, I:156). From one standpoint, of course, Durkheim and Fauconnet merely wish to balance the excessive specialization of the social sciences with a more synthetic "principle of interdependence of social facts" derived from sociology (Durkheim 1982, 205; 1975, I:157). However, they present their argument in a form which once again reiterates one of their main themes: the whole and its parts, especially in relation to the problem of encyclopedic or synthetic knowledge. The open identification of society with the category of the whole is particularly striking. It is a trope which animates much of Durkheim's work.

The essay's critical remarks are directed primarily at the work of German social scientists. Whether this reflect's Durkheim's desire to distance himself from German thinkers, from whom he was thought to have taken so many leads, is open to question. The essay contains material important to my present argument. That is my main concern, not Durkheim's other possible motives. I do think the German connection, argued in his time and reiterated today in new forms (Deploige 1938; Hall's remarks in Durkheim 1993), is greatly exaggerated. For present purposes (i.e. the problem of totality in Durkheim), the German writers are not decisive. The notion that Arthur Schopenhauer strongly influenced Durkheim's work on religion is unsupported by his texts and irrelevant to my concerns (Meštrović 1991; also Nielsen 1996d). The conceptions of the whole found in the work of, for example, Johann Fichte and the Socialists of the Chair (Deploige's main choices) differ markedly from Durkheim's main emphases. They are passed over for that reason.

First Essays on Totemism, Kinship, and Primitive Society

Around the turn of the century, Durkheim wrote several essays dealing with totemism, kinship, and primitive society. The monograph of 1898 on the incest taboo (Durkheim 1963; 1969b, 37–101), the lengthy 1902 statement on the nature of totemism (Durkheim 1985; 1969b, 315–52), and an essay of 1903–4 on primitive matrimonial regulations (Durkheim 1969b, 483–510) all circle around these common themes. They reflect his increasing interest in such topics. They also express his growing sense that the problems which interested him could best be addressed through the study of primitive society, totemism, and through the use of religion as a primary explanatory reference point. While these essays are only occasionally revealing about the problems of interest to me in this work, they do shed some light on the ways in which Durkheim employs the problem of totemism in his evolving theory and, as a result, on some of his favorite conceptions.

These essays also have an added interest for the study of the categories. Although they do not consistently address the problems developed in the essay (with Mauss) on primitive classification, they do lay a foundation for the later study of the categories. Durkheim and Mauss argue that the first notions of genre or classification are modeled on the kinship groupings. Thus, in discussing the moral order of primitive society through the study of the clan, kinship, matrimonial rules, incest, and so forth, he wants to lay the foundation for his study of the categories. Indeed, these essays already are, in a sense, studies of the categories, those which determine the rules regulating relationships among members of primitive society, although they have not yet taken the further step of focusing on the category of genre or relation (or those of time, space, causality, etc.).

His essay on the incest taboo focuses on an explanation of exogamy, the most primitive form of that taboo in his view. It should be added immediately that Durkheim does not view clan exogamy as the most primitive form of kinship organization or society (Durkheim 1963, 105). In this essay, he accepts Lewis Henry Morgan's idea of a undifferentiated primitive "mass" without rules of exogamy existing before the development of the incest taboo. This corresponds to his earlier argument in *Division* about the primal quality of the horde as a social unit. It is interesting to see this hypothesis reappearing in this work. It is also worth noting that this analysis was written before he began to develop his interpretations of the evidence presented in the books of Baldwin Spencer and F. J. Gillen (1968). He already adopts the general strategy, familiar to readers of his later work on religion, of locating the most primitive manifestation of his problem (i.e. exogamy and incest taboo). In this way, he thinks it possible to say something about the essense of the topic. Yet, it is far from clear that he wants to explain the absolute origins of society. However, he does thereby insist that exogamy and the incest taboo represent the most primitive forms of organized society. This methodological move will seem less puzzling if we recall our earlier contention that Durkheim seeks out the problems of totemism and religion and the setting of so-called primitive society in order to establish a line of attack on his central philosophical problem, the nature of the whole or totality. He does not need, or want, to establish the absolute origins of kinship structures or society. Although he retains a variant of the primitive horde hypothesis in this essay, it is not emphasized any more than it was in his earlier book.

Durkheim sees religious origins for the incest taboo. The totem is a god and totemism is a cult. This sufficiently warrants a search for the religious origins of exogamy (Durkheim 1963, 70; 1969b, 72). Sexual prohibitions are like ritual prohibitions and are explicable in the same way. He finds the religious institution of the taboo (a universal one, in his view) to be the key to these prohibitions. The force or power residing in certain persons or things makes them taboo to normal contact. It is of interest that Durkheim already identifies this power or force with an "energy" which is simply in want of a proper social recepticle (Durkheim 1963, 71; 1969b, 73). The primitive horror at shedding blood is, in his view, linked to the woman's menstrual flow and women come under a taboo during this period. The magical properties which come to be associated with blood in general are explained by the nature of totemism itself.

The substantive identity of the clan member with the totem is emphasized strongly by Durkheim. The ancestor of the clan is the true being to whom are tied both the living members of that clan as well as the existing animal species with which it is identified (Durkheim 1963, 85–87). The "substantialism" of the primitive, allows him to unite disparate things: the living clan and animal and mythological ancestor. The ancestor is the principle unifying force, containing within his power the species and the clan. "All that one contained is retained in the other. That is to say, the living substance, even though divided, retains its unity" (Durkheim 1963, 87; 1969b, 83). This living substance is identified particularly with the blood. The blood is the "common substance" (Durkheim 1963, 88; 1969b, 84) which binds together and identifies all of the members of the community as beings of a common nature, those adopted through blood rites as well as those born into the clan, its human as well as its animal members. The totemic being is "immanent to the clan" and each of its members individually (Durkheim 1963, 89; 1969b, 84). These early references to the category of "substance" are striking and are developed further by Durkheim and the members of his school.

From Durkheim's sociological standpoint these ideas express the collective unity of the clan itself, where there is a strong collective consciousness and very weak individuation. Indeed, in this essay, the clan is given a rather interesting description, not only in keeping with his earlier discussion in *Division*, but with our overall theme. Durkheim writes that the clan itself is a "homogeneous and compact mass," with "no differentiated parts." Each clan exists "as a whole, resembling all others" (Durkheim 1969b, 84; 1963, 88). However, the sociologistic outlook which informs his later theories of primitive classification and religion is still underplayed in these pages. He places a certain emphasis on the emotions of revulsion and veneration which enter into the social process of constructing this taboo and also emphasizes the emotional contagion of primitive society which allows the transfer of sentiments readily from one object to another. He also insists on the importance of the opposition of values, especially the sacred and profane, in the evolution of the incest taboo. He restates the idea found in his contemporaneous essay on individual and collective representations, that ". . . everything which is social consists of representations," that is, of course, "collective representations," which are the very "matter even of sociology" (Durkheim 1963, 114; 1969b, 100). However, these claims are made in a complex context, where Durkheim is analyzing both the developmental processes by which social differentiation of sexuality and the kinship group takes place and through which collective representations are liberated from their social structural settings and take on a certain independence of their own. Without using these precise phrases, Durkheim restates his argument about collective mental phenomena of the "first" and "second" degree. He argues that later representations can be derived from both the direct reinterpretation of earlier representations (i.e. the representations the "second degree") as well as from new ideas gestated directly out of the changes in the social substratum, especially changing social morphology (i.e. representations of the first order) (Durkheim 1963, 114–15, especially notes 1 and 2; 1969b, 100–1). This entire discussion strikes me as part of a transitional phase in Durkheim's work. On the one hand, there is the underdeveloped "double theory" of representations (i.e. those of the first and second degree). On the the other, there is Durkheim's general idea that the fundamental transition from one social type to another involves the reorganization of the "social substance" and the release of social energies which are the basis for new representations.

For present purposes, this essay has several important features. One is Durkheim's identification of the origins of the incest taboo with totemism and, thus, with both religion and a particular theory of nature. Another is his interjection of the rhetorics of substance and energy (most especially the former) into the analysis to express his sense of primitive mentality. Durkheim needs totemism to achieve his philosophical aims. One begins to suspect that the "primitive" view which he has identified is largely his own philosophy imported into his study of primitive society. Finally, we once again see Durkheim developing the relationships between collective representations and the "social substratum." Here, he seems to combine the "internalist" and "externalist" views already broached (if rather ambiguously) in his contemporaneous essay on individual and collective representations. He argues both that new representations develop directly out of old ones, but also that the transformation of society from one type of kinship system to another brings about the creation of new collective representations suitable to the new social form.

The two essays on matrimonial customs and totemism were published within a few years of each other and are of a piece. Many of the same issues are raised in each paper, in particular, both focus heavily on the transition from "uterine" descent systems to ones reckoning descent through the male line (Durkheim 1969b, 497).

Both papers also demonstrate Durkheim's interest in "mixed" forms of social organization, ones which combine characteristics of earlier and later social types. Indeed, matrimonial groupings are largely to be explained, in Durkheim's view, as a by-product, so to speak, of the transition from female to male oriented systems of descent. In the essay of 1903–04 on matrimonial groupings, we also see Durkheim making more explicit reference to the relationships between social and logical categories. He even plays briefly with the question of the mathematical quality of the primitive matrimonial systems (Durkheim 1969b, 510). As with the contemporaneous essay on *Primitive Classification*, ". . . the clans and phratries are not only social categories, but logical categories" (Durkheim 1969b, 510).

When we consider Durkheim's 1902 essay on totemism, we note his increased reliance on Spencer and Gillen, whose work, in his view, demonstrates the irrefutable empirical reality of totemism as a religion. At the essay's outset, we already see the appearance of the notion that totemism is an actual religion. Its beliefs and practices "form a whole," now an identifying feature of a religion, and their totemic nature is incontestable (Durkheim 1985, 91; 1969b, 315). The earlier essay on the incest taboo was based, in his own view, on much less adequate evidence. The essay on totemism repeats many of the main ideas of his earlier essays on incest and on matrimonial classes. The image of totemism which emerges continues to focus on the "substantive identity" of the individual and his totem. However, the emphasis is now also placed on the rituals used to periodically renew this "substance," one which is "simultaneously material and mystical" and which binds the two together (Durkheim 1985, 112; 1969b, 345). This theme is to play a large role in the mature theory of 1912. However, this essay also contains several passages of more immediate interest for our purposes.

Durkheim contrasts the legends and traditions of the Australian tribes (especially the Arunta) concerning the orgins of their matrimonial customs with, in his view, their real historical origins. He views their own account as historically suspect, largely a mythological view of changes which themselves were not clearly understood. These legends are collective representations created by the popular imagination to explain existing religious practices (Durkheim 1985, 100; 1969b, 328). They are to be contrasted with the laborious collection of precise facts about the subject.

A particularly interesting aspect of this problem is Durkheim's contrast between the Arunta's own account of the origin of its phratries from the combination of preexisting clans and Durkheim's view that the phratrie is too closely associated with the totemic cult to have been such a late introduction. In his view, there is an error of fact at the basis of their myths of origins, one which is easily explicable. There are several causes of this error, but one cause is especially relevant to my concerns. Durkheim writes that the human mind, because of its "native simplicity," always imagines "the part as anterior to the whole, the individual as prior to society." In the same way, it also tends to see "elementary societies" as historically prior to "the more complex societies of which they form a part" (Durkheim 1985, 100; 1969b, 329).

It is fascinating that Durkheim should introduce such general philosophical musings, and in this precise manner, into a paper devoted to the development of totemism. He combines several of his major concerns in this sentence. His assumption that the human mind is naturally prone to see parts as prior to wholes reveals one of his main strands of thought. The imputation of such a tendency to the human mind is entirely in keeping with Durkheim's sense that sociology, as he conceives it, is far from being a "natural" mode of thought. He couples this cognitive assumption with his more familiar notions about the relations of both individual and subgroups to society. This not only broadens his image of this general problem, it also helps suggest why sociology is so vital a field of study. It alone combates a powerful and misleading tendency of thought. As such, it shatters fundamental illusions and substitutes a new revelation about reality: the priority of the whole to the part at every level of historical and social existence. It is odd that Durkheim should introduce a philosophical assumption about the tendency for human nature to emphasize the part (over the whole) in an essay which describes primitive mentality as dominated by collective rather than individuated consciousness. He seems to imply that even primitives are born "individualists," when it comes to examining the reasons for their own social arrangements. In any case, it seems that the problem of whole and part was never far from Durkheim's thoughts, even when he was thoroughly immersed in the intricacies of primitive kinship systems.

Durkheim and Rousseau

Durkheim's lectures on Jean-Jacques Rousseau's social and political thought are from the year 1901–02, but were published posthumously only in 1918. Durkheim had lectured on Rousseau, especially his *Émile*, as part of his courses on the history of pedagogy, at Bordeaux and later at Paris (Durkheim 1979). These latter lectures on education (often in little more than outline form) also contain some interesting, if highly fragmentary and inconclusive remarks on the problem of the whole.

Durkheim always admired Rousseau's work and found it challenging (Durkheim 1965, 142–43). He evidently grappled with Rousseau's ideas from an early date, although it is not clear when he shifted his emphasis from Rousseau's pedagogical ideas to a wider study of his political and social theory. The substantial manuscript of 1901–02, drafted after a course on Rousseau at Bordeaux, comes at a point in Durkheim's own intellectual development when he was moving from the earlier position on the problem of the whole or totality, articulated most fully in his first three books, to his later view. This suggests that Durkheim's interest at this time in Rousseau might itself have had something to do (among other things) with the problem of redefining his own view of totality. In this respect, Rousseau was a good choice. His social theory qualifies as one of those most concerned with the problem of totality. Durkheim would naturally be interested in this theory, as he had been involved earlier with Rousseau's conception of the whole in his own pedagogical lectures. Rousseau's *Émile* contains references to the whole/part problem which had attracted Durkheim. He quotes Rousseau in a lecture outline, for example, where Rousseau writes: "The citizen is but the numerator of a fraction, whose value depends on its denominator; his value depends on the whole. . . ." He adds that social institutions should create dependence from independence, so the individual "no longer regards himself as one, but as a part of a whole . . ." (Durkheim 1979, 167; Rousseau 1911, 7). He also relates the whole/part problem to the society/individual issue, roughly equating the two problems in a manner familiar to readers of *Division*. The whole/part or society/individual problem is also linked to another question which haunted Durkheim's work throughout his career: the "duality" problem in moral, religious, and social life. It seems that Durkheim largely equated these three perspectives in his early work, although, as I shall later demonstrate, he modified this equation in some crucial respects as his thinking developed. As we have seen, Aristotle had already conceived of the whole/part problem as identical, in one of its aspects, that pertaining to life in the *polis*, with the society/individual issue. At times, when discussing this question, Durkheim sounds a good deal like Aristotle. However, the problem of duality does not entirely mirror the whole/part problem. As we will see later, the whole/part problematic is a broader one, only one facet of which can be identified with the society/individual issue or with the question of "the duality of human nature."

When we turn to Rousseau's political and social theory, as seen through the lens of Durkheim's treatment, we discover that the question of whole/part or totality is central. Durkheim argues that Rousseau does not think society is natural, but emerges because men need one another, a mutual assistance which for Rousseau is not naturally necessary (Durkheim 1965, 81; 1966a, 135). Only under the press of external circumstances does society arise through the modification of human needs and, as a result, a change of human nature, one which develops a human's latent, but as yet unrealized perfectability.

Even this increased mutual association does not create society. For that, human relationships must not merely exist, but be truly organized. Durkheim quotes Rousseau's *Geneva Manuscript* to the effect that there must be a "connection between the parts, that constitutes the whole" (Durkheim 1965, 82; 1966a, 135; see Rousseau 1978, 159). According to Durkheim, Rousseau is saying that society is a moral entity with qualities distinct from the individuals that compose it. Rousseau uses a number of different metaphors to capture this idea. Society is like a chemical compound different from its elements. Durkheim again quotes Rousseau's idea that a true society would be a "social body" (*corps social*) which would have a "common sensorium that would oversee the correspondence of all the parts" (Durkheim 1965, 82; 1966a, 136). Here, we see Durkheim once again entertaining the notion of a "common sensorium." It is an idea which he had already identified from Saint-Simon, probably absorbed from Charles Renouvier, and which he also used to characterize religion in his letter to Gaston Richard. For Durkheim, such remarks demonstrated that Rousseau understood the "specificity of the social order" and saw that "society is nothing if not a single definite body distinct from its parts" (Durkheim 1965, 83; 1966a, 136–37). Indeed, he quotes Rousseau to the effect that society results from a "liason" of parts which constitute the whole (Durkheim 1965, 83; 1966a, 137). Despite what Durkheim sees as the contradictory quality of many of Rousseau's basic formulations, he clearly finds much of interest in him concerning the problem of the whole. In these pages, I want to focus on the problem of totality in Durkheim and, therefore, must pass over

Durkheim's many analyses, comments, and criticisms of Rousseau. Instead, I want to pick up a strand of thought in Rousseau which was relevant to Durkheim's interest in totality: the problems of the general will, the will of all, sovereignty, and so forth.

Durkheim sees Rousseau's theory in the following terms. For there to be a civil state which overcomes the nonsocial state of natural man, there must be a moral force which transcends the individual will. The moral order is something added "synthetically" to the evolving social facts and cannot be found in them. This "synthetic connection" requires a new force, namely, the general will. However, for individuals to respect the general will, it must be something outside them, a being sui generis. This being is, in fact, society and it is only through the creation of a "social body" that the moral order, the general will, realizes itself in nature. Sovereignty, in turn, is only the collective force in the service of the general will. This sovereignty is inalienable and indivisible, but it is not coherent by virtue of being an organic unity. Its unity is that of a homogeneous force which emanates from the entire people (Durkheim 1965, 110–11; 1966a, 168–69). Durkheim remarks that this idea is rooted in a "vitalist and substantialist conception of life and society" (Durkheim 1965, 112; 1966a, 170). The "parts" of the social body resulting from this conception are not parts of a organic system of mutually supportive functions, and, as a result, they are hardly "parts" at all in Durkheim's view. Even if the sovereign creates distinct powers such as magistrates, "[T]he powers which are thus born are not parts, but emanations of the sovereign power . . . finding their unity in it and by it" (Durkheim 1965, 112; 1966a, 170). Throughout this passage, Durkheim echoes the findings about social solidarity from *Division* and implicitly compares Rousseau's theory with his own. In effect, he argues that Rousseau has hit upon what Durkheim himself has called "mechanical" (rather than "organic") social solidarity.

This sovereign is "the people in an active state; the people is the sovereign in a passive state" (Durkheim 1965:114; 1966a, 172). If the sovereign were to deal with individual or private matters, rather than public ones, it would cease to express the general will "for it is no longer the will of the whole. The whole minus a part, is no longer the whole. There is no longer a whole, but unequal parts" (Durkheim 1965, 114; 1966a, 172). From this standpoint, the object of the laws is "to express the relation between the whole and the whole, that is, between the totality (*ensemble*) of citizens regarded as sovereign and the totality (*ensemble*) of citizens regarded as subjects" (Durkheim 1965, 122; 1966a, 181). This ingenious formulation of Rousseau's theory is rather unusual in Durkheim's discussions of the problem of the whole. I cannot think of another passage where he so deliberately identifies two corresponding wholes in precisely these terms. He does do something similar in his last book on religion, where religion, totality, and society are mutually identified as different expressions of one and the same notion. However, the contexts are vastly different, one the problem of sovereignty and social-political theory, the other the study of religion, the categories, and society. I would therefore be wary in identifying the two discussions, although it is certainly suggestive to see Durkheim develop such ideas and images in his discussion of Rousseau's work.

This set of passages, focused on the whole/part problem in Durkheim's reading of Rousseau, do shed a certain new light on Durkheim's own conception in *Division*. What sort of whole is constituted by a society characterized by "mechanical solidarity?" From Durkheim's remarks on Rousseau, it would appear that it is a whole without true parts, or, at least, one whose parts are little more than "emanations" of the whole. It is worth noting that the discussion has hardly turned away from the identification of the whole/part relation as one of the relationship of society and individual, or, in Rousseau's terms, between the individual and the general will. There is no hint in Durkheim's reading of Rousseau that he thought the latter had anything important to say about the other whole/part relations which are central to *Division* and to the lectures on professional ethics. This whole/part relation is not that of society/individual, but of society and the groups which compose it.

Where does this leave us? In omitting any reference to this latter whole/part problem (i.e. society/subgroups), one so central to his earlier formulation in *Division*, is Durkheim breaking new ground, or is he merely suggesting an implicit criticism of Rousseau? Durkheim clearly admires Rousseau's attempt to conceptualize, in rather sophisticated terms, the specific reality of society. It is of interest that he does not criticize Rousseau on this particular point, but rather on the more general issue of Rousseau's tendency to see humankind as, by nature, nonsocial, with society emerging only later in his conjectural history of humanity. In the end, for Durkheim, the individual is never the starting point and all the contradictions of Rousseau's system result from the fact that he tries to wed an individualistic conception of human nature with an emerging sociologistic conception of society, that is, one which recognizes society as a "whole" with priority over the parts. This contradictory formulation can only be avoided and the fuller sociologistic theory asserted if the individual is, in effect, eliminated from the picture entirely, at least as far as early society is concerned, that is, society with mechanical solidarity. One either accepts Rousseau's formulation about the general will, in which case the parts (i.e. the individuals) emanate from the whole (i.e. society), or one recasts the whole/part problem (as Durkheim did) as a question of the relationships between society and its subgroupings, with the society/individual complex now a second form of the whole/part problem.

In his own early work, Durkheim ends with two whole/part problems, rather than one (or, more accurately, given his discussions in the lectures on professional ethics, several whole/part problems). Perhaps he meant to do so. In light of his later work, I think that this formulation is a sign of conceptual ambiguity, rather than clear deliberation, and reflects his need to "stretch" the whole/part notion to fit all his theoretical needs. However, I also think that there is already a hint of a new starting point in Durkheim's comments on Rousseau. The notion of the parts "emanating" from the whole can be viewed critically or constructively. As noted above, there is no indication that Durkheim was directly critical of this part of Rousseau, as far as it went. Indeed, it is strange that he does not more directly link it to his argument about mechanical solidarity in *Division*. My sense is that Durkheim is already moving toward a conception of the whole which is more dependent on the role of religion, and this is signaled in a small way in the issues he chooses to raise in his treatment of Rousseau. Rousseau's use of mathematical analogies in describing the general will, his treatment of individual/society relations in terms of "forces," and his use of the term "effervescence" to describe his own personal transformation are additional reasons why Durkheim might find him attractive (Rousseau 1978, 31, 53, 61). In this treatment, he revisits, and, I think, begins to revise the conception of totality found in his first book.

The Problem of the Whole in Durkheim's Lectures on Education

Moral Education

Durkheim's sociology emerges within the institutional interstices, and, to a certain extent, within the intellectual context, of pedagogy, or the study of education. His original position at Bordeaux was as Chargé de Cours in pedagogy and the social sciences (Lukes 1973, 95). While at Paris, he continued to teach and write regularly about education. Several of his most extensive posthumously published series of lectures were in this area, one on moral education and another on the development of secondary education in France. Both of these works, as well as several shorter essays and unfinished manuscripts not only reveal Durkheim's views about education and society, but also provide information concerning our subject: the problem of totality in Durkheim's social theory.

The lectures do pose problems in the chronology of Durkheim's ideas. We are told by Paul Fauconnet that the lectures on *Moral Education* are from the year 1902–3, and were the first in that field that he gave at Paris, and that they were repeated in 1906–7. However, he also remarks that Durkheim had already sketched his ideas on this subject earlier while still at Bordeaux (Durkheim 1961:v). Similar comments could be made about his work on the development of educational thought, which were delivered in 1904–5, and again in subsequent years afterwards until World War I (Durkheim 1977, xi). As a result, it is not easy to locate the precise beginning points of the ideas found in them, especially if the lecture series subsequently published were developed in continuity with earlier lectures by Durkheim. Also, they were not published by Durkheim himself, and represent either manuscripts published after his death or works reconstructed from notes taken by students and colleagues. However, they do tell us a good deal about Durkheim's thought at the time the particular lectures were delivered. As a result, they can be very helpful in fleshing out Durkheim's developing thought on the problem of totality, especially as it emerged within particular substantive fields, like education (as with other topics like socialism and professional ethics). This is especially true of the lectures on the development of education in France, which contain some extraordinarily interesting passages relevant to our present concerns.

It is worth noting at the outset that the whole/part problem is featured rather prominently in the lectures on *Moral Education*. Durkheim makes the now familiar judgment that a human is a limited being, a part of a larger whole, both morally as part of society, and physically, as part of nature (Durkheim 1961, 51; 1974b, 44). Society itself is an "enormously complex whole" (Durkheim 1961, 251; 1974b, 213). It is not primarily the individual's idea of it, but a complex of collective ideas and sentiments. He sees society primarily in terms of consciousness, in particular, a "consciousness of the whole" (Durkheim 1961, 277; 1974b, 236) and reiterates his idea that, without exception, a whole must be something beyond "the sum of its parts" (Durkheim 1961, 61; 1974b, 53). The interaction and association of the elements naturally gives rise to new phenomena. While Durkheim is concerned to promote individual autonomy, his predominant posture is to favor the collective over the individual. In defending the use of collective sanctions in the classroom, a practice which might seem to violate our sense of individual responsibility, he argues that the child must be made to feel a contributing and responsible part of a larger solidary group. Such collective penalties provide the unique opportunity to instill in the child "the feeling (*sentiment*) that we are not a self-sufficient whole, but the part of a whole (*la partie d'un tout*) that envelops and penetrates us, and on which we depend" (Durkheim 1961, 245; 1974b, 208).

The child's sociological education can also be advanced by the study of biology and chemistry, where the examination of the combination and association of elements to form larger unities is an established fact, one which, by analogy, will help the child better understand the reality of society. Such studies will help the child better comprehend the fact that a "whole is not identical with the sum of its parts" and, by analogy, that "society is not simply the sum of individuals who compose it" (Durkheim 1961, 264). It is worth calling attention to the fact that Durkheim's interest in the pedagogical value of chemistry and biology is specifically related to his emphasis on the use of analogy, the whole/part problem, and the sui generis quality of the societal whole. He argues for their inclusion on this basis alone and not out of a desire to advance natural scientific education or the understanding of scientific method. Durkheim calls attention to the "Cartesian" orientation toward the rational analysis of things into their elements which possesses the French. However valuable this approach to reality, it has the disadvantage of overlooking "the complex and living unity that these elements of concrete reality form when they are joined together, when they interpenetrate or fuse" (Durkheim 1961, 253; 1974b, 215). Language and analysis itself alert us to the simple. The character which "the totality takes on as a totality . . . that which makes its unity, continuity, and life, it (i.e. language) is in large measure uninterested" (Durkheim 1961, 253; 1974b, 215). Continuing in the same vein, Durkheim argues that the reduction of society to nothing but the individuals composing it leaves us with a "vertible social atomism. Society becomes only a collective noun, a spurious name given to a sum of individuals externally juxtaposed" (Durkheim 1961, 257; 1974b, 218). Here, Durkheim employs a form of argument familiar in his mature work. He rejects the idea that society is merely a "collective noun," "a spurious name" or a mere "mental construct." This is in keeping with his general rejection of all nominalism regarding society's reality. Society is much more than a "level of analysis" or a creation of reason. It is an ontological reality, perhaps even a "substance."

While discussing two faces of morality, duty versus the good, Durkheim argues that this moral dualism is overcome in society. These two elements of morality are only two aspects of the same reality. Society both commands us and penetrates us, it forces us but also inspires us. Their unity is that of a "real entity," even "a real being of which they (i.e. duty and the good) express different modes of action" (Durkheim 1974b, 84). These passages reveal Durkheim's repeated effort to transcend dualisms in favor of a more unified perspective. They also give us a clear indication that he had come to see the two dimensions of morality (duty and the good) as "modes" of a larger whole, that is, society (a fact badly obscured by the existing translation). Both reflect the operation of social forces which "constrain" as well as "expand" the individual. This is one of the few places where Durkheim speaks explicitly about the "modes" of society. However, as we have seen, such a view is implied in *Suicide*.

Society must have a unity in which individuals are devoted to the pursuit of collective ends. The spirit of discipline alone is not enough, especially during periods of moral crisis, like the contemporary one. It is also necessary to engage and inspire. Society must have a unity resulting from an exact regulation between its parts and a harmonious relationship among its various functions. This can be obtained through effective discipline. However, society also must have a unity which results from a common commitment, one directing wills to a common objective. Otherwise, "it is no more than a pile of sand . . ." (Durkheim 1961, 102; 1974b, 87). This comparison of a disintegrated society to a mere "pile of sand" recalls his earlier critique of Spencer and points toward Aristotle's distinction between wholes with uniform versus nonuniform parts. A morally ill society has become one with uniform parts, subject to egoistic disintegration.

As he later wrote, in an essay of 1911 on education, an ideal of humankind is found in every society and is differentiated for each social milieu found in the society. This ideal, which is the focus of education, has as its function to arouse in the child a set of physical and mental states appropriate to both the child's existence in society and in the particular groups to which he is attached (e.g caste, class, family, profession). The ideal set forth in education must emerge from both "society as a whole" as well as "each particular social milieu" (Durkheim 1956, 70; 1966b, 40). Indeed, a class is a small society and not an agglomeration of independent subjects. In a class, there emerge the varied phenomena of "contagion, collective demoralization, mutual overexitement, wholesome effervescence," all of which must be understood if one is either to combat them or utilize them (Durkheim 1956, 112; 1966b, 79). It is remarkable to see Durkheim describing the school class in terms very similar to his contemporaneous discussion of the dynamics of religious effervescences. This certainly gives pause to anyone wishing to limit Durkheim's conception of the dynamic and creative quality of society to purely religious or sacred settings. This and other passages also point to the fact that Durkheim saw many group settings as potentially generative of what he would usually describe as "religious" dynamics. I would recall that Durkheim had even used the notion of "effervescence" in *Suicide* to describe the pathological overexcitement which accompanied anomie (Durkheim 1995a, 284). We need to be careful not to automatically identify this idea of collective enthusiasms solely with the development of sacred religious forces. Durkheim seems to have used it more broadly to describe collective forces generally, whether their outcomes were socially beneficial or pathological. Indeed, the general interchangeability of these terms at different points in the analysis, for different purposes, seems to imply a more abstract conception of social energies accompanying social assemblies, that is, unbound concentrations of the social substance.

In this same essay, Durkheim argues that homogeneity and diversity are both necessary for society to flourish. There exist two beings in each of us, the individual being with the mental states peculiar to each, and the collective one, expressed through the system of shared ideas, sentiments, and practices. These include the religious, moral, national, occupational, and other beliefs, practices, and currents of opinion of society or its various subgroups. "Their totality (*ensemble*) forms the social being (*l'être social*)" (Durkheim 1956, 124; 1966b, 92). Durkheim sees the personality in its social aspect as a refraction of a variety of group settings, in sum, the total social involvements of the individual. Indeed, it is not clear what the content of the more purely "personal" mental states would or could be apart from the societal ones. Durkheim never tells us, and, in any case, is uninterested in them. Moreover, he sees these groups and their collective mental states as parts of a larger "social being" and identifies this being with his notion of totality. We once again see the whole/part analogy operating in two different ways.

In *Moral Education*, Durkheim rejects the idealistic view that morality is part of a transcendent realm separate from the world or nature. He argues that "[T]he universe is one." The end of moral conduct is "beings (*les êtres*)." These are superior to the individual, yet equally "empirical and natural," just as natural as "minerals or living beings: these are societies" (Durkheim 1961, 266; 1974b, 225–26). Underneath the symbolic exterior, the formulas, in which morality is expressed, "there are real forces" and these are "the soul (*l'âme*)" of society (Durkheim 1961, 92; 1974b, 77). Collective sentiment and public opinion lie behind the moral symbols. This sentiment and opinion is a "force as real and actual as the forces that fill the physical world" (Durkheim 1961, 92; 1974b, 78). This notion of the real complexity of things must itself become a "category" of thought for the child (Durkheim 1961, 261; 1974b, 221). Here, we see some of Durkheim's central ideas: the ontological reality of society; its existence as a force or system of forces which constitute its "essense"; the identification of these forces with "sentiment" or "public opinion"; finally, the rejection of ontological dualism in favor of the the idea that "the universe is one." We will see how far Durkheim takes this latter idea in his last writings.

The Evolution of Educational Thought

Maurice Halbwachs informs us that the lectures on the development of secondary education were delivered by Durkheim in 1904–5 and repeated in following years until World War I (Durkheim 1977, xi; 1969a, 1). This places them at a particularly important point in Durkheim's intellectual development. They represent a stage in his thinking well after his shift in focus toward religion and the study of the categories, yet before the full fruition of this move in the work of 1912. They fall shortly after he and Mauss published the essay on *Primitive Classification* and contain a good deal of material which has a bearing on Durkheim's logical interests. They are a substantial and important work in their own right, quite apart from their relationship to our problems. They cut a wide path through the intellectual and cultural history of Western Europe, from the Middle Ages to the nineteenth century. They provide important evidence for our discussion, even though—precisely because—they were not designed to focus explicitly on our particular concerns.

Toward the very end of the lecture series, Durkheim notes the omnipresence of an "encyclopedic" perspective in French educational history and affirms the value of this educational orientation in a fashion familiar to students of his work. Since the ideal of encyclopedic culture has been a persistent, developing feature of French educational evolution, "it is impossible that it should be a mere fantasy" (Durkheim 1977, 347; 1969a, 398). Durkheim uses the same mode of reasoning here, in the affirmation of the value of encyclopedic education, that he employs in his demonstration of the reality of religion. The persistence of a cultural outlook is a guarantee that it cannot be an illusion. Earlier in the lectures, he had already referred to the truth of Christianity in a similar way (Durkheim 1977, 336; 1969a, 386). In the *Forms*, he reiterates this view in more general terms (Durkheim 1995b, 226–31). This amounts to the idea that no traditional belief which is so persistent in the history of a society can be based on an illusion. The *consensus gentium* must contain some truth. It must have some reality behind it, even if that reality is not to be understood precisely in the terms in which it was originally expressed and even if sociology alone can recover its true nature and meaning. Durkheim even suggested that it was somehow "monstrous" to think that people throughout history could have consistently been deceived by false ideas or deceived themselves about reality. The role played by this methodological commitment in Durkheim's work is considerable. It marks the distance of his critical reappropriation of religion from any purely skeptical or Enlightenment Age critique.

It is of the greatest interest that Durkheim immediately follows the sentence quoted above, about the importance of encyclopedic education, with the following remark: ". . . [I]t (i.e. encyclopedic education) responds to that very profound idea that the part (*la partie*) cannot be understood if one does not have a conception of the whole (*le tout*) from which it emerges" (Durkheim 1977, 347; 1969a, 398). By now we are familiar with Durkheim's repeated and varied uses of this notion, but I can think of few other places where he refers to it in such glowing terms. Its frequent appearance in his work should lead us to think that he always believed it to be such. It is particularly interesting that Durkheim links the notion of the whole/part relation with his deepest intellectual intuition about the reality of such perennial phenomena as encyclopedic culture and religion, in effect, anticipating his later identification of the notions of divinity and totality. The traditional commitment to encyclopedic education rests on an experience similar to that at the root of religion. Neither are entirely illusory. Each in its own way is an intuition of the whole. Aspects of the fuller argument in the *Forms* were already emerging at this time, but in entirely different intellectual contexts. This is not the only aspect of that later argument which appears in the lectures.

Durkheim also ties humankind to nature in a way characteristic of his later treatise. Only a mutilated and unreal being exists if humankind is abstracted from Nature. He argues that an individual "is not a self-sufficient whole, but a part of the whole of which he is a function" (Durkheim 1977, 337; 1969a, 387). After this enhanced conception of the whole/part problematic, he goes on to argue that even the most idealistic religions have some sort of cosmology which locates humanity within Nature. Durkheim and Mauss were already examining some of the elements of cosmology, those having to do with primitive classification, and Durkheim later expanded these investigations, very much in the manner suggested in these lectures on educational thought.

Durkheim also presents a view of the categories and their role which is congruent with his later work. In a remarkable sequence of claims, he argues that everything in the universe can be comprehended in the main categories of understanding. This is possible because the categories are merely "higher-order classes which include all things and outside of which there is nothing." Thus, the understanding of these fundamental concepts, their interrelationships and operation in reasoning and judgment, leads simultaneously to an understanding of "reality as a whole" and does so with a "maximum generality." Durkheim writes: "The mind . . . is a microcosm, a universe reduced to scale and portraying in miniature the greater one outside." Therefore, from one perspective, when we understand the mind, we understand the world. Those various sciences which study the mind therefore "constitute an abridged kind of encyclopaedia" (Durkheim 1977, 50–51; 1969a, 63). Durkheim traces the development of this interest in the categories from the study of grammar in the Carolingian era, where the properties of words led in a beginning fashion to the study of ontology, to the more rigorous debates over the nature of universals in the twelfth century period (Durkheim 1977, 57–60; 1969a, 70–73).

We cannot now pause to ask how this extended description of

the role of the categories and the mind, as well as the sciences of the mind, is related to the special function fulfilled by humankind in the universe, nor does Durkheim tell us in any direct way. But these remarks are enormously suggestive. They raise the question of humanity's ultimate place in the world, its purpose, so to speak. Moreover, the references to the microcosmic quality of thought and the role of the categories in this process are soon repeated in an even less guarded fashion in the section of Durkheim's essay of 1909, which was omitted from the *Forms* (Durkheim 1982, 237–39). The reference to the historical antecedents of this problem in the medieval period, especially the debate over universals, is also of considerable interest. While this discussion is not directly connected with the whole/part issue, or even with his conception of society as a reality *sui generis*, it does confirm the sense that Durkheim was willing to bring the medieval debates over the "reality" of universals into the intellectual mix. More noteworthy is the fact that this is one of the few places where he does so.

I will argue later in these pages that Durkheim does, indeed, move toward a particular view of humankind's place in the wider scheme of things, one which is at the center of his sociological metaphysics. For the moment, I would add only that these various quotations of the lectures on educational thought once again reaffirm Durkheim's commitment to an investigation rooted in the problem of the whole/part relation and that, even in these lectures, he sees the whole/part problem as having several different facets.

A close reading of these lectures immediately makes clear that Durkheim's history of educational thought is also structured in terms of his other key sociological concepts. For example, a central guiding thread is the conflict between religious and secular thought in education, or, in Durkheim's own terms, the conflict between sacred and profane. The problem emerges, in part, from the fact that Christianity inherited secular learning from pagan antiquity. Moreover, although education begins in the medieval world primarily in religious institutions, it becomes increasingly secular, indeed, carries within it a "principle of secularity" (Durkheim 1969a, 33; not "circularity" as in Durkheim 1977, 25). This principle was "innate" in these institutions and, as a result, they carried within them the germ of "that great struggle between the sacred and profane" (Durkheim 1977, 25–26; 1969a, 33).

It is also remarkable that Durkheim continues to employ one of his key concepts, the idea of social concentration, so central in *Division*, the *Rules*, and elsewhere. Durkheim notes that the emergence of important cultural centers first requires "an energetic movement of concentration" (Durkheim 1977, 37; 1969a, 47). He adds that education results from concentration and that, for education, "dispersion means death" (Durkheim 1977, 118; 1969a, 137). The Carolingian court school provided the beginnings of such a concentration. This process was taken further in the cathedral schools and, especially, with the emergence of the colleges and universities after the twelfth century, when a vast amount of "force," "moral energy," and "vitality" were "concentrated" (Durkheim 1977, 66–69; 1969a, 79–81). In fact, the Carolingian era, the twelfth-century developments, and what has been called the Renaissance in the sixteenth century were all only "an uninterrupted series of renaissances" (Durkheim 1977, 34; 1969a, 44). Here, Durkheim identifies his own notions of increasing "moral density" and "collective effervescences" in the intellectual, cultural realm, with the inherited notion of a "Renaissance." It is particularly interesting that the actual sociological process is conceived as one of "concentration" in which the society undergoes modifications through the reorganization of group life into new centers. Durkheim continues to insist that this "concentration" requires the physical movement of populations and is by no means only a collective mental process within the realm of representations. His references to the "nomadism" of the twelfth century era confirms this fact. These modifications of society through "concentration" of previously unassociated social groups serves to gestate "forces" and release "moral energy." The concentration of this energy allows it to be channeled into new cultural forms.

In his treatment of the twelfth-century Renaissance, Durkheim also reveals one of his strongest negative orientations: his unwillingness to grant any importance to the individual, even the "great individual," in his theory of cultural revival. This idea reflects his general view of the individual in society. This attitude is already implicit in one of his very first written works, his speech at the prize ceremony at the Lycée of Siens in 1883 (Durkheim 1975, I:409–17, esp. 416). The individual can only refract the collective forces that play upon him and "incarnate the ideal here on earth," but never be a truly independent source of change. In the lectures on the evolution of education, Durkheim speaks at length about Abelard's great significance during this period, but views him only as a focal point for the coalescence of collective moral energies. Abelard was an "incarnation" of the twelfth century's ideals. The twelfth century admired Abelard, like the eighteenth century

admired Voltaire. In doing so, both centuries were admiring themselves (Durkheim 1977, 70; 1969a, 85). Durkheim knows of
Abelard's great importance, and, therefore, cannot entirely omit a
discussion of him. But his treatment is most revealing of his theoretical intentions. The individual, even the extraordinary one, is
always only a mode of a more inclusive social substance. It is the
process of social concentration which forces the social energy into,
and out of, the individual. Everything important or creative about
the individual is always and everywhere the reflection of collective
processes.

These lectures are enormously revealing. They bridge the
period between Durkheim's first book and his last one and contain
theoretical notions from both, but focus them now on the historical
development of education. Social concentration, force, energy, cultural revivals, the derivative character of individuals, the
whole/part relation, the role of the categories in summarizing reality, the sacred and the profane, and a number of other Durkheimian
ideas all find expression in these pages. The lectures are a good
measure of the continuity as well as the transition in his thinking.
They demonstrate that he never relinquished his commitment to a
philosophy which would link transformations in the social substance with the evolution of the highest cultural ideals.

Fragments of The Problem of Totality in Durkheim's Essays II: 1905–1912

The period between about 1905 and 1912 sees the increasing
development of the themes which become central to Durkheim's
last book. Several of the essays published during this period contain particularly important discussions. They also add some new
images, which expand Durkheim's metaphorical range and enrich
his rhetoric.

In an essay of 1906 on "The Determination of Moral Facts"
and the discussion which followed it, Durkheim raises some issues
of concern to us in a manner both similiar to as well as different
from what we have come to expect of him. Durkheim opposes the
Kantian concept of duty as the center of morality and argues that
both duty and the good need to be seen as equally important
aspects of the moral life. He notes that this duality in the concept
of morality is also found in the notion of the sacred, which is simultaneously loved, yet also forbidden and feared. Durkheim rejects

the idea that morality can ever be identified with the egoistic actions of the individual. Neither I nor any other individual can be seen as the locus of morality in society. He concludes from this that the object of morality must be the numerous associated individuals considered as a single personality "qualitatively different" from its constituent individuals (Durkheim 1974a, 37; 1967, 42). This idea is reaffirmed later in the discussion when Durkheim argues that morality cannot be attached either to acts of the individual or even to those of one individual towards others (although he does not entirely deny the possibility of labeling as "moral" those acts directed to the welfare of others). He insists that the number of individuals is not the central issue. If the single individual cannot endow conduct with a moral character, a "total sum (*le total*) of individuals" added together numerically will also be unable to do so. Only a new subject, sui generis, can constitute the object of morality. For a system of moral duties and obligations to exist, society must be a "moral person qualitatively distinct from the individual persons" which compose it and from whose synthesis it results. Durkheim claims that this argument is analogous to the one used by Immanuel Kant to demonstrate the existence of God. Kant postulates God, while Durkheim postulates society as the necessary root of morality (Durkheim 1974a, 51–52; 1967, 58). Disinterestedness and devotion are the two core features of morality and the only object other than the Divinity which can instill these responses is society. For Durkheim they are identical. As he notes, in one of the most forthright statements of his view, "Between God and society lies the choice." Both hypotheses are coherent. Durkheim is indifferent to the choice between them, since in God he sees "only society transfigured and symbolically expressed" (Durkheim 1974a, 52; 1967, 59). He adds that society, the object of morality, simultaneously transcends us, yet is immanent in us (Durkheim 1974a, 54; also 55; 1967, 62).

I want to call attention to several features of Durkheim's argument. First, we see Durkheim employing the opposition between society as a collective "personality" and the sum of individual subjects who compose it. Although this usage is hardly unique in his work, here Durkheim comes as close to reifying society into a living personality as he does anywhere. This usage testifies once again to the strength of his sense of society's separate "reality." Second, and more central to our concerns, is the way he rather obliquely raises the question of number and uses the categories of quantity and quality. These notions serve not only in his comparison of the individual and society, but also in the comparison of a sum of individuals with society. Quantitative increase in the number of individuals is insufficient in itself to bring about moral life. Only a qualitative transformation of these individuals when they are associated in a particular way can do this. Society is this qualitatively transformed quantity of individuals. We have already discussed Durkheim's use of the notions of quantity and quality in *Suicide*, both in connection with the whole/part analogy as well as with the problem of causality. It is interesting to see Durkheim once again addressing our problem from this standpoint. This time he uses both categories, quantity and quality. He especially emphasizes the notion that quantitative change, at a certain point and under certain conditions, becomes qualitative change. This fits better into his overall image of whole/part and society/individual relations, with fewer of the difficulties which emerged when he tried to amalgamate the quantity/quality distinction with the more linear notion of causality. Although we once again see Durkheim using the quantity/quality distinction as a rationale in the explanation of society's very nature and reality, the precise character of this qualitative transformation remains unclear.

Durkheim also raises the question of number. Number appears as a category in Durkheim's short list in the *Forms*, although he says little directly about it in those pages (or anywhere else). Number clearly was implicated as a reality (but not a category) in his explanation of the rise of organic solidarity in *Division*. His various references in his subsequent writings to the precise role of population density and volume point to it as a sticky problem in his work (Durkheim 1982, 136–37; 146, fn.21). Problems of quantity are also central to *Suicide*, where he attempts to quantify the outcomes of social forces, and, thereby, indirectly measure them. Indeed, number is at the very heart of his proofs and implicates many other issues, including the idea of concentration, the precise nature of collective effervescences, and the role of social morphology or the distribution of groups in social space. The fact that this essay distinguishes a mere additive process from a qualitative transformation is therefore of considerable interest. A total sum (*le total*) is distinguished implicitly from a true totality, a whole, a qualitatively transformed sum. Here, Durkheim's precise choice of words promotes a certain ambiguity. Durkheim never comes to an entirely satisfactory or consistent resolution to questions concerning the role of number, or the categories of quantity and quality in social life. The category of number eluded him, even while the problem of populations, their movements and distribution, remained important to him and his school (Mauss 1966, chap. 7). As I have already suggested, this may be a by-product of his commitment to a conception of the whole as a social substance which contains both "material" and "ideal" elements.

Durkheim's use of the notion of God or Divinity in this context is also noteworthy. He thinks his notion of society occupies the same place in his theory as God did in Kant's. This essay is concerned with the determination of moral ideas and, within this context, it is not strange that he should have recourse to a Kantian analogy about a topic so intimately related to Kant's work. However, Durkheim departs from a strictly Kantian emphasis on the idea of duty. Also, his discussion concerns only the legitimation of morality through God (or society). This hardly exhausts Durkheim's conception of religion and its role in society and nature.

In a related exchange among Durkheim, Gustave Belot, and Jules Lachelier, published in 1908, Durkheim responds to the discussion by agreeing that there is a duality between the individual, animal life, and both the moral life and life of the mind. But he notes that this duality raises problems only if it conceived as a "linear series" in which one becomes a means to the other as an end. But the problems disappear if we adopt the image of a "circle" and view one aspect of the duality as "the part (the individual) of which the other is the whole (society)." In a fascinating, if rather confusing formulation, Durkheim argues that the parts and the whole are mutual functions of one another. He adds that the whole is, in a sense, the end for which the parts provide the means. This is because the whole cannot exist without the parts. However, from another standpoint, the parts are themselves the end and Durkheim cites as evidence the idea that society's aim is to actualize the individual's potentials. Therefore, he concludes, everything is equally means and end, and there is no need to insist on an absolute reference point (Durkheim 1979, 54; 1975, II:343).

Durkheim's brief comments are immensely revealing about his mode of thought. There is nothing surprising about the reappearance of the familiar whole/part: society/individual correspondence. However, Durkheim now puts this notion to another use. He analogizes it to a circle and uses this new analogy to escape from the means-ends problem which haunted Kant's moral theory and poses problems for any theorist, like Durkheim, interested in the relationship between individual and society. We will recall the implicit appearance of means-ends problems as early as his critique of Tönnies' work. At that point, he was much less explicit about the new metaphor to be used in escaping the dilemmas of means-ends thinking, which haunted German social theorists such as Wilhelm Wundt, Ferdinand Tönnies, Max Weber and others. Is the individual a means to society's ends, or is society the individual's means to its own self-realization? Durkheim sees this as a false "linear" way of posing the problem and substitutes the circle image, to which he equates the whole/part problematic. Means and ends, individual and society, disappear as elements in a series, and are now mutually implied as coexistents in the whole/part complex.

It is noteworthy that Durkheim does not use the organismic analogy often thought to be his fundamental metaphor. Instead, the image of a circle shadows forth his whole/part perspective, further evidence of this perspective's centrality in his thinking and his willingness to capture it in other than organismic terms. We also see Durkheim stepping away from the Kantian way of posing the problem and moving toward a more Aristotelian one. In fact, there is no movement at all in Durkheim's position. All along, he has repeatedly adopted the Aristotelian whole/part problem as his own. Despite the Kantian trappings of his work, Kant's way of solving these problems was never Durkheim's (although Durkheim's way of initially posing them was sometimes similar to Kant's and he certainly drew on problems inherited from Kant's work). In the end, it is neither Aristotle nor Kant, but rather Spinoza who provides the best point of comparison with Durkheim's perspective.

One of the most important essays published during this period is on religious sociology and the sociology of knowledge. This essay, minus the third brief section, was later reprinted as the introduction to the *Forms*. Later we will discuss the material from this essay which found its way into the book. I want to focus now on the remarkable section of the original essay of 1909 which was omitted from the book. It treats the relationships among sociology, psychology, and philosophy.

He first states his familiar position on the relationship between sociology and psychology, that humans are a social product and, to understand them, we must understand society. He goes on to make an assertion about the relations between sociology and philosophy which is integral to our entire thesis. For methodological reasons, sociology has attempted to remove itself from the tutelage of philosophy, yet it is far from hostile to the latter, although it should not also be identified too closely with a shallow empiricism. Durkheim insists on the axiom that the perennial questions may be transformed, but never forgotten. This is true even of the metaphysical problems that have taxed philosophers. At the same time, they must be examined in new ways, and, for this reason, sociology is in a unique position to renew them (Durkheim 1982, 237; 1975, I:185–86). These remarks reveal one of Durkheim's central intentions: the hope of resolving the perennial problems of metaphysical philosophy (not merely moral philosophy or epistemology) and religion by sociological means.

Durkheim goes on to suggest that the philosopher's attempt to encompass the totality of things needs to be replaced by a sociological attack on this problem, one which cannot be resolved, in the nature of the case, by any of the specialized sciences. It is necessary to find a science which can be absorbed by the individual mind, yet has a central enough relation to "the totality of things" to establish the foundation of a "unified and philosophical speculation." Only the sciences of the mind or spirit (*l'esprit*) qualify. Durkheim writes that "the world exists for us only in so far as it is represented," and, as a result, "the study of the subject envelops that of the object." This makes it possible to take in "the universe as a whole (*ensemble*)," yet avoid having to ceate an encyclopedic culture, which is an unrealistic goal (Durkheim 1982, 238; 1975, I:186). Only the collective consciousness can perform this task, since it is "the true microcosm" (Durkheim 1982, 238; 1975, I:186). In it are found all the specialized intellectual accomplishments of an era. The unity of things, sought by philosophers, can only be achieved if they adopt the perspective of the collective mind. The further corrolary is that, for philosophy, sociology becomes the most helpful prolegomenon (Durkheim 1982, 238; 1975, I:187).

Sociology and philosophy are further linked by the centrality of the categories to both fields. The categories dominate thought by summarizing it and condensing the entirety of civilization. The human mind synthesizes the world and, in turn, "the system of categories is a synthetic expression of the human mind" (Durkheim 1982, 238; 1975, I:187). The study of the categories is increasingly the centerpiece of philosophy. This has been noted especially by the neo-Kantians, who have focused their efforts on creating a system of categories and attempting to discover the law unifying them (Durkheim 1982, 239; 1975, I:187). Since these categories are collective, historical products, the individual has little role in their development. To understand them, sociological investigations are required. We must grasp the poorly understood realities which lie behind them, including their nature, causes, and functions. Only then will we be able to create a philosophical system, enabling us "to philosophize about things rather than words" (Durkheim 1982, 239; 1975, I:188). For Durkheim, sociological reflection is called upon to extend in a natural progression the form of philosophical thinking (Durkheim 1982, 239; 1975, I:188). Finally, in an important footnote to his remark about Kant's recent disciples, Durkheim adds that these philosophers think the categories play a constitutive role in shaping reality, while he and his school think that they sum up reality. The neo-Kantians view them as a natural law of thought, while Durkheim sees them as "the product of human artifice." Despite this difference, both emphasize their role in synthesizing thought and reality (Durkheim 1982, 240; 1975, I:187, fn. 1).

We have provided a lengthy summary of this brief essay for several reasons. It states the philosophical aims of Durkheim's sociology as unambiguously as possible. It locates sociology as the most viable candidate to answer perennial metaphysical questions, ones which can never completely disappear. It raises questions about the categories, some of which are resolved in the *Forms* (and in the writings of his school). It also distinguishes his own view of the categories from that of the neo-Kantians. For them, the categories are a constitutive element in human nature, while, for Durkheim, they are a collective human artifice which sums up reality. It provides insight into his sense of sociology's role as a synthesizing science, one which can take in the world as a whole through its account of the categories, yet be mastered by the individual mind. It is a miniaturization, so to speak, of the cosmos. Durkheim's urge for totality finds its boldest expression in this brief statement.

I would dwell for a moment on the issue of Durkheim and the neo-Kantians. While they surely shared much in common, the differences are also crucial. The issue here is not that Durkheim offers a sociological account of the categories, while retaining a Kantian image of their operation. Instead, he distinguishes his sense that they sum up reality and are human artifices from the Kantian view of them as constitutive, a priori, rules. This view of the categories not only fits into his sociological theory, but also into his relationship with Aristotle and Bacon. It distinguishes his position from any sort of "idealism." As he noted later in the *Forms*, the categories are like tools (Durkheim 1995b, 18). In the terms of this essay, they are a product of human artifice. This capacity to sum up reality allows the human mind to have access to the totality of the cosmos through the categories. Durkheim's formulation is actually somewhat ambiguous. The categories are not precisely a synthetic expression of the human mind, if by that is meant the individual mind, but a synthetic expression of the collective mind. This is already implied in *Primitive Classification*, where the categories are modeled on the organization of society. It becomes even clearer in *Forms*, where the implications of this idea are drawn out more subtly and in greater detail by comparison with the present essay.

Durkheim's philosophical intentions are also expressed clearly in this brief statement. The problems of metaphysics are perennial. They never disappear, nor should they. This parallels the notion expressed in his lectures on the history of education about the persistence of the idea of encyclopedic education as well as his notion in the *Forms* that religion is a perennial phenomenon which captures an essential truth about reality. Sociology is the heir to all these efforts and, moreover, constitutes a natural progression and extension of philosophical and religious thinking. Sociology extends them to new horizons. This ambitious goal takes Durkheim far beyond any more modest effort to create an intellectual "niche" for sociology (and himself) through the creation of a sociology of knowledge (Schmaus 1994). Durkheim's sociology aims at unification and takes on the entire universe.

The remarkable references to the collective consciousness as the "true microcosm" which can take in the whole of the cosmos may help explain why Durkheim omitted these passages from his later book. They were perhaps too bold an expression of his standpoint. Yet, the present essay merely states unequivocally what is buried in the larger work. The collective, not the individual consciousness is the true microcosm. This is an important, if characteristically Durkheimian distinction, and forms a part of our conception of his sociological monism. This microcosmic quality of the collective mind brings the macrocosm, in some sense, within society. It is clear from this brief statement that the collective mind can be a microcosm because of the categories. They sum up reality and open up the possibility of the human mind knowing the totality of the cosmos without necessarily knowing all of its detailed operations. Encyclopedic culture, no longer possible for any individual, is displaced by knowledge of the cosmos through the categories. The categories of the collective mind are like a vortex, a funnel, so to speak, whose narrow end captures all of the cosmos within the categories and which in turn fans out into an infinitely wide and diffuse reality. The vortex of these categories, this microcosm, flows into society, itself a part of nature, as Durkheim repeatedly tells us. Society is therefore adequate to the task of creating such a microcosmic shunt through which flows the whole of reality.

I have fleshed out Durkheim's ideas with images (i.e. the vortex) which appear infrequently in his writings (e.g. Durkheim 1994b, 64). However, I do not think that I have distorted his meaning. The central images are all Durkheim's own: totality, the cosmos, the collective mind as microcosm, the categories as a summary device, their social nature, even elsewhere, the vortex. They are all worked out in much greater detail in his analysis of religion and knowledge in primitive societies.

I conclude this section with reference to Durkheim's essay on morality of 1910, where he combines several of his favorite images. There he argues that morality is a system composed of forces. These forces are not physical, but mental and moral. Their power emerges from the combined effects of action, representation, and consciousness (Durkheim 1979, 65; 1975, II:373). Durkheim's distinctions are worth noting, as is his partial tautology. Moral forces are not physical ones, but moral ones and mental ones. These moral forces derive their power from actions, representations, and states of consciousness. However, actions do take us into the realm of the "physical," as Durkheim himself emphasizes repeatedly in the *Forms*, where the role of collective assemblies and ritual practices are central to the theory. Although representations and conscience are "mental" processes, they are also in the later work, in their collective dimensions, viewed as thoroughly dependent on action, therefore, on the "physical." Indeed, I would strongly urge that, despite his disclaimer, Durkheim's moral forces are partly, perhaps preeminently, "physical" ones or dependent on them, and are such precisely because they are social. I see no easy way of separating Durkheim's conception of society from the actual physical movement and assembly of persons, even if such assemblies do not tell the whole story about society. Indeed, one of the biggest challenges for Durkheim's sociology is to convincingly link actions and representations, the physical and the mental, into a larger unity. In my view, he does so by creating a sociological monism rooted implicitly in the idea of social substance.

8

THE PROBLEM OF TOTALITY IN THE EARLY DURKHEIM SCHOOL: THE WORK OF DURKHEIM, MAUSS, HUBERT, HERTZ, AND BOUGLÉ

The present work is focused on Durkheim's writings. His texts provide the main evidence for our interpretation of his theory. However, Durkheim worked closely with a number of colleagues. Together they formed one of the most coherent and productive schools of thought in the history of sociology. They shared a large number of ideas in common, ones derived, in large part, from Durkheim himself, a sufficient number to give the term "Durkheim school" a meaningful intellectual content. We need to examine evidence relevant to our argument in the writings of Henri Hubert, Marcel Mauss, Célestin Bouglé, Robert Hertz, and others.

The ideas developed by these writers are by no means identical with Durkheim's formulations. Each author had his own particular domain of research, with its own problems, and each developed his own variant of theory. They all shared a great deal with Durkheim, but also departed occasionally, sometimes significantly, from his ideas.

Also, we need to distinguish between the work done by the Durkheimians during Durkheim's lifetime and the perspectives developed by them after his death. I will backtrack a bit chronologically and discuss those major writings produced between about 1903 and Durkheim's death, which help shed light on his thought. In particular, we will want to examine the following: Durkheim and Mauss on primitive classification; Hubert and Mauss on magic; Mauss's essay on seasonal variations in Eskimo society; Hubert's piece on time; the separate preface to the Hubert and Mauss *Mélanges*; Hertz's essay on religious polarity; and Bouglé's study of the Hindu caste system. These constitute the central collateral writings which need to be examined in connection with Durkheim's work.

Durkheim and Mauss on Primitive Classification

One of the most important collaborative texts for our present study is the lengthy essay on primitive classification by Durkheim and Mauss, first published in 1903 in *L'Année Sociologique*. I have included it in this section only because it is a jointly written work. The essay's main arguments are congruent with Durkheim's other writings and we could just as readily have placed it at an earlier point in our discussion. The minor differences between this essay and the one by Hubert and Mauss on magic published in the same year point to Durkheim's predominant influence. We will mention some of these differences as we proceed. However, I would immediately add that it is immensely difficult, perhaps to some degree impossible, to make such distinctions among the different intellectual creations of the Durkheim school done during Durkheim's lifetime. As Hubert and Mauss themselves note, although the essays on time and magic were credited to Hubert and Mauss respectively, they are both the result of collaborative effort and constant communication.

Mauss mentioned years later that this essay dealt with the notion of genre or kind (Mauss 1966, 334). The central focus is clearly on this topic, with a good deal of emphasis placed on the problem of classification as a hierarchical system of concepts, genus and species being especially prominent in the discussion. The notion of a system of classification is defined in these terms. In addition, they argue that no model is provided for such classificatory systems by either our mind or the physical world (Durkheim and Mauss 1963, 8; Durkheim 1969b, 399). The mind does not bear the framework of classification innately within it. Neither can such a classification be derived from the empirical observation of nature, although the models for the categories are later said to be taken from society itself. Durkheim and Mauss note that in Australian totemic societies, the moiety and the marriage classes provide the basis for the classification, with the former serving as genus, the latter as species. Everything in nature is divided among these classes, which thus form a full system of nature. Moreover, the ranking of these classes and concepts demonstrates that we are studying not merely a system of dualistic oppositions, but a true hierarchy of concepts (Durkheim and Mauss 1963, 14; Durkheim 1969b, 404). Other Australian systems use moities and totem clans as the basis of classification and, in general, Durkheim and Mauss trace a series of increasingly complex classificatory systems from the Zuni and the Sioux, to the Chinese and others.

The development of these systems takes place against the background of both the existing social structures and the preexisting classificatory systems (Durkheim and Mauss 1963, 32; Durkheim 1969b, 27). While society still furnishes the model for the ideas of these later systems, it is also true that the collective mind is able to react against its own societal cause and bring about changes in its own organization (Durkheim and Mauss 1963, 32; Durkheim 1969b, 417). In an argument reminiscent of the theory in *Division*, they note that the increasing size of the society results in the segmentation of new groups from the the existing ones; these are created along the lines of the existing classificatory system. The attachment of these new groups, usually sub-totems, to their original society and, thus, their classificatory relation to the existing system, wanes in emotional strength. After a time, each group exists independently, with each animal species or other object tied to its particular totemic grouping. The systematic quality of the classification is increasingly dissolved, yet together these totemic groups include most of the objects of the world within their now less systematic and hierarchical system. Thus, social dissociation and segmentation lead to disintegration of the classificatory system and, despite its continued scope and coverage of nature, it no longer serves as a systematic, hierarchical classification. In sum, Durkheim and Mauss are concerned to note the close link between the social system and the logical system (Durkheim and Mauss 1963, 41; Durkheim 1969b, 425).

The authors' treatment of the Zuni and Sioux systems brings to the forefront the issue of the spatial and functional organization of society and its classification system. There emerges a correspondence between the physical distribution of the clans in space and the development of a comprehensive logical system of spatial orientation, within which the remainder of the world is located and organized. While there are variations in emphasis among the different tribes, in general, the more complex system of spatial classification evolves from the earlier one. The original classification of things was by clans and totems, but when clans became strictly localized, the things attached to the clans also underwent localization. From this point forward, all objects in nature are conceived as having a "fixed relationship to equally fixed regions in space." The ideas of the camp and the world, tribal space and cosmic space are identified. "The camp is the center of the universe, and the whole universe is concentrated within it" (Durkheim and Mauss 1963, 65;

Durkheim 1969b, 443–44). The hierarchy of totemic groups is replaced by spatially fixed groups, and the classification system changes accordingly. Thus, there are two different types of primitive classification systems, one modeled on the jural and religious organization of the tribe, the other on its morphological organization (Durkheim and Mauss 1963, 65–66; Durkheim 1969b, 444–45).

After a brief discussion of the Chinese system of classification—they emphasize its increased independence from any social organization and its subsequent intellectual elaboration (Durkheim and Mauss 1963, 73; Durkheim 1969b, 450)—they move on to a particularly important concluding section. There the authors develop the issues most closely related to our present theme. Primitive classificatory systems are hierarchized systems of notions, with a speculative purpose, which "unify knowledge." There is no break in continuity between them and the first scientific classifications (Durkheim and Mauss 1963, 81; Durkheim 1969b, 455). This idea of continuity is repeated in Durkheim's later work as well as in his review of Lévy-Bruhl's book, which argued for a more radical discontinuity between primitive mentality and civilized thought (Lévy-Bruhl 1910; Durkheim 1969b, 679). The center of the Durkheim and Mauss analysis, of course, is their sociological account of these classificatory systems. "Society was not only a model which classificatory thought followed; it was its own divisions which served as divisions for the system of classification. The first logical categories were social categories . . ." (Durkheim and Mauss 1963, 82; Durkheim 1969b, 456). Things were thought to be part of society and it was their place in society that determined their place in nature. Moreover, since human groups fit into each other in an organized way, the first classifications of genera and species were also modeled on the hierarchy of society. All things could thus be linked to the group structure of society. The "totality of things" can be seen as a "single system" only because society itself is one. "It is a whole (*un tout*), or rather it is *the* unique whole (*le tout unique*) to which everything is related." They add that "logical hierarchy is just another aspect of social hierarchy, and the unity of knowledge is nothing else than the very unity of the collectivity, extended to the universe" (Durkheim, and Mauss 1963, 83–84; Durkheim 1969b, 457).

They also make the fascinating remark, related to one of our discussions above, that there are good reasons why "concepts and their interrelations have so often been represented by concentric and eccentric circles, interior and exterior to each other . . . ," since these very concepts were conceived in the form of social groups with particular spatial locations (Durkheim and Mauss 1963, 83; Durkheim 1969b, 456–57). Here, once again, we see Durkheim and Mauss conceiving of philosophical processes, in this case classificatory ones, in terms of the metaphor of a circle. But they are even more specific. They argue that logical groups were modeled on the lines of the kinship group, that logical relations are domestic relations (Durkheim and Mauss 1963, 84; Durkheim 1969b, 457) and also relations of subordination politically and economically.

This argument refers us to Durkheim's essays on domestic systems, matrimonial rules, and kinship structures, which we have shown to be closely related to the work on classification systems and the categories. It also allows the authors to introduce the argument from emotion or sentiment. The same sentiments at work in social, including domestic organization have spilled over into the logical divisions. The affective relations obvious among humans is transmitted to the object world. They argue that the classification of concepts by pure understanding is not the only possible classification. Ideas, which are products of sentiment, rather than pure reason, can themselves be systematized only by reasons of sentiment (Durkheim and Mauss 1963, 85; Durkheim 1969b, 458).

Religious emotions are particularly important in this connection. They interject ideas of sacred and profane, pure and impure into the conception of the world. Thus, things change their nature from society to society, depending on how the collective sentiments of society effect them. While our modern civilization works with homogeneous ideas about space, other societies have given an "affective value" to regions of space. In these latter societies, ideas are connected and separated by virtue of the emotional values attached to them (Durkheim and Mauss 1963, 86; Durkheim 1969b, 459). Humans first conceive things by relating them to themselves. This appears to be "anthropocentrism," but is better designated as "*sociocentrism* (emphasis in the original text)," since the first classifications of nature are not centered in the individual, but in society (Durkheim and Mauss 1963, 86–87; Durkheim 1969b, 459).

They conclude that logical classifications were difficult to form, because they were classifications of concepts, notions of clearly defined groups, while primitive classifications were laden with emotion, which in its essense is "fluid and inconsistent" and "contagious." Such classifications had a collective, emotional basis, and therefore defied rational and critical examination, since they were sacred to individuals.

From their standpoint, "the history of scientific classification is . . . the history of the stages by which this element of social affectivity has progressively weakened, leaving more and more room for the reflective thought of individuals" (Durkheim and Mauss 1963, 88; Durkheim 1969b, 460). At the end of the essay, they call attention to the possibility of carrying out similar sociological studies of other basic logical functions or fundamental notions besides classification, including the categories of time, space, cause, substance, and the different modes of reasoning (Durkheim and Mauss 1963, 88; Durkheim 1969b, 461).

I want to relate the above presentation to my primary focus. The study of primitive classification fully confirms the emphasis on the role of the categories, including that of totality, in the Durkheimian program. This study focuses on the problem of genre or kind, as Mauss tells us, but it also has a good deal to say about space and its role in classification. It also places the problem of the whole near the center of its analysis, without explicitly elaborating it. It also yields another reference to Aristotle. They credit him with discovering the reality of specific differences, showing that means are causes, and denying that one could pass directly between one genus and another. They claim that Plato had a less clear sense of these problems, including that of hierarchical organization (Durkheim and Mauss 1963, 5; Durkheim 1969b, 396). Durkheim and Mauss also proclaim that their future program of research would include not only all the basic categories (time, space, substance, cause, etc.), but also the "different modes of reasoning" (Durkheim and Mauss 1963, 88; Durkheim 1969b, 461).

This takes us more deeply into the heart of their project, although it is not entirely clear what "modes of reasoning" they had in mind. They probably would have started with those found in Aristotle's *Organon*, as they had done with the categories, for example, the logical analysis of propositions in *De Interpretatione* and the *Prior* and *Posterior Analytics* (Aristotle 1941, 40–206). In any case, neither Durkheim nor any of his school ever completed a sociological study of the modes of reasoning, although, in keeping with his desire to create a "new sociological organon," in the spirit of Sir Francis Bacon, Durkheim surely hoped to do so.

This text is one of the first in which Durkheim attempts to develop an idea which was logically implied from the very first in his choice of totemism as an object of investigation. As noted earlier, this choice seems to have been calculated to produce the best possible yield for his sociology of religion and knowledge. It allowed him to combine both of these investigations into one.

Totemism allowed him to study the most "primitive" religion and also allowed him to examine a set of beliefs and practices which already linked society to nature. I think that it was also this perfect fit for his wider religious and philosophical concerns, along with the congruence of totemic clan society with his prior study of mechanical solidarity and segmental structures which drove Durkheim to choose totemism as his focus. It was congruent with his prior analyses and pointed toward the future resolution of his philosophical questions. Despite the later criticism of Durkheim and of the very idea that totemism is a "religion," no less the most primitive one (e.g. Stanner in Durkheim 1994a, chap. 16; Lévi-Strauss 1963), such a view certainly fit his emerging intellectual needs. Totemism was a perfect basis for social philosophizing on a grand scale about humanity, God, and Nature. We have already seen how far Durkheim could take such philosophizing in the section of his 1909 essay omitted from the *Forms*.

In the present essay, Durkheim already begins to do so in the most systematic fashion, although as yet his scope is still limited to a single topic and there is little development of the importance of religion, except through the medium of the problem of collective sentiment or emotion. However, at this point in his work, the problem of emotion is still linked to the structure of kinship relations and only tangentially connected with religious beliefs and practices. In his final work, the role of religion increases, while the place of the kinship structures, as primary centers for the gestation of collective emotion and sentiment, is rather diminished. If we look at his earlier work on totemism, we discover that the place occupied by kinship analysis is much greater. Durkheim moves imperceptibly from the incest taboo, totemism, kinship structures, and matrimonial groups to the problem of classification, where kinship and religious sentiment are seen as mixed and produce intellectual outcomes. From there he moves toward his final work, where religious beliefs and practices take center stage as the gestating point of collective sentiment and thought and the kinship system is now embedded more firmly in religious processes.

Another issue central to this essay is that of the whole or totality. Durkheim's explicit reference to this problem toward the end of the book is telling. Society is not only a whole but "the unique whole" to which all other things are related. Durkheim's addition of "unique" points to the increasing centrality he accords to human society within the larger scheme of things, one which reaches its apex in his final work on religion. While the essay by Durkheim and Mauss is on the problem of genre or kind (i.e., classification), it also clearly broaches the question of the whole within which classificatory schemas operate. He already needs the notion of the whole of society in order to account for the hierarchically ordered concepts of primitive classification systems, but he does not yet develop an account of the category of totality itself, as the most comprehensive one. This remains for his later work.

Why did Durkheim and Mauss introduce the notion of collective sentiment and emotion into the theory? In Lévi-Strauss's view, this was an unfortunate theoretical turn, which closed off the very possibility of a scientific theory of classification, since emotion— even less collective emotion—was recalcitrant to scientific analysis (Lévi-Strauss 1987, 56). We need to account, within Durkheim's own intellectual evolution and within the logic of his theory, for the emphasis placed by him on these emotional forces. Perhaps this last combination of terms (i.e. emotional forces) takes us in the right direction. Only a focus on collective emotion or sentiment would allow him to fully capitalize on his conception of society itself, including his notions of dynamic density and social forces, social concentration leading to enthusiasms and cultural creation, and the collective effervescences related to religious ritual. Such concepts as collective social action or, as he often prefers, "association," allow him to link social processes directly to collective emotional states. Association leads to or generates enthusiasms, along with other cultural creations.

But this argument is still incomplete, since it omits a link in the chain, so to speak. This link is provided by the notion of force or power, a concept which is oddly absent in this study of primitive classification, yet featured prominently in the Hubert and Mauss study of the same year. What explains this disparity? Why do Hubert and Mauss, in examining magic, introduce the notion of *mana*, force or power, an idea even more fundamental in their view, than the notion of the sacred, while Durkheim and Mauss, when studying classification, do so only with the idea of collective sentiment, tying sentiment primarily to the domestic organization and kinship sensibilities of primitive societies? The notion of *mana* does play a much more central role in Durkheim's later work on religion and knowledge. It would seem that Durkheim was slow to arrive at his final synthesis, in which social association, power, emotion, culture, and nature could be linked together in a relatively seamless web. It would appear that Hubert and Mauss have one key in *mana*, a key which, however, is usually placed in a second level of signficance by Durkheim, below the notions of the sacred and profane. Hubert and Mauss's analysis implies that force, power, *mana* is the central collective experience. Durkheim does not entirely disagree with the vital importance of this experience of force, but he seems to locate it within the context of the sacred and profane distinction.

Mauss on Social Morphology and Eskimo Society

The essay on seasonal variations in Eskimo society, published in 1904–5 by Mauss (written with the collaboration of Henri Beuchat), is of enormous interest. Despite its brevity, it contains some of the most important Durkheimian formulations about our subject. Its emphasis on social morphology and its effects on every aspect of Eskimo society and culture raises particularly interesting questions. It also yields some unsuspected dividends concerning the problem of the categories in the Durkheim school.

Mauss argues that, in addition to the constant features of Eskimo social morphology, there are also seasonal variations between winter and summer. These result from the impact of the seasons on social life. It is the change in the dynamics of social life, rather than the climatic changes themselves, which really bring about the modification in social and cultural practices (Mauss 1966, 474). The seasons serve as collective ideas, a sort of classificatory system with two great categories, which divide everything about society and nature between them (Mauss 1966, 448). In particular, the winter brings about a concentration of society, while summer results in a dispersion of the population. This alternation of concentration and dispersion is the central dynamic which effects all other aspects of social life (Mauss 1966, 440). In winter, family life is concentrated in collective living arrangements with an emphasis on sexual communism, property is communalized, laws and customs are modified accordingly, myths and stories are transmitted to solidify the generations, and, especially, religious life undergoes an increasing intensity.

Mauss conceives of social life in the winter as a lengthy collective festival, subject to "paroxysms" of the collective religious conscience (Mauss 1966, 445). By contrast, the summer results in a dispersion of society into smaller family units, an increased differentiation, and a general weakening of the collective bonds, including a diminished level of religious enthusiasm (Mauss 1966, 462). In a particularly interesting summary statement, Mauss writes that "the qualitative differences which separate the two successive and alternate civilizations emerge above all from quantitative differences of very unequal intensity in the social life of these two moments of the year. Winter is a season when society, strongly concentrated, is in a chronic state of effervescence and superactivity" (Mauss 1966, 470). During this latter time, there are many social actions and reactions, ideas emerge and are exchanged, sentiments are reinforced, and the group's existence is visible to each individual.

In a comparative expansion of the scope of his argument, Mauss argues that this "rhythm of dispersion and concentation" is found in many other societies (Mauss 1966, 473). In a series of concluding remarks, Mauss notes a "rule of method" in such investigations. All social life, moral, religious, juridical, and so forth, is a "function of its material substratum" and "varies with this substratum, that is to say, with the mass, density, form and composition of human groups" (Mauss 1966, 474–75). In this connection, he notes that Durkheim had already demonstrated this general rule of method in his first three books. He adds that his own study of the Eskimo is a "rare example of what Bacon called a crucial experiment," one which illustrates a "law of extreme generality" in social life (Mauss 1966, 475).

This study is certainly one of the most remarkable ever produced by the Durkheimians. Its extraordinary quality emerges, in part, from the fact that it contains in miniature many of the ideas central to Durkheim's own work. I would call attention especially to the following ideas. First, Mauss's essay reiterates what we already know more generally from the *Rules*, that Bacon's method of "crucial experiment" was central to the Durkheimians. It is particularly interesting to note that Mauss has already produced such a crucial experiment based on a limited and well-studied set of facts, and done so well before the appearance of Durkheim's *Forms*. Second, Mauss has identified the general societal rhythm of concentration and dispersion which is central to the entire analysis in the *Forms*. Third, in 1904–5, Mauss was still arguing for the causal influence of changes in social morphology on beliefs and practices. This argument is presented in a fashion entirely congruent with Durkheim's earliest emphasis on the outcomes of social density and concentration. Moreover, as we have seen, this emphasis remains central to Durkheim's own writings of this period, and will reappear as a crucial feature of his last book. Mauss's strong case for social morphology certainly gives pause to anyone who would argue that the Durkheimians ever, at any point in their work, separated collective representations from their social substratum. Fourth, we see the reappearance, in the setting of Eskimo society, of the classificatory problems raised in the nearly contemporaneous essay by Durkheim and Mauss. This essay by Mauss is also a study of "primitive classification." Finally, I would draw attention to Mauss's summmary statement quoted above, in particular, the way Mauss engages the categories of quantity and quality.

Quantitative changes (i.e. increased social concentration) lead to qualitative ones (i.e. changes in societal beliefs and practices). Durkheim had hinted at such issues in *Suicide* and pursued a similar line of argument concerning quantitative and qualitative change in his essay of 1899–1900 on "Two Laws of Penal Evolution" (Durkheim 1978, 153–81). Mauss's emphasis on the "intensity" of social life resulting from quantitative changes is particularly fascinating. It reinforces the sense that the Durkheimians thought of social concentrations, and the forces and emergies emerging from them, as potentially measurable quantities. The appearance in this context of the quantity/quality distinction, which emerges on and off in Durkheim's writings, adds to its importance for the school.

Hubert and Mauss on Mentalities, Magic, and Society

Henri Hubert and Marcel Mauss collaborated on several important writings. They published studies of both sacrifice (1899) and magic (1904) in *L'Année Sociologique* (Hubert and Mauss 1964, 1972). Hubert also published a separate study of time. These studies were collected, with the addition of an extremely interesting preface, and published in 1909 (Hubert and Mauss 1929). In this section, we will examine their analysis of magic. In the two following sections, I will look at the essay on the collective representation of time and comment on their preface to the collection. This preface directly addresses some of the problems of the present work. Let us turn first to the essay on magic.

Their study of magic is central to the issues raised in this book. It covers ground related to Durkheim's own work on religion. It also touches directly on the problem of the categories and, especially, the notions of the whole, force, power, and so forth. Moreover, there are some revealing differences between their discussion and

Durkheim's own work on religion. Their essay was published in *L'Année Sociologique* in 1904, around the time of Durkheim's and Mauss's study of primitive classification, which we have already examined. Indeed, the comparison of these two texts is particularly revealing.

One of the first questions in their study concerns the relationship between religion and magic. Durkheim later distinguished in general terms between religion, which involved beliefs and practices relative to the sacred which unite their followers into a moral community (i.e., a church), from magic, where no "church" exists and practices emerge from individual magicians serving clients (also usually individuals). Religion is of the society, magic of and for the individual (Durkheim 1995b, 39–42; 1991, 103–6). Hubert and Mauss present a more complex picture of this relationship. Magic and religion have a great degree of continuity for Hubert and Mauss. Indeed, they wish to stress the mutual involvement between magic and religion, and explain it later in their study (Hubert and Mauss 1972, 22; Mauss 1966, 14). They do cover ground rather similar to Durkheim's later analysis. Religion and magic have different agents (priest and magician). Religion generally forms part of an obligatory public cult, while magic is often the private action carried out by individuals in secrecy. However, there are some magical cults and also cults which are not public, and the line between the two is often blurred. They preliminarily define a magical rite as one which is not part of an organized cult and emphasize the private, secret, mysterious, and even prohibited quality of magic (Hubert and Mauss 1972, 24; Mauss 1966, 16). To this extent, their opening emphases approximate Durkheim's later treatment.

For present purposes, the differences among these authors on this topic are less important than some other aspects of the Hubert and Mauss study. Their analysis of the categories is more relevant. They discover in magic one of the early forms of the idea of causality. For them, magic seems to be a "gigantic variation" on the theme of causality (Hubert and Mauss 1972, 63; Mauss 1966, 56). This not surprising, since magicians always concern themselves with contagion, harmony, opposition, and contiguity (Hubert and Mauss 1972, 76; Mauss 1966, 69).

Hubert and Mauss tie magic directly to the collective life of the community. Collective beliefs are necessary if both impersonal representations of magic as well as the personal ones are to operate. Neither the impersonal forces in the world nor the personal spirits and demons could be influenced by magic without the collective belief in the existence of these forces and the efficacy of the magician's spells (Hubert and Mauss 1972, 86; Mauss 1966, 79). The lines separating magic, religion, and technology are difficult to establish. Despite the diversity of magical practices, they are united into a whole, a system, and ". . . magic does form a real whole" (Mauss 1966, 80, correcting the misprint in Hubert and Mauss 1972, 87). In a familiar statement, Mauss writes that, in magic, a variety of incompatible ideas are joined together, without "the whole (*le total*) losing anything of its incoherent and dislocated aspect. The parts do . . . form a whole. At the same time the unity of the whole is more real than each of its parts." They suggest that the magical elements actually appear "simultaneously," although they have had to present them "consecutively" (Hubert and Mauss 1972, 87; Mauss 1966, 80). The "living mass, formless and inorganic," which is magic contains "constituent parts" and these "have neither a fixed position nor a fixed function" (Hubert and Mauss 1972, 88; Mauss 1966, 81). Magic has no specialized functions and, unlike religion, gives rise to no fixed institutions. It is a whole, more than the sum of its parts, and a reality, a collective one, dependent on the shared beliefs of the magician and the community (Hubert and Mauss 1972, 97; Mauss 1966, 90). Behind this common belief is the notion of a power, a force, not physical, but magical, which can be used to bring about results, and a milieu where this power resides (Hubert and Mauss 1972, 107; Mauss 1966, 100).

At this point, Hubert and Mauss draw on the notion of *mana* as the most characteristic variant of this force found in ethnography (although they also discuss the related ideas of *wakan, orenda, manitou,* etc.). This notion helps to account for a fundamental feature of magic: the confusion of actor, rite, and object (Hubert and Mauss 1972, 110; Mauss 1966, 102). *Mana* is simultaneously a quality possessed by something, a substance, or essense which can be handled and communicated, yet is independent, and a spiritual force (Hubert and Mauss 1972, 109; Mauss 1966, 101–2). It is both natural and supernatural, and immanent in the world, operating over distances, as through a kind of "ether" (Hubert and Mauss 1972, 112; Mauss 1966, 105). In sum, they argue that the notion of magical power is omnipresent in primitive and archaic societies. Its center is the idea of a "pure efficacy." This is a material power and can be localized, yet it is simultaneously spiritual and is a "substance," which can operate over distances as well as through direct connnection. It is mobile and fluid, without having to move, imper-

sonal, yet expressed in personal forms, and divisible, but also continuous (Hubert and Mauss 1972, 117; Mauss 1966, 110–11). This
power seems to work in a "fourth dimension of space." It exists a
priori, before all experience and ". . . functions as a category." It
makes magical ideas possible, just as the categories make human
ideas possible (Hubert and Mauss 1972, 118–19; Mauss 1966, 111).
Indeed, *mana* is an idea of the same order as that of the sacred. In
fact, it is more general than the sacred. The sacred is inherent in
the notion of *mana* and, in fact, is derived from it. For Hubert and
Mauss, the sacred is probably best viewed a species of the genus
mana. By studying magical rites, they have discovered the true root
of the sacred (Hubert and Mauss 1972, 119; Mauss 1966, 112).

Hubert and Mauss go on to see *mana* as the fundamental form
of magical judgments, a form which operates as a synthetic a priori
category and makes magical judgments prior to experience, and
experience only an a posteriori confirmation of the collective sentiments and beliefs already enbodied in the category of *mana*. This
category also serves to synthesize cause and effect, a synthesis
which takes place only in collective opinion (Hubert and Mauss
1972, 122–26; Mauss 1966, 115ff.). These facts mark the influence
of society on magic.

Magic is not an obligatory practice, like religion, but draws on
the detritus of religious rites. It constitutes a set of negative rites
which draw individuals in and transform them into ritual actors. As
such, it is highly collective in its operation. Here, group psychology
is at work, in bringing a variety of affective social states, especially
hope, into play. It is only because society is activated that magical
belief can make its influence felt. In turn, magical belief allows the
activation of society (Hubert and Mauss 1972, 133; Mauss 1966,
127). Not individuals, but a believing group, living in a given state,
is the core of magic (Hubert and Mauss 1972, 137; Mauss 1966,
130). It is only when religion and magic later become separated
that magic becomes an exclusively individual, rather than a collective phenomenon (Hubert and Mauss 1972, 139–40). In its origins,
it is collective, and within it we find the undivided roots of many of
our central ideas of causality, force, and substance.

Hubert's and Mauss's theory of magic is complex and has an
ambiguous relationship to Durkheim's ideas, yet it has an important bearing on our subject. Indeed, few texts are more central to
an understanding of the issues raised in the present work. Several
points brought out in this discussion require further emphasis.

First, we should note the great effort of Hubert and Mauss to demonstrate the collective, social origins of magic, even though they initially defined it in terms which were quite "individualistic" (i.e. private). Here, we cannot help but see a real difference of emphasis between Durkheim and his colleagues. It might be argued that their qualification concerning the later, individualized trend of magic, once differentiated from religion, would bring their argument into line with Durkheim's view. However, this is not obvious, unless we assume that Durkheim's case study of religion dealt with a later evolutionary phase of religion. Durkheim would surely have rejected this idea, given his claim to be analyzing the most elementary form of society, therefore, of religion (and by implication of magic). Despite this difference, Mauss reinforces Durkheim's emphasis on the reality of society when he writes that the unity of the whole, in fact, is more real than any of its parts.

Second, Hubert and Mauss give priority to the notion of *mana* over that of the sacred, and, by implication, the distinction between the sacred and the profane. *Mana,* or other ideas like it, is the primary concept, indeed, the primordial one. The sacred is probably a subset of the more inclusive category, *mana.* It is also interesting that the distinction between the sacred and the profane occupies no central place in their analysis. This seems particularly noteworthy, given the fact that Durkheim had been using the distinction for some time, and it appears briefly in the Durkheim and Mauss essay on primitive classification, published in the same year (Durkheim and Mauss 1963, 86).

Third, *mana* is identified as a power and force in their theory, albeit not a physical, but a moral one. They discover in it not only the primitive notion of causality, but many other things. Here, it is important to see not only an anticipation of an aspect of Durkheim's later theory, but also the ways in which the other members of the Durkheim school used the notion of force in their work. They also identified it with its operative substratum of collective emotion. More important, the notion of force or power is identified with the idea of *mana.* Hubert and Mauss placed the notion of force or power at the very center of their theory and, indeed, tended also to identify in with the notion of substance, a subject on which Mauss had prepared some incomplete and unpublished investigations (Mauss 1966, 334; Mauss 1968, III:161ff). At this point, we need to recall the fact that Mauss had worked extensively in the 1890s on Spinoza's philosophy, where it would have been impossible to avoid a full confrontation with the category of substance. I would suggest that Mauss's research on substance was related to his study of Spinoza's work.

Fourth, the role played by the notion of *mana* in their analysis is quite astonishing, especially in relation to the problems being discussed in the present work. In the category of *mana*, they have found the substratum of the whole. *Mana* is the whole as it is expressed in primitive thought or collective representation and, as such, it is also a primitive notion of substance.

Finally, since collective beliefs, especially emotions, sentiments, and affective states, lie behind the notion of *mana*, it is to society itself that we must trace this category. Hubert and Mauss do not tie up the argument with the same elegant philosophical sweep later used by Durkheim in his treatment of the relations of society, deity, and totality. They prefer to stay closer to a neo-Kantian way of expressing their sense of how *mana* operates (i.e., as a synthetic a priori category of the understanding). However, it is clear that they have taken a long step toward the identification of society, *mana*, and the whole. As the prime category, *mana* serves as a matrix from which other categories emerge, especially those of cause and effect, and substance. It is truly the substratum of the whole for Hubert and Mauss. Claude Lévi-Strauss thought the idea of *mana* did play the role of a mysterious power in the Durkheimian system, if not in the lives of the primitive peoples they studied (Lévi-Strauss 1987, 57). In a sense, rather different from Lévi-Strauss' own meaning, this comment hits close to the mark. What is critical is the fact that Hubert and Mauss identify the notion of *mana* with the notion of the social whole. In doing so, they also confirm the centrality of this problem for their theory as well as for the Durkheim school.

Hubert on the Collective Representation of Time

Henri Hubert's interest in time goes back to the turn of the century. His 1909 *Mélanges* essay lays the foundation for Durkheim's later treatment of this topic, but also stands as a contribution in its own right. It draws on evidence from his special field (i.e., the ancient Germanic peoples) as well as from other ancient cultures. From my present standpoint, the essay has several important features. First, there is his critical engagement with Henri Bergson's ideas. Second, there is Hubert's sociological analysis of time itself, one which contains a number of fascinating perspectives relevant to the present study.

One of Hubert's aims is to criticize Bergson's philosophy of time (he cites Bergson 1960, 1988; Hubert and Mauss 1929, 212 ff.). The Durkheimians carried on an intermittent debate with Bergson and his followers about such topics as time, memory, evolutionism, religion, and philosophy more generally (Halbwachs 1980, 1992; Durkheim 1975, I:64–70; Vialatoux 1939). Bergson's philosophy distinguished between the inner duration of experienced time and the various forms of "objectively" measured time, which generally subordinated temporal to spacial perspectives. Hubert notes that Bergson has succeeded in transporting time from the domain of quantity to that of quality and that his own study of time seems to confirm Bergson's emphases. It reveals a distinction between the association of time with the facts of natural phenomena, with which human activities must be coordinated, and its association, on the other hand, with successive representations which correspond to a qualitative duration. However, it is precisely the "artificial" schematism of time (the one that repels Bergson) which is of interest to Hubert. In general, time is marked by a rhythm which is itself a sign of collective activity and social collaboration. The rhythm of time does not necessarily have as its model the periods naturally established by cosmic experience. Society itself has the needs and means of instituting these divisions (Hubert and Mauss 1929, 219). Any actual system of time reckoning combines a conventional numerical index with a phenomenal index. The conventional measures of time actually precede and result in the development of the more phenomenally based (e.g. astronomical) calculation of time. He notes that some primitive cultures derive their numbers not from a division of the natural periodization of seasonal processes, but from the addition of the various points of social space and, in general, from a subjective synthesis of representations shared by entire societies. For Hubert, the division of time involves a "maximum of convention and minimum of experience" (Hubert and Mauss 1929, 217). Bergson's philosophy of qualitative duration is too individualistic and, thus, inadequate to understand the social origins and complexity of qualitative temporal distinctions themselves.

Hubert argues that the associations, which define the qualities attached to different segments of time, are sacred ones. Hubert uses the term "sacred" in an extensive sense, to include the sacred in magic and religion, as well as in relation to *mana* and other related ideas. A common quality lies behind the distinctive qualities attached to the various parts of time. When we abstract from these special associations connected to particular dates and periods, we find that they can all be reduced to the common quality of the sacred (Hubert and Mauss 1929, 221). In following this line of argument, Hubert arrives at the idea of essentially religious time. This time is both "dangerous and solemn." It is a concrete representation of a "pure duration, existing in itself and altogether objective . . . a true eternity . . ." (Hubert and Mauss 1929, 222). Just as the idea of *mana*, as a notion of the order of all forces, has risen from the consciousness of social powers, in a parallel fashion, the general notion of time, as the order of all possible concordances, has emerged from the awareness of changing social circumstances. In a particularly important passage for us, Hubert notes that the qualities attached to the parts of time emerge from this notion of a pure duration at the heart of all possible times. The parts of time are "diverse modalities of a quality common to time" (Hubert and Mauss 1929, 209). This common quality would seem to be the sense of the sacred gestated within the social process itself.

In characteristically Durkheimian fashion, Hubert argues that the sacred is formed in settings of "collective agitation," where primitive, exceptional, and momentary emotions have left behind a residue of belief. The key categories which capture this belief are able to revive certain of these emotional effects even when the cause has been attenuated. The logical power of the categories and concepts serves to prolong the influence of these emotions (Hubert and Mauss 1929, 224). Indeed, Hubert seems to imply that the categories of time carry a residual emotional "charge." This emotionally gestated sense of the sacred justifies a variety of qualitative temporal distinctions to which time is itself already susceptible. The sacred objectifies itself in qualitatively distinct, yet internally homogeneous durations which become inviolable and governed by systems of taboos. These symmetrical parts of time are not equivalents by reason of their resemblance, but become really and substantially identical. The "part of a duration" is capable of serving as "the whole." This is because the qualities of an overall time period are localized in a portion of it and, more importantly, "because substantially, the quality of that duration is able to be detached and fixed on the part" (Hubert and Mauss 1929, 225).

The emerging temporal framework takes the form of a calendar. The true original function of calendars was religious or magico-religious. The calendar is the periodic order of rites and, also, the code of the qualities of time (Hubert and Mauss 1929, 228). The institution of calendars does not have as their unique object the measurement of time considered as a quantity. Calendars derive from qualitative time, rather than pure quantitative time. This qualitative time is made up of "discontinuous heterogeneous parts" (Hubert and Mauss 1929, 228). In fact, the notion of an objective and abstract time follows after the detachment of a qualitative time from the objective world. The central dates of a calendar all have the quality of festivals, covered by interdictions and the presence of the supernatural. As a result, the times during which religious practices take place become sacred like the religious things themselves (Hubert and Mauss 1929, 223). These festivals have the effect of transfering the dangerous sacred forces from the totality of time to a part of it. This essential convention presides over all the other temporal divisions.

Hubert emphasizes that the calendar serves primarily not to measure, but to put rhythm into time (Hubert and Mauss 1929, 195). This latter distinction is critical for Hubert, since this rhythm is not only religious, but essentially social. It allows him to separate the construction of calendrical time based on observation of nature, especially the movements of the moon, planets, seasons, and so forth, from the more socially constructed time which emerges from myth, ritual, and the calendrical divisions created from them (and which, in turn, make them possible). The religious and magical notion of time differs regularly enough from the common one to make it a separate object of investigation (Hubert and Mauss 1929, 197). The succeeding parts of religious and magical time are not uniform. They are considered homogeneous and equivalent only because of their location in the calendar (Hubert and Mauss 1929, 197). As a result, the notion of time is not a pure quantity, but more complex. The "parts of time" derive their properties from their relationships with "the concrete durations" for which they provide the framework (Hubert and Mauss 1929, 197).

The cycle of calendrical time is a system of critical intervals and dates. The crucial dates interrupt the continuity of time. As a result, the time of magic and religion is discontinuous and nonhomogeneous. The intervals comprehended between two crucial associated dates are each continuous and indivisible, because the rites observed during the intervals create a solidarity among the parts of the rites and the intervals of time. Moreover, the crucial dates are equivalent to the intervals which they limit (Hubert and Mauss 1929, 202). They carry the same names. Movement and duration, fact and duration, are identified in a synthetic mental operation. Similar parts of time are also equivalents: the week, the month, the season and so on are given as similar among themselves. This equivalence of similar parts of time permits the repetition of the same events, to which are attached the same representations (Hubert and Mauss 1929, 205). When these possible equivalencies are all put into operation, time is represented as a series of equivalent points. It becomes a "succession of parts" with unequal value, each nested inside the other. Each of the points and periods can count respectively for "the whole" (Hubert and Mauss 1929, 206–7). In such a situation, the unequal quantitative durations are equalized and equal durations made unequal.

From the standpoint of religion and magic, the issue is not so much that time is not a quantity, or susceptible to being treated as one. Rather, it is not seen as a pure quantity, homogeneous in all its parts, always comparable to itself and exactly measurable (Hubert and Mauss 1929, 208). The qualities that define time periods are thought of as equally distributed homogeneously throughout all the parts of the duration. The homogeneity of time ends with the completion of that period and a qualitatively new differentiation emerges. Time is not a pure concept, a sort of geometrical locus, abstracted from the mass of particular durations.

Hubert's text is complex and thickly illustrated. The topic's intrinsic difficulty is further enhanced by Hubert's novel, sociological approach. Yet, the essay has several features of interest.

First, it clearly establishes the main lines of Durkheim's own later theory about time, with its emphasis on the social roots of temporal rhythms, the importance of calendars and sacred festivals, and the general unwillingness to locate the origins of the category of time in any experiences other than those of society. Second, we once again see the strong Durkheimian emphasis on the categories of quantity and quality, this time in the context of the critique of Bergson. The quantity/quality pair are central to the analysis. Indeed, it is implied that the categories of time and quality are somehow linked (as, by implication, are space and quantity). Third, we see the whole/part notion operating in yet another context, that of the relationship between the qualitatively distinct parts of time and their relationship to the notion of an undifferentiated temporal whole, a pure duration, or "eternity," in Hubert's own words. The Durkheimian critique of Bergson's notion of duration takes shape in an alternate idea of pure duration as a socially gestated form of "eternity." Nowhere else in the Durkheimian corpus is there such an explicit, sociological discussion of the idea of "eternity." Finally, we see the identification of temporal durations as "modalities" of a more pure, qualitative, collectively rooted time, comparable in its functioning to that of *mana*.

It is interesting to see Hubert designating the social divisions of time as "modes" of this more inclusive notion, which itself is the result of social processes. This provides further evidence, not only of the general philosophical thrust of these essays by Hubert and Mauss, but also of their Spinozist echoes.

Reason and Society: The Hubert and Mauss Preface to the *Mélanges d'Histoire des Religions*

The preface of 1909 to the *Mélanges* reviews the book's main findings and places them within the setting of the Durkheimian problematic. It makes a number of important points relevant to our discussion. It contains sections which not only summarize the central ideas of the essays on sacrifice, magic, and the collective representation of time, but also provides a more general treatment of the problem of reason, the relationships between general ideas and myth, and the roles of religious sentiment as well as social structures in religious psychology. Let us examine the issues raised in this preface, especially those concerning reason and the categories, which do not emerge as directly in the individual essays.

One of the main points of the preface's treatment of magic concerns the notion of *mana* and cognate conceptions. Hubert and Mauss are quite clear that they conceive of it as an undifferentiated entity capable of being thought of in a variety of ways. It is simultaneously identified with power, cause, force, quality, substance, and milieu. As a term, *mana* is also simultaneously substantive, adjective, and verb. It designates attributes, actions, natures, and things. It can be applied to rites, actors, substances (*matières*), and both magical and religious spirits (Hubert and Mauss 1929, xix). They continue to equivocate somewhat about the relationships between such concepts as *mana* and the notion of the sacred, whether they are identical or merely analogous.

They also offer an appreciative criticism of their *L'Année* colleague, Paul Huvelin's essay on the role of magic in primitive law, especially in the rise of individual law. They suggest that Huvelin has rested his argument too heavily on a rigid antinomy between religion and magic (Huvelin 1907; Hubert and Mauss 1929, xxix). Huvelin unearths a paradox concerning the role of magic in the gestation of nonetheless obligatory legal institutions, one which questions the Durkheimian distinction between obligatory religion and optional magical rites. Hubert and Mauss argue that although magical rites are not obligatory, they remain social. They claim that social things, acts, and sentiments are not defined primarily by the notion of obligation (Hubert and Mauss 1929, xix). The magical rites are social because they take their form from society and their reason for existence only from connection with society. The distinction made by Hubert and Mauss is a particularly interesting departure from the earlier established position of Durkheim, in which social facts, including religion, could be identified by their obligatory character (Durkheim 1994a, 93; 1982, chap. 1). However, by 1912, Durkheim himself has come to question the definition of religion in terms of obligation and constraint as excessively "formal." He supplements (but did not claim to entirely replace) it by a new one, which focuses on the social group character of religion and places a greater emphasis on the content of the religious representations (Durkheim 1995b, 44, fn. 68). We might view the statement of Hubert and Mauss as a step in the direction of this renovated Durkheimian definition. It is also worth noting that this shift moves religion away from the purely "moral" orbit implied by the earlier notion of obligation, yet emphasizes even more strongly the purely social character of religion (and even of magic). For those who would see Durkheim's work as exclusively preoccupied by the problem of morality, this is a troubling shift of emphasis. It features a new sense of the social besides that of obligation.

One of the most interesting sections of the preface deals with the problem of reason. Primitive thought rests on conscious judgments, judgments of value, but ones strung out on a thread of hopes, fears, desires, and, more generally, sentiments. By contrast with individual sentiments, which can attach themselves to chimeras, collective sentiments can connect themselves only to the sensible, the visible, the tangible. That is why magic and religion concern the body and real beings generally. They are related to experience and the actions of *mana* are, for the believer, susceptible to verifications. It is clear that Hubert and Mauss are laying a firmer groundwork for Durkheim's notion (already broached in his earlier essays) that collective representations, especially the categories, must be connected to the physical world if they are to operate at all. Indeed, they are adequate to the understanding of nature precisely because they are collective and attached to the material world. In a fascinating related remark about magical action at a distance, they note such an idea rests on the notion that *mana* is simultaneously "extended and unextended" (Hubert and Mauss

1929, xxix). This description of *mana* evokes early modern philosophical conceptions of extended and unextended substance as found in Descartes, Spinoza, and others. *Mana* is the matrix from which collective representations are disengaged and socially relevant, physical objects demarcated. In this sense, it is extended and unextended (i.e. material and mental).

Hubert and Mauss treat *mana* as one of those philosophical categories on which judgments and reasonings ultimately rest. Such categories are found in language and are unconscious, yet are directive forms for consciousness. But *mana* is not only a category of primitive thought, it is also the source of our notions of substance and cause. In a brief overview of the notion of genre, already studied by Durkheim and Mauss, they note that the notion of genre has for its model the human family. In general, the classes in which the images of concepts are distributed are the same as the social classes (Hubert and Mauss 1929, xxx). It is an example of how society serves the formation of rational thought and itself furnishes the categories ready made, which are the clans, phratries, tribe, camp, temple, regions, and so forth. In these passages, we see Hubert and Mauss entering into not only a clarification of the social roots of the notion of genre, but beginning to develop the subject of the social and religious roots of reasoning itself. However, they do not pursue it very far.

In a brief discussion of the ways in which the categories of time and space are shaped, they note that the spaces and times are identified with actual temples and festivals (Hubert and Mauss 1929, xxxi). The calendar serves to create the abstract notion of time, if not the concrete notion of duration. This notion does not describe a quantity, but qualities. These qualitative notions of time and space represent parts which are not evenly divisible ("not aliquote"). Each of these parts is opposed to the others, but can be interchanged with them because of their specific qualities. "The harmonies and qualitiative discordances of the parts of time are of the same nature as those of the festivals" (Hubert and Mauss 1929, xxxii).

In an important summary of their relationship to established philosophical positions on such issues, they write that with the empiricists, they recognize that judgments are not possible except after a minimum exposure to the experience of things. However, with the nominalists, they also recognize the "omnipotence of the word" and with the rationalists, they recognize that judgments of value are coordinated by constant and constantly perfected rules, although these rules are not given by pure reason alone, but by social forces, traditions, and language. While they generally accept the pietistic theologians' concept of value judgments, they resist the idea that such judgments emerge from practical reason and a noumenal realm of freedom. Sensations, collective needs, and movements of human groups lie behind these judgments (Hubert and Mauss 1929, xxxiii). Hubert and Mauss call attention to the "pietistic" orgins of these ideas, mentioning Søren Kierkegaard as their source, but clearly implying by their references to the noumenal and practical reason that they include Immanuel Kant in this statement. At the same time, they also convict a variety of other thinkers of the error of suggesting "individualistic" origins of religious ideas of the soul, spirits, and so forth, including Wilhelm Wundt, who is said to have made a "grave error" in placing the idea of soul before that of *mana* (Hubert and Mauss 1929, xxxiv). This leads to a fascinating discussion of the relationship between the ideas of soul and *mana*. The latter is the more primitive notion and contains a variety of ideas about shadows, organic souls, exterior souls, totems, genies, and so forth within itself. It is from this complex that *mana* becomes specialized and individualized in a variety of representations and for a variety of ritual purposes.

In a remarkable summary statement, they argue that the idea that the soul has power requires the prior notion of power itself, whose origins cannot be accounted for if we assume soul to be elementary. The qualities of the spiritual and of power are not given simultaneously in the idea of soul. However, they are found together in a "natural synthesis," in the idea of *mana*. The notion of a power joined to the spiritual must first exist before the idea of an active soul can emerge. One must first have "the idea of a quality" before this quality can be made into "an attribute" (Hubert and Mauss 1929, xxxv).

In a footnote to this passage, they extend their argument to the concept of God and the category of religion generally. These obey the same rules as other "concepts and categories." They must first operate as a "predicate" before figuring as "subject" (Hubert and Mauss 1929, xxxv). Primitive notions, of which *mana* is the type, are highly concrete. They coordinate a swarm of representations, including those of sensations, emotions, desires, needs, volitions, objects, and qualities (Hubert and Mauss 1929, xxxvi). However, it is difficult, if not impossible to trace two distinct moments in which the original *mana* is later succeeded by other spiritual notions. They are merely suggesting that the general idea of *mana* is the logical and chronological condition of mythical ideas in the same way that time, marking a rhythm, is the condition of rhythm (Hubert and Mauss 1929, xxxvi).

Hubert and Mauss conclude their preface with a discussion of religious psychology and religious sentiments. Arguing in favor of a sociological account of such religious phenomena, rather than of a social psychological one (as that term was then understood), they state that they never consider the ideas of peoples in abstraction from those people. In sociology, the facts of social psychology and social morphology are joined by intimate and indissoluble ties. They cite Mauss's study of Eskimo society. In a particularly telling passage, they add that ". . . all religious phenomena are the product of a certain social mass endowed with a certain state of spirit and animated by certain movements" (Hubert and Mauss 1929, xxxix). Indeed, it is this mode of analysis which constitutes their sociological approach as opposed to the abstract and inadequate conception of the human group in Wundt's *Volkerpsychologie*. They close the preface by noting that there is no specific religious sentiment (and criticize William James and other psychologists who make this claim). There are only normal sentiments of which religion is the product and object (Hubert and Mauss 1929, xli; also Ribot 1896).

The preface by Hubert and Mauss is immensely revealing. We see them giving the notion of *mana* a greater place of prominence in the analysis than the idea of the sacred. They continue to remain ambiguous about the priority of these two ideas, but their treatment focuses almost exclusively on *mana* and its relationships to the social and much less on the sacred, an emphasis almost directly reversed in Durkheim's later book on religion. Hubert and Mauss srongly suggest that it is the primary category from which others are derived (logically and perhaps chronologically). They also suggest the social itself is the matrix from which the notion of *mana* emerges, especially society assembled in its ritual activities (although their repeated references to "the social" seem to clash in rhetorical tone from Durkheim's more frequent use of the more substantive notion of "society"). This is particularly striking in their discussion of soul and *mana*, where the two are further related to the quality and attribute distinction. The quality of power is associated by them with the substance, *mana*, as a logical prerequisite for its further assertion as an attribute of soul. We will later see Durkheim making a similar, though not identical argument about the origins of the soul in *Forms*. In their analysis, *mana* clearly serves as the logical matrix from which qualities are disengaged. When we add the essentially social roots of *mana*, we also can see how other categories (genre, time, space, etc.) become disengaged from *mana*, with the social process and social sentiments generated within them becoming the "occasions," so to speak, for the differentiation process. They seem to subordinate the category of God, or religion itself, to this same logic, with their insistence (against the Danish philosopher Harold Höffding) that this category (i.e., God) must first have served as a predicate before being seen as a subject. This seems to imply the same subordination of the conception of God to the more basic, undifferentiated category of *mana*.

In general, Hubert and Mauss locate the philosophical traditions about the role of the noumenal, practical reason, and judgments of value within their religious settings (i.e., what they call "pietism"). This designation seems evidently to include not only Kierkegaard and James, but also all the theorists of animism (Tylor, Wundt, etc.) and, by strong implication, Kant himself as well as other Protestant thinkers (see Nielsen 1987a). This religiously oriented "sociology of knowledge" strongly implies an alternative religious and philosophical conception of their of own, one which I have been calling "sociological monism."

Their analytical stragegy is interesting in another respect. They not only seem to stay closer to a Kantian or neo-Kantian mode of expression, but they also employ language drawn from philosophy and logic as much, if not more than Durkheim himself. In their discussions of *mana* and its relationhip to magical rites and other aspects of the religious life, Hubert and Mauss do seem to be keenly interested in modes of reasoning. Perhaps we are justified in seeing these discussions as a partial, if sketchy payment of the promissory note about the study of "modes of reasoning" in the closing paragraph of *Primitive Classification* (Durkheim and Mauss 1963, 88). In their sociological account of "substance," "predicate," "attribute," "subject," "quality," "quantity," and a variety of other terms (which we have examined in our earlier discussion of the other essays), they betray a strong attachment, if not demonstrably to Aristotle's logical writings, then at least to philosophical logic in general. I find strong echoes here of the themes developed by Aristotle, especially his discussion in the *Categories* and *Topics* (Aristotle 1941, 3ff; 187ff.). However, their conceptual usages are also generally compatible with the early modern philosophical discourse of Spinoza, Leibniz, and others.

Robert Hertz on Religious Polarity

Hertz was one of the rising stars of the Durkheim school. His death in World War I at the front in 1915 cut short the life of a promising thinker who one day would have rivaled the master in originality. Two important essays published during his lifetime, on the collective representation of death and on religious polarity (or left and right), have become classics in their respective fields and helped gestate a large critical literature discussing and extending their insights (Hertz 1970). The study he began, but did not complete, on sin, expiation, and religion promised to be the most extensive study of religion after Durkheim's own work. Only the introduction was published posthumously by Mauss in 1922 (Hertz 1922; on this study and Hertz generally see Nielsen 1986, 1987a; also Parkin 1996).

Published in 1909, the essay on religious polarity is of greatest relevance. We are informed by Alice Hertz, in her preface to his collected essays, that the piece was meant as a contribution to the sociological study of space and its representation. In a particularly suggestive comment, she writes that this space can be considered in two different senses: ". . . space profoundly asymmetrical, living, and mystical, with the primitive; abstract, empty and absolutely isotropic with the geometers, from Euclid to the moderns" (Hertz 1970, xiv). The essay has a strong bearing on our concerns: the problem of the categories (e.g. space) as well as the whole or totality in Durkheim and his school. The study is an analysis, as the title indicates, of the "preeminence of the right hand" and of "religious polarity." What do these terms mean and how are they related to our present concerns?

Hertz uses the fact that favor is typically shown to the right hand, and things associated with it, as a way of attacking biologically based theories of this phenomenon and introducing a sociological explanation. Organic asymmetry exists, but is coupled with evaluative asymmetry. The latter is more significant. The right hand is favored as an ideal, and has a sacred quality, as does everything associated with it. In primitive societies, right and left are collective representations which form the basis of a comprehensive system of dual symbolic classification. They form the matrix of a veritable cosmology in which everything finds its place. Hertz sees this system of dual symbolic classification rooted in primitive notions of the sacred and profane and being linked in turn to the basic features of social organization. The ideas of sacred and profane are linked to the mutual relationships between the two phratries, or clans, in which the society is organized. Right and left, sacred and profane, form a reciprocally opposed and mutually implicated pair which compose the whole. The groups are linked by exchange of wives, goods, and so forth, but are divided along evalutive lines between right and left. Religious polarity combines with reciprocal engagement to produce a social whole with internal oppositions.

The argument is concise and brilliant. It is familiar to students of the Durkheim school. Hertz tends interestingly to emphasize the priority of religious polarity and dualism in primitive mentality as the primary features in the organization of society and culture, rather than insisting, as Durkheim and Mauss did, that the social structure decisively formed the basis for the religious distinctions and categories of thought (contrast Hertz 1973, 8, 22 with Durkheim and Mauss 1963). Hertz's evident desire to define the whole through the analysis of the spatial orientations or metaphors created by the dual system is also fascinating. Alice Hertz's remark was accurate. The study is clearly oriented to the question of space and spatial metaphors in the organization of society. The system's reference points are spatial (i.e., right and left). In segmentary societies, organized space operates in an asymmetrical, "horizontal" matrix, to the left or right, with the cultural values of the society loaded in turn into this horizontal division. If there is a sacred quality to the right side of the classification, and a profane one to those things on the left, the sacred/profane distinction defines the opposition, even while it displays these two sorts of realities on a horizontal plain. This plain is the one on which the two subgroups, or clans, of the overall society work out their mutual relationships of cooperation and conflict. The whole or totality of society, everything of significance in its world, is contained in either side of this dualistic plain.

Hertz's essay contains hints of a more inclusive, evolutionary theory, which is not fully developed by him. He suggests:

> [T]he evolution of society replaces this reversible dualism with a rigid hierarchical structure: instead of separate and equivalent clans there appear classes or castes, of which one, at the summit, is essentially sacred, noble, and devoted to superior works, while another, at the bottom, is profane or unclean and engaged in base tasks. (Hertz 1973, 8; 1970, 90)

He adds that the assignment of rank and function in this later society still results from religious, social polarity. The "reversible dualism" of the "primitive" society is replaced by the exclusive, hierarchical structure of thought and social organization of "civilization." The spatial matrix which defines the orientation of the whole has been turned ninety degrees, so to speak, with the right, sacred or good now representing "higher" values of a higher world, and the left, profane or bad being the manifestation of a "lower" world. The whole has been spatially reoriented. There has been a "transvaluation of values." The implied reference to Nietzsche is not fanciful. As I have shown elsewhere (Nielsen 1986, 16–17, 35–36), Hertz knew Nietzsche's work and owed something to him. His writings on "The Four Great Errors" , in *The Twilight of the Idols*, particularly interested Hertz (as Mauss noted in Hertz 1922). I would add that Hertz's interest reconfirms the debt of the Durkheim school (and Nietzsche) to Bacon.

From the standpoint of our present problem, Hertz has made a major contribution to the collective representation of space and the whole through his analysis not only of dual symbolic classification in primitive societies, but also by his undeveloped suggestion that evolutionary change in society transposes the whole and its moral valences. Hertz's essay also offers a glimpse into a mature, yet never completed Durkheimian theory of sociocultural transformation. It gives an indication of how Hertz might have rewritten Durkheim's *Division* in accordance with the insights of his essay on religious polarity. From a study, through the medium of changing legal sanctions, of the transition of the whole from mechanical to organic solidarity, via the mechanism of increasing moral density, it would have become a study of the whole as it moved from a moral and cosmological order based on dual symbolic classification to one based on a new ontology, the hierarchy of being.

I would once again call attention to Alice Hertz's remark concerning primitive qualitative versus Euclidean geometrical space. The movement is from a horozontal space, defined by dual symbolic classification of right and left and a related whole defined by this opposition within duality, to a spatial metaphor rooted in a hierarchical conception of the whole, in which totality is now constituted by a metaphysical hierarchy of Being and the concomitant social representatives of this hierarchy. This conception reverberates strongly with the historical transition in Ancient Greece from an early Pythagorean world view to more Platonic, Aristotelian, and Euclidean ones. Indeed, it was later investigated by others working in the Durkheimian spirit (Cornford 1912; Lloyd 1992). Hertz's pioneering study certainly belongs within the setting of our problem: the study of the categories and, in particular, the whole in the Durkheim school.

Bouglé on the Hindu Caste System

While Hertz was completing his analysis of dual symbolic classification (published 1909), Célestin Bouglé published the first Durkheimian treatise (published in 1908) on a total society, the first Durkheimian study, after Durkheim's *Division*, on the whole in a particular historical setting. Bouglé's study is both an analysis of one historical variant of the second developmental level of Hertz's emerging, if briefly articulated theory and also a study of a developed civilization based on an expanded variant of mechanical solidarity. It is an ambiguous text, valued in its own right by Indologists (Dumont 1980), but developed conceptually in the interstices between the early Durkheimian formulation of the whole and the later one, based on religion.

Bouglé's text and others which followed it within the Durkheimian orbit (Granet 1934; Dumont 1980) also illustrate the difficulties of retaining a notion of the whole in studying more complex civilizations. In a discussion of 1907 (with René Worms and others) concerning the role of ethnography in the development of sociology, Durkheim noted that the so-called primitive societies are of special interest to sociologists. The separated, yet organized social forms found in complex societies thoroughly interpenetrate one another in primitive societies and this fact makes their unity more visible (Durkheim 1982, 210; 1975, I:258). Moreover, the more advanced societies cannot be understood unless we know about the more primitive ones. This emphasis on the unity of social life in the less developed societies needs to be juxtaposed to Durkheim's better known reason for studying primitive societies: that they constitute a crucial experiment. Indeed, they serve as a crucial test case precisely because of their "unity." Once again, we see the notion of the whole placed at the forefront of the reasoning, from which other arguments can be derived, including the emphasis on a "primitive" test case. Let us turn to Bouglé's text of the interim from the standpoint of our problem.

Bouglé focuses on the principle of hierarchy, defined by the opposed notions of pure and impure, as the central orienting notion in Hindu civilization. Despite some ambiguities in his discussion, he clearly gives priority in his analysis to the notion of the whole. Along with the principle of hierarchy and the pure/impure distinction, he adds that castes are related in terms of a principle of separation/interdependence, and that they correspond to a complex division of labor which gives each caste a function in the system (Bouglé 1969; the helpful summary in Dumont 1980, 43–44; 355–56). In sum, the whole is defined in advance by reference to hierarchy, separation/interdependence of parts, and functions of parts within the whole system. The notions of pure/impure are particularly central in defining the hierarchical organization of the whole. As Dumont has noted about Bouglé's conception, "The whole is founded on the necessary and hierarchical coexistence of the two opposites. One could think of a synthetic a priori opposition" (Dumont 1980, 43).

Bouglé's theory of the Hindu caste system is highly congruent with Hertz's contemporaneous analysis of the transition from segmental to civilized conceptions of the whole and its constitution. The primitive notion of sacred and profane has been replaced by the distinction pure/impure which now reorients the spatial structure of the whole, but in a hierarchial rather than a horozontal or segmental fashion. However, Bouglé notes that, within this system, separation and interdependence continue to operate and reproduce elements of the "horozontal" spatial structuring of relations from the earlier type of society. Moreover, the detailed division of labor itself is now developed within the complex whole defined by hierarchy. There is no hint of "organic solidarity," despite the complex division of labor possible in this context.

Bouglé appears to have merged several different theoretical elements in his analysis. Without identifying the source of these theoretical tensions in Bouglé's work, Dumont notes that Bouglé tends to separate the three aspects of his analysis (i.e. hierarchy, separation/interdependence, division of labor) from one another (Dumont 1980, 43).

I think that the tensions emerge from Bouglé's combination of various Durkheimian theories in his analysis. The text merges Durkheim's perspectives in *Division* with the idea being developed by Hertz (undoubtedly a general Durkheimian intellectual property at this time) of a shift towards hierarchy in more advanced civilizations of the "axial age." Bouglé adds strands of thought taken from various other sources. These include the interest in Indian civilization already found in Mauss and his teacher, Sylvain Lévi, as well as the theoretical and ethnological studies of Durkheim on primitive kinship systems, matrimonial classes, and so forth. Bouglé had written a study of equalitarian ideas, and, therefore, had his own reasons for wanting to study such a contrasting hierarchical civilization (Bouglé 1899; Vogt's comments in Besnard 1983, 238ff.). He was not an Indian specialist, in the way that Marcel Granet was a sinologist (although comparison of Bouglé's work with Granet 1934 would certainly be a revealing task). Bouglé's study was the first book published in the series founded by Durkheim, *Travaux de L'Année Sociologique*, and is the first work by any Durkheimian (save Durkheim himself) on the complexities of an advanced civilization from the standpoint of the problem of the whole. The Durkheimians produced few comparable studies.

9

THE SECOND APPROACH TO TOTALITY: SOCIETY, RELIGION, AND THE CATEGORIES IN *THE ELEMENTARY FORMS OF RELIGIOUS LIFE*

In a letter of 1908 to Xavier Léon, Durkheim writes that he has begun the revision of his book, *Elementary Forms of Thought and Religious Practice* (Durkheim 1975, II:467). He adds later in the letter that he has been preoccupied with this question of the social origins of the categories of thought for a long time. I am less concerned about the implication that Durkheim already had a draft of his book worked out in 1908 or had long been thinking about such matters than about the earlier proposed title. It features both of the topics treated in the actual book, but places emphasis first on the forms of thought and, regarding religion, emphasizes the problem of "religious practice." It is unnecessary and perhaps unwise to read too much into this change of title. The final book does all these things and more. However, one is almost led to wish that Durkheim had retained the earlier proposed title. In my view, it does capture the tenor of his actual theory better than the final one.

However we judge this question, one thing is certain: the logic of Durkheim's emerging standpoint reaches its zenith in the *Forms*. Although many issues raised in this book are clarified by reference to his other mature writings as well as those of his school, this book contains the fullest statement Durkheim ever achieved of his theory of society, religion, and the categories. We see the completion of the shift in emphasis from the whole/part metaphor to an analysis of the category of totality itself. Despite the book's length, it contains relatively few direct uses of the whole/part rationale in ways with which we have become familiar (Durkheim 1995b, 156, 268, 299, 342, esp.442–43). Indeed, it now identifies the whole explicitly with the category of totality and, at the same time, offers the fullest discussion of the nature of this category, including a sociological account of its origins. I take this to be one of the book's main aims. To be sure, Durkheim never entirely relinguishes his use of the whole/part metaphor. It appears in its customary role two years later in his essay on the dualism of human nature (to be examined below). Despite this, his analyses of religion, totality, and society ground the discussion in a way not found in his earlier work. Through its treatment of the categories and their relation to religion and society, the book also displays some notable modifications of his sense of how the whole/part problem is to be resolved.

Any reconstruction of Durkheim's argument about society, religion, and totality assumes a form which necessarily differs from the topical order of Durkheim's own text. I will not pursue a sequential treatment of his definition of religion, his critique of other theorists, his analysis of elementary beliefs and practices, and so forth. Only by first presenting the key concepts which provide the foundation of his philosophy, and in a logical order which allows us to judge their varying degrees of significance in his system, can we provide a coherent picture of Durkheim's standpoint, its emerging direction and its ambiguities. This is especially true if one wishes to understand Durkheim's philosophy and clarify the role of the notion of totality in his work. The book contains not only separate treatments of religion, the categories and social processes (i.e. discernible sociologies of religion and knowledge and a general social theory), but through its synthesis of all three accomplishes the creation of a social metaphysics. Even with such a systematic approach, ambiguities remain in Durkheim's work. These cannot be ignored if we are to locate the sources of tension in his philosophy.

At many key points in his argument, Durkheim makes what appear to be the most sweeping philosophical statements. They seem incredible coming from a thinker who is associated with a spirit of logical rigor and strong empirical commitments. However, we have already encountered such remarks often enough not to be surprised. These daring statements sometimes appear explicable, in part, by the historical, analytical, and rhetorical contexts in which they occur (e.g. most frequently where he is polemicizing against "individualistic" accounts of religion and cultural processes and arguing for the "reality" of society). However, just as often, they make important claims which are apparently expected to stand on their own. In fact, they look like fundamental principles of thought which have broken away from the constraints established by other key ideas to which he is also committed. These sorts of remarks caught the attention of earlier critics (especially Richard, translated in Durkheim 1994a, 228–76; Richard 1943). They are an index to the reach and suggestive philosophical quality of Durkheim's thinking in its most mature phase.

My sense is that Durkheim was still on the road to a philosophy whose terms he never fully articulated—perhaps, was hesitant to articulate. Many of its key horizons remained undeveloped, if not necessarily in a state of disarray. With these preliminary thoughts in mind, let us examine the logic of Durkheim's argument as it appears in his last book. I will begin with some brief references to Durkheim's conception of nature and society, and then examine his view of the category of totality, and its relationships to religion and society. I will next examine those particular categories comprehended by the notion of totality (e.g. space, time, causality, the person, substance). Finally, I will show how his analysis of the categories and religion is rooted in his understanding of society and how his overall theory amounts to a new social metaphysics of a fundamentally monistic type.

Nature and Society

The problem of the relationship between nature and society was central to Durkheim's work from the beginning. The problem is not only, or even primarily one of "relationship" as it is increasingly of "participation," if a phrase associated with Lévy-Bruhl might be allowed (see Fields' remarks in Durkheim 1995b, 9). From the very beginning of his labors, Durkheim insisted that sociology needed to overcome all metaphysical dualisms that placed humankind outside of Nature, as an "exception" to its laws. Society had to be seen not only as a reality in its own right, but as a "natural" phenomenon, one equally as real as the empirical individual. As he repeatedly argues, there can be no science if there is no distinctive object for that science to study. Society must exist if sociology is to exist. It was his "mission"—this word is not too strong—to bring this reality within view of the sciences. While the whole/part rationale serves many purposes in Durkheim's thought, one of its primary functions is to legitimize the natural quality of society as a real existing being.

Durkheim's view of society as an aspect of nature evolved considerably. In particular, as his notion of totality and the whole/part relation was modified, his conception of society's relationship to

nature also changed. We have already remarked on this problem in
the context of his early work. The emphasis there is on human society as a fact of nature, subject to distinctive laws of organization and
transformation specific to itself. In examining the problem of nature
and society in his last book, we will see more clearly a development
from a naturalistic theory of society to a theory which places society
at the epicenter of existence and reality. As we have seen, large steps
in this direction had already been taken well before 1912.

The greater "methodologial" emphasis on the reality of society
in his early writings was already linked to other ideas, implying
that he was also committed to the notion that society does, in some
sense, exist as an ontological realm, perhaps even as a "substance"
in nature. In his later writings, especially the *Forms*, the ontological emphasis adds claims for society, as a realm of nature, which go
far beyond a mere "methodological" assertion of its reality. He has
fully integrated society with nature, indeed, has gone a long way
toward a complete integration of his conceptions of nature, society,
religion, and knowledge. The position which emerges is a sociological monism whose overall architecture is strikingly like that of
Spinoza's philosophy.

His essay on "Judgments of Fact and Judgments of Value,"
published in 1911, contains important indications from this period
about Durkheim's view of these problems. Durkheim writes that,
although part of nature, society also dominates it. All the forces of
nature converge on and are synthesized by society. This synthesis
results in a new creation. This new creation is more complex and
powerful than the elements which went into its formation. Society
is a higher form of nature, in which nature concentrates its energies and transcends itself (Durkheim 1974a, 97; 1967, 109). We will
recall Durkheim's earlier argument for sociological naturalism, but
against materialism. This approach defines social life by its "hyperspirituality," yet also views this latter phenomenon as a assembly
of "natural facts" to be explained by "natural causes" (Durkheim
1974a, 34; 1967, 37–38).

The extraordinary claims for society found in these remarks,
as well as the juxtaposition of naturalistic and spiritualistic
images, are characteristic of Durkheim's sociological rhetoric. In his
view, even society's highest moral ideals are formed within nature
and from nature and are similar to other forces in the universe
(Durkheim 1974a, 93–94; 1967, 106, 105). Indeed, a central aim of
his entire theoretical effort is to fold the ideal into nature, translate
sacred morality into rational terms, while simultaneously retain-

ing, and not destroying, its most distinctive characteristics (Durkheim 1974a, 69, 96; 1967, 79, 109). As we proceed, we will need to remember this triple effort by Durkheim to retain the essense of the religious and moral realities, naturalize them, yet transcend them in a new sociological form. In the end, this strategy is what allows him to overcome many of the dualities which run throughout his analysis and move toward what I am calling a monistic perspective.

When we examine the problem of nature and society in the *Forms*, we see Durkheim's argument shifting. Durkheim sees society as part of nature, yet, in some sense, transcending it. Society is part of nature, its highest expression, and distinctive only because of its enhanced complexity (Durkheim 1995b, 17; 1991, 66). Toward the end of his work, in discussing the reality of society versus the individual, he writes that the individual has hitherto been taken as "the *finis naturae*," but now it must be realized that society transcends the individual and that society is a real "system of active forces—not a nominal being, and not a creation of the mind" (Durkheim 1995b, 448; 1991, 739). Not only is society part of nature, but it is, in fact, its highest manifestation. In a remarkable statement, Durkheim argues that, in fact, society is the most "powerful collection of physical and moral forces . . . in nature" (Durkheim 1995b, 447; 1991, 739). It has a power of creativity that "no observable being can equal" (Durkheim 1995b, 447; 1991, 739). While these remarks are made in connection with a critique of individualistic forms of analysis, their sweep and importance in Durkheim's theory transcend the polemical context.

Durkheim refuses to see society as a nominal construction. It is not, in contemporary language, merely another "level of analysis." There is little in Durkheim of Talcott Parsons' (or modern sociology's) analytical dissection of distinct system levels, a model developed by Parsons, I would add, primarily under Bronislaw Malinowski's influence (Parsons 1957). There is no understanding Durkheim's emerging position unless we accept the fact, however troubling, that he saw society as a real, active force of nature and likened it to a variety of phenomena such as energy, power, electricity, and so forth. It is particularly interesting to see these physicalist images of force most fully expressed in his final book on religion, the work which many see as the apex of his sociological "idealism" and his interest in symbolic representation and culture, allegedly at the furthest remove from the "positivism" or "scientism" of his earlier writings.

Totality and Society

The power and creativity of society extend to the furthest reaches of the world. Durkheim repeats a point which he had already made in the section of the 1909 essay later omitted from the *Forms*. According to Durkheim, the existence of the universe depends on the fact that it is the object of thought. It is thought about in its "totality only by society," and, as a result, the universe, "takes its place within society." It becomes part of society's inner life. Society is "the total genus, outside of which nothing exists" Durkheim 1995b, 443; 1991, 732). This notion of totality is central to the structure of Durkheim's mature work. Totality is the most essential category. The categories encompass all other concepts, and the notion of totality, in turn, encompasses all the categories, as the most comprehensive one (Durkheim 1995b, 442; 1991, 730–31, where "totality" is emphasized in italics). All of nature is folded into the categories and, as a result, into the notion of totality. In a particularly striking phrase noted earlier, Durkheim writes that ". . . the concepts of totality, society and deity are in all probability only different aspects of the same notion" (Durkheim 1995b, 443, fn.18; 1991, 732, fn.1; Nielsen 1987a, 290–91).

Despite the ambiguous phrasing—"aspects of the same notion"—this statement is perhaps the key to Durkheim's mature thought. We will need to examine the links in Durkheim's work among these three ideas. First, I want to recall Mauss's remarks discussed above, concerning Durkheim's emphasis on the whole or totality as his focus of study. Also, as we have shown, Durkheim's writings from beginning to end are replete with references to the problems of the whole and the whole/part relationship. As we have also seen, Durkheim felt compelled to discuss a variety of monistic theories, although he and the members of his school went out of their way to distance themselves from monistic theories generally and from the idea that his position was itself, in any sense, "monistic" (Durkheim 1970, 321; Bouglé's remarks in Durkheim 1974a, xxxviii–xxxix; Davy's comments in Durkheim 1957, xxxiv). However, far from providing evidence that he was, in fact, not a monist, these preoccupations with monism and defensive reactions against it are tokens of their very awareness that Durkheim's theory could easily be taken as a monistic one. Indeed, many of his remarks could hardly be understood in any other way and remain philosophically meaningful. Before examining his system as an integrated philosophy, let us discuss each of the central catgories treated in Durkheim's book and their relationship to the notion of totality.

The Categories, Totality, and Society

Durkheim's list of categories is brief: time, space, cause, person, substance, number, and nothing else. It should be contrasted with Mauss's later call for the study of as many categories as possible (Mauss 1979a, 32). This takes us back, to some extent, to the philosophical issues raised by Kant and Renouvier. What are the basic categories? I think Durkheim is trying to stay within the older philosophical orbit, with his concentation on "essential" categories and their relationship to religion and society. Mauss and the Durkheim school clearly intended to go further (probably with Durkheim's tacit agreement). Thus, we might distinguish between the perennial categories, addressed by all societies (probably time, space, cause, person, substance, number) and the larger number of variable categories which emerge at different historical periods or in different cultures.

Toward the end of his book, Durkheim summarizes the relationship between the categories and society by stating they not only emerge from society, but they express social things (Durkheim 1995b, 441; 1991, 729). The category of genre is, at first, indistinct from the the notion of the human group. Time has the rhythm of social life at its base. The category of space is modeled on the division of space occupied by society. Collective force is the prototype of efficacy, an aspect of the notion of causality. The categories do not apply only to society, but to reality as a whole. Since they "govern and contain" all other constructs, they must be based on a reality of an equally wide scope. Durkheim offers his familiar critique of the idea that such categories could have an origin in individual experience. This is especially true of the "notion of the whole." It is the foundation of all these classifications and cannot emerge from the individual, who is merely "part of the whole" and confronts only a limited part of reality (Durkheim 1995b, 443; 1991, 730).

This argument is reminiscent of Pascal's remark, "How could a part possibly know the whole" (Pascal 1966, 93). It is a familiar rationale in Durkheim's work. But there is now an added emphasis on the origins of the category of the whole or totality itself. Indeed, the whole is now seen as a category, one which encompasses all of the other categories. As such, it can be explained sociologically like the others. Only a sociological account of it can be adequate, and for quite logical reasons. Since it is inaccessible to the individual, it can be a product only of society. Moreover, since it is the most synthetic category, comprehensible only by a sociological science, sociology is placed in a unique position. It is the science most capable of a totalizing, synthetic understanding of all reality. All things become unified through sociological understanding. Auguste Comte would have recognized (and perhaps applauded) Durkheim's strategy. It is not surprising that Gaston Richard thought Durkheim's theory to be metaphysical, specifically monistic, if by metaphysical monism is meant the idea that "the subject and object are fundamentally identical" (Richard in Durkheim 1994a, 230). For Durkheim, they seem to be identical. The collective knowing subject, in the form of sociology, can know society, namely, itself, in which all other realities are absorbed. Durkheim's monism is more comprehensive than even Richard implies.

We need to go beyond such a shorthand description, which tells us little about the articulation of the elements in Durkheim's system. Let us instead examine each of the central categories and establish both their social origins and their relationships to totality. I would strongly emphasize that both of these tasks need to be completed. It is not enough to examine the social roots of each of the catgories separately. This is clear from Durkheim's own work (with Mauss) on the notion of genre as well as from an examination of the other Durkheimian statements about other categories. These other analyses offered fragments of totality, so to speak, while Durkheim's study offers the whole. The full task is completed only when they have been linked together via the notion of totality, and, in turn, tied to a further analysis of religion and society. Only then is the system complete (or well on its way to completion). This is why Durkheim's *Forms* accomplishes much more than any of their other writings on the categories and also why it represents a recapitulation on a new basis of the early attempt at understanding the whole in *Division*.

Space. The category of space occupies a particularly important place in Durkheim's work, much more than might be suspected from an examination of the citations to this concept in the index to the *Forms*. He does treat it (along with time) as a category, in opposition to Kant and in agreement with Renouvier. Indeed, we generally see Renouvier's influence in Durkheim's willingness to treat all these notions as categories. Space also figures in quite a few of the other Durkheimian writings, including his essay with Mauss on classification. Moreover, it is a complex category, with many different facets. It had been treated from an entirely different, "individualistic" standpoint by Durkheim's opposite, William James. James argued that all sensations had a spatial orientation or aspect (James 1890, II:135, chap. 20 generally). Durkheim referred to this idea with a certain grudging agreement (Durkheim 1995b, 441; 1991, 730), but also opposed this individually formed experience of space to his own theory of the collective origins of the category of space.

Even after he has disposed of this opposing standpoint, Durkheim's analysis of space remains complex. First, as we have seen, the organization of groups in society (i.e. kinship groups or clans) forms the basis of the classification of things into genres. Moreover, this organization "is naturally passed on to the space it occupies" (Durkheim 1995b, 444; 1991, 734). Each group must be assigned a specific location, and thereby space becomes "divided, differentiated and oriented" (Durkheim 1995b, 444; 1991, 734). Space is not only linked to social morphology, but to his notion of the rhythm of society through periodic concentration and dispersion (Durkheim 1995b, 443; 1991, 733). Both of these latter ideas (really a single dynamic process) play a vital role in his last book. As a result, it is difficult to entirely separate the categories of space and time. The periodic renewal undergone by society as well as its more mundane collective activities (e.g. hunts, military expeditions, etc.) point to a temporal rhythm which is socially established, but also to population movements of concentration and dispersion which are connected with the dominant conception of space. This notion of space, when related to collective renewals and assemblies, also implicates Durkheim's central idea of the sacred.

One of the facets of this complex notion (i.e. the sacred) is its spatial connotations. In connection with the study of negative rites, Durkheim argues that religious and profane life "cannot coexist in the same space" (Durkheim 1995b, 312; 1991, 523). Religion's development depends on special spheres set aside for it. Sacred entities are kept from mingling with profane ones. They are set apart and kept from contact with the ordinary reality. Moreover, insofar as the sacred is conceived as transcending the mundane reality, it is also actually localized in "another world" spatially. Thus, the sacred has some important spatial connotations. From an undifferentiated force (e.g. like *mana*), which can be within society, but must not physically contact or spatially mingle with its profane elements, it is differentiated into special spaces, times, and objects and gives rise to further social differentiations.

Space also involves a coordination of experiences, which would be impossible if space were entirely homogenous, as Kant thought, without qualitatively distinct parts. The zones of space are thought of in the same way by all of society's members and its varied dimensions emerge from the different "affective colorings" which have become attached to regions (Durkheim 1995b, 10–11; 1991, 55). In primitive society, in particular, spatial organization "replicates" social organization, taking the latter as its mold (Durkheim 1995b, 11; 1991, 56).

Time. The category of time is equally central, and, like space, is treated as a category by Durkheim. He draws on Hubert's earlier work and emphasizes that the rhythm of collective activity finds expression in the calendar, while the calendar, in turn, guarantees the continuation of that rhythm (Durkheim 1995b, 10; 1991, 54). Like Hubert, he focuses often on the interdictions imposed during sacred periods. However, Hubert's distinction between the system of measurement of time rooted in the observation of cosmic processes and those more qualitative divisions of time, resulting from religious (and therefore social) practices is much less central to Durkheim. He is more interested in the reanimation of collective life through periodic religious gatherings for the observation of positive cults. All religions, therefore all societies, divide time into two separate and alternating parts (Durkheim 1995b, 313; 1991, 524). These particular cults constitute a rhythm which, in fact, expresses and results from the rhythm of social life (Durkheim 1995b, 353; 1991, 588). Durkheim seems to emphasize even more than Hubert the social and religious character of the category of time. In almost the exact terms used to describe space, Durkheim notes that religious and profane life "cannot coexist at the same time" (Durkheim 1995b, 313; 1991, 524). The regular alternation of sacred and profane times results from the fact that collective assemblies cannot last forever, but must be balanced against the (equally robust) needs of profane existence. The temporal periods of concentration and dispersion differ from society to society. In general, the larger the period of dispersion, the more intense the emotionality of the ceremonies (for an earlier variant of this thesis, see Mauss 1966, chap. 7). When the two phases of life follow each other more closely, there is less of a emotional contrast between them. Durkheim notes that societies become more intolerant of pronounced interruptions as they become more developed (Durkheim 1995b, 354; 1991, 589). This last argument is noteworthy, since it points to a developmental perspective concerning the social phases of time and the rhythm of concentration and dispersion, including the place of intense emotions in these alternations. In effect, Durkheim gestures in his own way toward what Max Weber called the progressive "rationalization" of social life in which widely separated, yet highly intense periods of social activity are replaced by closer, but more uniform and less emotional rhythms. This insight would presumably be applicable in different ways to all of the categories if we were to attempt a fuller developmental study of them and their societal settings.

Durkheim's analysis of time also involves his idea that myth and mythological personalities are secondary developments from more vague and primitive beliefs and practices. Individual mythical personages always presuppose the more basic idea of an abstract, impersonal force, or energy (e.g. *mana*). Even these individual beings continue to retain a vague impersonal form, which allows them to combine with one another. For Durkheim, religious forces, by their very nature, cannot be fully individualized (Durkheim 1995b, 203; 1991, 356). Durkheim adds that he arrived at this conclusion only by the study of totemism (Durkheim 1995b, 203; 1991, 356). It is fascinating to see Durkheim make this reflexive remark about the role of totemism in his work in the very midst of his study. He thus gestures backwards to the period of 1895, when he first discovered the way of dealing with religion through a focus on totemism and had to begin his studies all over again.

Durkheim's discussion of myth demonstrates that he sees the conception of time lengthened into a mythological past, connected more or less to the present, via the conception of *mana*, or impersonal force. History is created and time stretched out backward, so to speak, by the individualization of mythological personages and events from the matrix of collective force or power. Thus, not only is the rhythm of time linked to a conception of impersonal force, which is social at base, but the very possiblity of escape from the immediate present depends on similar social forces (although only later will the collective power cast forth a future temporal panorama populated with events and personages).

Cause. As we have seen, one of the central concerns of Hubert and Mauss was to discuss the primitive conception of cause by examining magical efficacy. Durkheim's view closely parallels theirs. Although Durkheim sees magic and religion as different phenomena, he also argues that magic is full of religious elements because it is born of religion. The forces of the universe are all originally conceived as sacred forces and the contagiousness and communicability of these sacred forces is extended to them in turn. The principle that like produces like, at the center of magic, was initially religious, but could be detached from its ritual origins for other uses by magical practitioners. But faith in the effectiveness of magical rites remained rooted in shared religious beliefs.

The same collective ideas about sacred forces and their contagion became the core of the category of causality. Cause implies efficacy or effective power, active force. In an analysis strongly reminiscent of Aristotle (Ross 1995, 181–84), Durkheim argues that cause is force as a potential power, prior to its manifestation. "Effect is the same power, but actualized" (Durkheim 1995b, 367; 1991, 609). Both cause and effect are differentiated aspects of a more inclusive notion. The idea of force was sacred in origin but this sacred force was, in turn, of social origins and corresponds to the force exerted by society on its members. The only forces which we can touch directly are inward ones (i.e. moral forces). Moreover, these forces must be impersonal in character. Only social forces, only society, can provide experiences which have the twofold character of being moral, inward forces, but which are also impersonal (Durkheim 1995b, 369). The sense that there are forces of ascendancy, domination, dependence, and subordination in the workings of natural things, that is, dynamic processes of causality at work in nature, comes from the relations of society. In a particularly important remark, Durkheim argues that the earliest powers conceived by the human mind were "those that societies instituted as they became organized" (Durkheim 1995b, 370; 1991, 614). Since it is of social origin, the idea of cause itself changes both with the transformations of society and with the application of the category of cause to new phenomena (Durkheim 1995b, 373; 1991, 619). In a footnote to this passage, Durkheim adds that the idea of cause is not the same for a scientist and for the scientifically uneducated, and perhaps differs among scientists themselves (e.g. biologists, physicists, etc.).

I would call particular attention to Durkheim's idea that the first powers conceived by humans were discovered when societies first "became organized." It is an extraordinary claim, one which is central to his philosophy. We will return to this important idea momentarily, for it points to a key, yet neglected element in Durkheim's theory. The latter remark about causality and the sciences again gestures toward the societal processes which would need to be examined if the social theory of causality based on "primitive" evidence were to be extended into the study of modern society. Indeed, it is quite congruent with the earlier analysis in *Division* and with my suggestion above that Durkheim would ultimately need to study the categories in their modern manifestations, including their place in different occupational groups. This was clearly an item on their agenda (even if they never carried it through consistently). These remarks also imply the idea that new categories are gestated by fundamentally new societal arrangements. Here we need to briefly consider the problem of the immediate societal foundations of the categories, which seems to be Durkheim's own general view, versus the idea that the categories of later societies can only build historically on those of previous ones. Are the categories of time, space, cause, and so forth gestated once only, that is, in their primitive forms, under totemism, with all other later variants developing upon this foundation, or do new types of societies gestate new categories of their own, in the same way that the primitive one did?

Commentators have held differing views of this topic. In his critique of David Bloor's (1983) claim that, for Durkheim, there always exists some link between society and knowledge, Warren Schmaus has opted for the latter hypothesis about Durkheim's theory. He thinks the Durkheimians imply that all subsequent classificatory systems are minor variants of a primitive scheme modeled on primitive social organization. The categories are only invented once and Durkheim provides little more than a history of their later formation (Schmaus 1994, 257). Without necessarily supporting all of Bloor's contentions, I find Schmaus' view fundamentally flawed. It is difficult to imagine Durkheim accepting the limitations which Schmaus' reconstruction imposes on the scope of his sociology. It also goes against the comparative emphasis of the school, which implies the diverse development of categories in different societies (Nielsen 1991). It especially contradicts Durkheim's insistence that totemism was not necessarily universal and that its lack of universality does not contradict his theory of it's elementary quality or his view of the categories. Moreover, it fits poorly with Durkheim's earlier theory of the development of different societal types (Durkheim 1982, chap. 4). When combined with his thinking about the origin of the categories, this theory strongly implies a reorchestration of the categories for each social type. As we have seen, such a view emerges in his lectures on the development of educational thought, where changes in societal composition and concentration are related to changing forms of thought (Durkheim 1969a).

Schmaus' view of the categories is congruent with his very great underestimation of Durkheim's reliance on morphological and other social processes as an explanatory reference point in his work. It also fits his exaggerated emphasis on the idea that Durkheim, from the beginning, conceived of societal or collective phenomena strictly in terms of collective representations. Indeed, these two emphases are bound together in his interpretation of Durkheim. I find both emphases questionable. Schmaus overlooks a central aspect of Durkheim's theory, hinted at above: its rather indirect emphasis on the origins of "organized society" and the categories from the primitive horde. As we noted above, Durkheim had hypothesized in *Division* that the clan, especially the system of opposed clans, was the most simple form and origin point of organized society, but that this organization had emerged from the yet more primitive horde. This latter type of group was a hypothetical construct of a society formed by complete identification of its members as a homogeneous mass in which the parts would be indistinguishable. It is from this horde type that the segmentary society based on clans emerges (Durkheim 1984, 126–27; also 1982, 113–19). His intermediate essays on primitive kinship structures repeatedly deal with the origin of the clan system from some earlier, indeterminate or undifferentiated social mass (Durkheim 1969b).

In the *Forms*, Durkheim starts once again with the clan type as the most primitive known form of organized society and makes no direct mention of the horde hypothesis. But everything he says about the origins of religion and the categories, as well as his references within the *Forms* to *Division*, implies that these forms of human culture emerge simultaneously with the clan type of society, from the more primitive state of the horde (Durkheim 1995b, 93; 1991, 186). His references to the idea that the first powers experienced were those related to society as it "became organized" points in the same direction. There seems at first glance to be a "circular" quality about Durkheim's general theses in the sociology of religion and knowledge. He argues simultaneously that religion and the categories originate from society, yet constitute society, and that religious rites create the emotional setting for the creation of categories, yet also presuppose those very categorial divisions. This dilemma can be avoided only if we assume that all three phenomena—organized society, religion, the categories—emerge together in the transition from the homogeneous horde. It is Durkheim's version of the transition from nature to culture (and also his parry to Rousseau's hypothetical, individualistic "state of nature"). Without the horde as the tacit backdrop of the analysis of clan totemism, his entire theory becomes impossibly circular. With the horde, it becomes an intelligible account of the whole. In my view, many of the debates over the logical and chronological priority in Durkheim's theory of collective representations (including religion and the categories) versus society (including social morphology and social concentration) result from the fact that Durkheim's last book starts with totemist clan society as the most primitive type and makes no direct reference to the (hypothesized) prior existence of the horde. Yet, his argument about the origin of organized society logically imples such a group, even at this late date in his work.

Neither Bloor nor Schmaus offer satisfactory views of Durkheim, although Bloor's standpoint has the advantage of retaining the essential link between the categories and society. Both miss the fact that Durkheim's emerging sociological monism avoids the dilemmas of priority in the discussion by linking society, religion, and knowledge together into a single system. Durkheim's mature system implies that changes in society, religion and the categories take place together as aspects of one total transformation. Durkheim's emphasis on the fundamentally creative power of society involves the view that major transformations to new social types would necessarily involve the creation of new categories molded by the new realities, even if elements of the older ones continued to play some role in connection with the newer categorial forms.

The Person. The category of the person, or personality, was on Durkheim's short list and was also of interest to other members of the school (Mauss 1966, 333–62; Carrithers et. al. 1985). Durkheim's treatment of this topic is brief by comparison with the space allotted to other topics in the book. Except for the new emphasis on the religious sources of personality, it is also entirely in keeping with his earlier treatment of the relationship between individual and society. His basic view is that the clan's animating religious force is individualized, by "incarnating" itself in the individual (Durkheim 1995b, 426; 1991, 705). Secondary sacred beings are thus formed (e.g. the soul, the individualized totem, and the protective ancestor). The idea of the soul was and generally remains the most common form of the idea of personality (Durkheim 1995b, 272; 1991, 465). The individual totem can be either an animal or plant who protects the individual and whose fate is tied up with the individual (Durkheim 1995b, 282; 1991, 479). Individual totemism is a central part of collective totemism. The former emerges from and operates within the setting of the latter (Durkheim 1995b, 181; 1991, 322). The individual totem is not the motive force in public religion, but a product of it. It is the collective cult adapted to the individual's needs (Durkheim 1995b, 182; 1991, 323). In keeping with his earlier emphasis on the non-binding quality of individuated religious forms, Durkheim notes that the possession of an individual totem is seen as desirable, but not obligatory (Durkheim 1995b, 166; 1991, 296). As individuals become more differentiated within society and the value attached to the individual grows, the individual cult takes on an increasing significance in religion (Durkheim 1995b, 426–27; 1991, 706). To complete his sense of the gradations in the differentiation of religious objects, he also notes that there exists in some primitive communities an intermediate sexual totem, between the entirely collective and purely individual ones (Durkheim 1995b, 167; 1991, 298).

In general theoretical terms, two sorts of elements produce the idea of the person. The first is the impersonal spiritual principle, "the soul of the collectivity." Durkheim reveals one of his main assumptions when he writes that this principle is, in fact, the "substance of which individual souls are made" (Durkheim 1995b, 273; 1991, 465) and, through it, individual "consciousnesses commune." On the other hand, if there are to be separate personalities, there must be a differentiating principle. This is found in the body. Bodies are separated from each other, each with its own location in time and space. Collective representations are refracted and assume a particular coloration through the milieu provided by each individual body (Durkheim 1995b, 273; 1991, 466). Durkheim introduces a reference to Gottfried Leibniz's notion that each individual monad experiences one and the same object (i.e., the world) from its own particular standpoint. He also notes Kant's division between universal reason and individual will, rooted in bodily desires, as a related formulation of this general relationship. He goes on to note that his theory of the relationship between the collectivity and the individual captures the truth identified, yet also veiled by these earlier philosophical formulations.

It is interesting that Durkheim explains the philosophical intuitions of Leibniz and Kant with a sociological theory of the individual which itself bears a striking architechtonic resemblance to Spinoza's philosophy. In particular, we once again see Durkheim's parallellistic thesis at work. Individual representations become variants of the collective ones which have been individuated through the medium of bodily existence to individual situations in time and place. As with Spinoza, the soul is the idea of the body, but this idea is made available to the body only through the spiritual principle of the collective being whose "substance" is appropriated to individual needs. On closer inspection, we also note a certain "asymmetry" in Durkheim's formulation, especially when compared with his other discussions of individual and collective representations.

For example, in his essay of 1898 on this topic, he argued (not without a certain ambiguity) that individual representations were not merely an epiphenomena of the organism, but represented a distinct level of psychological processes. In the same way, he argued that collective representations were, in some ways, independent of their substratum in society. This earlier essay was aimed largely at analyzing these relations between types of representations and their respective substrata.

However, in the book of 1912, Durkheim not only speaks of the emergence of collective representations from collective assemblies, but also argues for the "incarnation" of collective representations directly in the individual, via the differentiating medium of the body. In fact, he is working with two types of parallelism:(1) the parallelism between individual representations and the body, and (2) the parallelism between collective representations and collective assemblies or associations (or what he sometimes, with his organismic analogy, calls the "social body"). However, his inherited metaphor, never entirely abandoned, of the relationship between whole and part, constrains him to continue speaking about direct relationships between the collective representations and the individual body. This crosscutting analysis, so to speak, is rather confusing, although it is understandable.

It has been observed that Durkheim does not adequately explain the emergence of collective representations from the alleged combination of individual ones. While this is true, it also misses the equally notable absense of any explanation of how the collective representations are actually individuated. His reference to the body as the differentiating medium establishes the relationship, but does not explain it. In slightly different terms, despite his extensive writings on education, Durkheim has no real theory of "socialization" or "internalization" of collective ideas. Both of the lacunae in his theory emerge from his commitment to parallelism, which resolves these problems in advance.

Durkheim's language of religious forces "incarnating" themselves is provocative in another respect. It is very much in keeping with his clearly stated view that society and deity are identical terms. If deity is the force of society symbolically expressed and transfigured, it is perfectly logical to think of this deity being "incarnated" in individuals, that is, individual bodies, literally bestowing a "soul" upon them. Durkheim's mixture of metaphysical and religious images in his sociological theory of the origins of personality is in keeping with his intention to bind together the truths latent in traditional religious thought and metaphysical philosophy with the insights of scientific sociology. This theory represents his sociological reconstruction of inherited Jewish ideas about the divine bestowal of spirit on humankind and, perhaps also, Christian ideas about the the two natures of Christ.

Substance. Having discussed the basic categories of space, time, cause, and personality, let us return to an examination of the notion of substance in the *Forms*. We would first note that Durkheim does include substance in the brief list of categories enunciated at the book's outset: space, time, number, cause, substance, personality (Durkheim 1995b, 8; 1991, 52). The list is intriguing. Space, time, causality, and personality are some of the book's central interests. As I will argue, substance is also literally at the center of Durkheim's analysis, indeed, one of his most important categories. However, we are puzzled by the mention of "number." Nowhere in Durkheim do we find an explicit treatment of number and not much more is found in the work of his school (e.g. Mauss 1968, II:308–13; III:185). In Kant, the problem of number fell within the category of quantity (which included unity, plurality, totality) while in Renouvier number replaces quantity as the general category, with the retention of its three moments as in Kant's philosophy. Indeed, number is central to Renouvier's entire philosophy. In the French language, the word *tout* can mean the whole, totality, or simply all of a collection of things, in the sense of a total numerical sum. As Durkheim himself mentions, totality as a category means one, inclusive of all things as well as other classifications (Durkheim 1995b, 443; 1991, 732). We are probably not far from the mark in thinking that Durkheim's analysis of totality implied an interest in number, even if he did not explore the origin of the category of number itself.

By contrast, while the notion of substance is central to his work, Durkheim does not directly thematize this category as Hubert and Mauss had done in their study of magic. Yet, it figures in a variety of ways in his study. It appears in connection with the primitive idea that the clan members share a common mystical substance with the totem figure (Durkheim 1995b, 271; 1991, 463). It is developed in connection with the notion of personality and the soul as the idea of common collective substance from which the individual person is differentiated or abstracted (Durkheim 1995b, 273; 1991, 465). Finally, it appears in the analysis of sacrifice in terms of the idea that the communion with the sacred principle in sacrifice periodically renews the mystic substance shared by the sacred being and the members of the clan (Durkheim 1995b, 341; 1991, 570). Behind these and other facets of the notion of substance lies the central reality of society. Society is the source of these ideas of common substance, especially insofar as it is also the source of the idea of a force or power (e.g., *mana*) which is at the core of the idea of substance. *Mana* is a power, force or energy, but it is also a substance, a kind of "ether," in the words of Hubert and Mauss (1972, 109). These notions are inseparable. In actuality, the category of substance is identical with society itself.

We need to be clear about this central idea. Society is at the root of the experience of power or force and is itself a particular force for Durkheim. It must be a real force and be experienced as such for it to be the source of our conceptions of force. If society is the origin—as it clearly is for Durkheim—of the notion of substance, then we need also to ask: is society itself a substance in Durkheim's view? The "representational" view of Durkheim's conception of society would deny this, as would all those who argue one or another case for Durkheim's "associational realism." But it is difficult to understand how Durkheim's theory of the categories could be internally consistent unless he did conceive of society as a substance, as having something of a substance about it. The category of genre is derived from the actual structure of human groupings. The category of space is molded on the spatial organization of society. Time is based on the actual rhythm of social life. The concept of causality was ultimately rooted in the collective force of the group. All the categories borrow their actual models from the organization of society, including the social morphology, religious, moral, and economic institutions, and so on, certainly one of the most theoretically charged et cetera clauses in sociology (Durkheim 1995b, 15, also 441; 1991, 62, also 729). If this is the case, then there must also be something about society that provides both the experience and the concrete model for the notion of substance. If it is separable in any way from the notion of collective force or power, and points instead toward a separate "essense," as the notion of substance did in the philosophical tradition, the category of substance must also be modeled on some feature of society. Yet, if society is in the end merely a set of individuals, what in society can gestate collective experiences capable of creating the category of "substance?" At this point, even the whole/part rationale fails. For Durkheim, it provides a useful account, but can offer no explanation of itself, that is, of the social origin of the notion of the whole.

I would suggest that the very experiences variously expressed by Durkheim in terms of concentration, dynamic density, copresence, assembly, and so forth are the model for the category of substance. This model requires the copresence of human beings—to be more precise, bodies in coaction and cofunctioning. Just as emotional assemblies gestate the sense of a power or force above the individual in which they are absorbed and on which they depend, so, too, social concentration generates experiences of a single substance which contains everything else. As with the other categories, this notion of a unitary substance is differentiated in a variety of ways in connection with social life, giving rise to other ideas and concepts. But within the consistently applied logic of Durkheim's analysis, this category of substance cannot be an "illusion." It must correspond to some reality, in the strong sense of taking its actual model from society.

The weaker thesis, that the experience and idea of substance derives from social concentration, needs to be supplemented by the idea that society must actually be a substance which provides a concrete model for the category. Just as there has to be a social division of space, a social rhythm, a social force, and a collective identity before there can be categories of space, time, cause, or the person, ones filled with social content, social substance must exist before there can be a category of substance. This social substance cannot be identified merely with "collective representation," since it is the originating source itself of all such collective representations.

Durkheim said as much all along, with his idea of society as a reality, sui generis, one which he repeated in various forms from the start to the end of his work. As we have seen, he even stated at various points that religion was the "sensorium" of society (an idea entertained by Saint-Simon and Renouvier). His last book provides a fuller statement of this view.

I can only conclude that Durkheim, without ever directly admitting as much, conceived of society as a substance, indeed, given the enormous power he associates with it, perhaps the ultimate substance. Such a notion is congruent with what I have been calling his "sociological monism," perhaps even with a sort of "sociological pantheism." Durkheim hardly confronts this issue of social substance in direct fashion. However, it lurks about in the suggestive, if fugitive references examined above from his earlier writings. It appears as an actual category in his final work, where it and the other categories are part of the agenda, but where the category of substance is still left in suspension. I see no other way of understanding him. Indeed, it is telling that substance appears on his list at all. In fact, it is analyzed in his book, without Durkheim consciously thematizing his actual practice. For Durkheim, society was no illusion, but perhaps the individual was. The crucial fact is that Durkheim simultaneously combines the representational and the morphological in a substantial societal whole. This takes him far from any Platonically inspired pan-psychism (e.g. of the sort associated with Jung).

In another sense, it is crucial to maintain the distinction between collective representations and society itself. The "representationist" view of Durkheim obscures the implications of this distinction and Durkheim's way of transcending it. It is mistaken in two respects. First, the notion of collective representations simply does not figure prominently in Durkheim's early work, up to the later 1890s. His references at this time to collective consciousness point in a very different direction, linking it quite clearly to social morphology and changes in moral density. Second, his own repeated references to social morphology, actual physical assemblies, and other manners of social concentration persist into his last work. They involve the real copresence of people in the creation of collective emotions and representations. Indeed, the creation of collective emotions is entirely a function of actual collective physical assemblies of people and cannot easily be understood solely in terms of collective representations. Even when he and Mauss develop their notion of "civilization," and go beyond the unit of society to identify cultural phenomena common to two or more societies, they explicitly tie these translocal phenomena to the concomitant expansion of society itself into new international forms (Durkheim and Mauss 1971). While no one would deny that the notion of collective representation plays a large role in Durkheim's theory, it is important to place this idea in the context of his entire philosophy. When this is done, it is clear that is only a piece, and not necessarily the most significant one, of a larger puzzle.

Society, Deity, Totality

After the turn of the century, Durkheim always emphasized the social nature of the categories and of concepts generally. In the *Forms*, he presents two different types of arguments about this problem. Concepts are necessary for communication among humans and language itself is a product of collective activity (Durkheim 1995b, 435; 1991, 719). More important is the fact that concepts are marked by universality (as opposed to generality), impersonality, and stability. They are thought *sub specie aeternitatis* (Durkheim 1995b, 437; 1991, 723), a phrase closely associated with Spinoza. What is true of concepts is especially true of the categories. They regulate and encompass all other concepts (Durkheim 1995b, 441; 1991, 729). Among the categories, that of totality, as mentioned above, has the particular function of enveloping all the other categories, since there is no category more inclusive than that of totality or the whole. Thus, Durkheim suggests a stratified conception of the human representative functions, once again strongly reminiscent of Spinoza: individual sensations, concepts, categories, and totality, as the most inclusive category.

If the category of totality envelops all other categories, and ultimately expresses one modality of a larger unity, one which is equivalent to both society and divinity, it is also the case that the other categories (time, space, cause, etc.) each conceptualize a particular mode of the total being. The language of "modes" does appear, if infrequently, in Durkheim's own terminology and that of his school. It is difficult to avoid using such terms if we want to adequately thematize his monism. Hubert had already discussed social time in such a language, and Hubert and Mauss had spoken of human reason in a similar fashion (Hubert and Mauss 1929). In effect, Durkheim argues that the categories point in two different directions: (1) toward unification within the notion of totality and, by implication, within the cognate notions of divinity and society; (2) toward dispersion out across society's processes which the categories, in turn, capture and express *sub specie aeternitatis*. Both directions need to be emphasized. To achieve its philosophical integration, Durkheim's system requires that the categories be comprehended in the notion of totality, yet also reflect societal processes, including those connected with religion. The categories are the bridge, so to speak, between totality and actually existing society. They touch ground on both sides, thought at its most universal level and material and social reality.

From the beginning of his new theoretical turn, Durkheim insisted on the social nature of the categories and systems of classification in the stronger, rather than merely the weaker form of that thesis. We have already discussed his idea that society provides a model for classificatory thought. Its classificatory divisions serve are the original divisions in the system of classification. "The first logical categories were social categories . . ." (Durkheim and Mauss 1963, 82). If this is true of all the categories, they are, in turn, all summarized, so to speak, in the notion of totality, which thematizes the whole (Durkheim and Mauss 1963, 83–84). Totality is, in fact, society expressed in its most universalizing form. From these observations, it is possible to conclude several things. First, Durkheim has created his own "New Organon," one with a sociological foundation, and evidently intended it to replace those of Aristotle and Sir Francis Bacon. We have already placed the Durkheimian project in relationship to Aristotle's list of categories and Bacon's quest for a new method and suggested that Durkheim did have such an aim. Second, the unification of the system of categories within the notion of totality becomes a sociological thesis when we consider that the differentiated processes of society, in particular, those connected with religion, are the realities collected in the categories, which are then also extended to the remainder of the cosmos. Here, I do not wish to mislead by using the Platonically tinged term, "collected." Perhaps Durkheim's own earlier choice, "summarize," would do better. It is not now possible to further compare either Plato's method of "collection" under the forms or Aristotle's system of categories with Durkheim's analysis (see Cornford 1957, 268–79). However, I would recall the above discussion of Aristotle and Durkheim, where it was argued that, for Durkheim, the categories are instruments and predicates which sum up reality. Durkheim is clearly operating with a system of categories, not with forms in any Platonic sense.

The seams of Durkheim's theory are so tightly and invisibly sewn that it is difficult to perceive the separate strands (societal, religious, categorial) composing the overall fabric. It is important to recall that, for Durkheim, the categories, like all major social institutions, ultimately have a religious origin. They emerge especially

out of the interstices of the system of religious ritual. But this originating point in religion turns out itself, on closer inspection, to be
social in nature. Society supplies both the mold for the categories as
well as the dynamic energies which go into religious practices;
together they are fused in society itself. The binding tie in this
seamless web is the social, society, or more accurately, collectively
gestated energies or powers. These energies seem to be the dynamic
reality behind all the representations, religious, or categorial.
Durkheim's social morphological emphases also merge with his
more dynamic associational ones. In the end, whether we are examining the category of totality, divinity, or society, we are examining
different modes of the same reality, one captured in a variety of
images of force, power, energy, and so forth. However, although
Durkheim's monism is ultimately sociological, its basic features are
so intimately connected with the dynamics of religion, its synthetic
as well as its generative influence, it would not be unreasonable to
suggest that his theory hints at a kind of "sociological pantheism,"
not entirely unlike that developed by the Saint-Simonians and discussed in Durkheim's lectures on socialism.

   Concepts not only forge consensus among minds, but they are
themselves also in agreement with nature, with things (Durkheim
1995b, 438; 1991, 725). Indeed, for Durkheim, the collective character of the categories validates the truth claims embedded in
them. The fact that they have a social origin does not bar them from
also being true. On the contrary, their social origin supports their
truth, since individual variations in perception and understanding
have been checked by others (Durkheim 1995b, 439). This social
process of mutual correction embodied in the categories guarantees
objectivity and truth, that is, their correspondence with things.
They are not only social products and applied to society, but
". . . extend to reality as a whole (*la réalité tout entière*)" (Durkheim
1995b, 441; 1991, 729). Here, it is not primarily social consensus
about the categories, in the sense of rational agreement, which
guarantees their validity. Social agreement alone could never
acheive such an objective, indeed, could never create the categories
in the first place. Durkheim evidently relies on the idea that nature
must be self-consistent among its varying departments, so that the
categories elaborated collectively by society will also be applicable
to nature. This is a corollary to his idea that moral and natural
forces are comparable, and both parts of a single universe.

   This fit between the categories and nature, the wider reality
of objects generally, emerges from another fact. Human activity,

especially religious ritual and symbolism, employs "tangible intermediaries" to embody collective mental processes which could otherwise not be publicly available or expressed (Durkheim 1995b, 232; 231–34 generally; 1991, 403–4, 402–6). Moreover, religious activities and their categories are added to and superimposed upon the objects of the material world and mold it to human thought. Religion sacralizes and socializes physical objects and brings them within the orbit of human thought. It serves as a "common sensorium" for society as it comprehends nature. As Durkheim notes, society is an immensely powerful creative force, and part of its creativity emeges from its classification and envelopment of the objective world. It is therefore not surprising that these categories should be true in relationship to a world they have, to some degree, created (Durkheim 1995b, 232).

I would separate these two strands of Durkheim's conception of the relationships among nature, society, and the categories. The one relies on the mutual harmony among the spheres of existence, the other on a more actively oriented notion that human agency, and its collective representational capacity, molds the world and therefore creates the very objective conditions necessary for the partial truth of its categories. These two conceptions are not entirely incompatible, yet also rest uncomfortably with each other. The former drives Durkheim toward a sociological metaphysics based on an assumed preestablished harmony (if not identity) between society and nature, while the latter points to some variant of a conception closer to that of Giambattista Vico, Karl Marx, and the Pragmatists, one emphasizing that human practice creates the very world which its intellectual categories, in turn, can truthfully comprehend.

In my view, while Durkheim was closer to the former perspective, he was hardly clear in simultaneously suggesting these two strands of thought. His explicit critique of the pragmatist emphasis on action as a central dimension in the vadidation of truth and his implicit critique of its pluralism (especially in James's version) supports the contention that his theory was less instrumentalist than harmonian, and harmonistic precisely because it is implicitly monistic. This may also helps explain why Durkheim devoted an entire course to the critical analysis of pragmatism at a time when he had just completed a major phase of his own constructive theoretical work. The fact that Durkheim, at this time, places such an emphasis on religion provides added support for my choice of the mutual harmony thesis as Durkheim's own.

All sociologists are familiar with Durkheim's idea that religion is not only a social institution, but also embodies symbolically the very nature of society itself. These two claims represent weaker versus stronger sociological views of religion. Few would object to the weaker claim that there is much social process embedded in religion. The "methodological agnosticism" of the contemporary sociology of religion has generally remained within the confines of this weaker claim that religion is a social institution and avoided anything which might appear to be a sociological challenge to the very essense of religion (but see Swanson 1966). It is the stronger claim that has always stirred objections, indeed, in Durkheim's day, even outraged some of his contemporaries. Yet, it is central to his main argument. Without it, his entire view becomes unintelligible. Despite the fact that this part of his theory has been widely examined, it remains one of the most difficult and confusing aspects of his work and has given rise to varied intepretations (Seger 1957; Evans-Pritchard 1965; Skorupski 1976; Pickering 1984).

Religious life is the "eminent form" and the "epitome" of group life. From religion is born everything essential in society and this is possible only because "the idea of society is the soul of religion" (Durkheim 1995b, 421; see also 208; 1991, 697, 365). Durkheim is quick to add that it is the real, actually existing society which is at the heart of religion, not an imaginary, utopian, or perfected society (Durkheim 1995b, 423; 1991, 699–700). As we have already seen, Durkheim argued in 1898 that divinity is nothing but the symbolic expression of transfigured society (Durkheim 1974a, 52). Indeed, in that earlier essay, Durkheim had also argued that an imperfect society can still give rise to experiences of divinity, because God is responsible for the same imperfect world (Durkheim 1974a, 73–74).

Sometimes Durkheim writes as though he were advancing an "idealist" thesis. In my view, his language has greatly misled commentators. Talcott Parsons (1937) thought that he had moved from a positivist to an idealist perspective. Through his references to the alleged "transfiguring" role of religion, others have smuggled much of the baggage of traditional religious thought, especially in its Protestant variants, into his theory (Bellah 1970; his introduction to Durkheim 1973, li–lii; Nielsen 1987a, 295–99). In general, omnibus conceptions such as empiricism, rationalism, positivism, idealism—or for that matter, structuralism, anti-structuralism, deconstructionism, postmodernism—and so forth badly muddy the waters about Durkheim's thinking. They force us into false compartmentalizations of his work. Durkheim himself is partly to blame. Caught between the "empiricism" and "rationalism" of his historical era, he repeatedly refers to "ideals" and "idealism" in a way which implies that he is a thoroughgoing "rationalist," yet also contradicts other seemingly "materialistic" aspects of his main thesis (Durkheim 1995b, 230, 425; 1991, 401, 703). Durkheim was more daring than his commentators have allowed. He demonstrates a willingness to break with the alternatives of materialism or idealism. The fault is not in his aims, or his basic ideas, as much as it is the ambiguity, resulting from his frequent hesitation in pursuing his deepest intuitions.

Durkheim's equation of divinity, totality, and society emerges from a theory which, at its explanatory center, combines reference to collective activity, collective sentiment and emotion, social force, energy, and several other terms which are not always mediated in a fully coherent fashion. As I have already stated, this theory can only be described as sociological monism, in particular, a monism shot through with powerful elements of a theory of "social energetics."

At the center of this theory is the analysis of rituals and collective assemblies. In my view (contra Jones 1986), ritual takes clear explanatory priority over belief in Durkheim's theory, even though he devotes a larger number of pages to the analysis of belief. Of course, the problem of religious beliefs is also central to his work. This preponderant textual emphasis on belief is also tied closely to his analysis of the categories, but both together are to be fully understood only in their relationship to ritual, and all that it involves as a social process. This is because rites focus on collective assemblies. Such collective assemblies gestate collective sentiments, emotions, and energies and disengage ideas and ideals. For Durkheim, the most critical fact is "that individuals are assembled and that feelings in common are expressed through actions in common" (Durkheim 1995b, 390; 1991, 646). He adds that the particular character of these sentiments and acts is of secondary importance. Here, Durkheim seems to distinguish betweeen a "pure" form of collective sentiment and social energy and the particular institutions and cultural forms in which it is expressed. He concurs with the earlier remark by Hubert and Mauss, that there are no specialized sentiments. Moreover, the preponderant role of ritual in religion results from the fact that society's influence cannot be fully exercised unless it is in action. However, it can be in action only if the individuals who compose society "are assembled and acting in common." As the result of common action, "society becomes con-

scious of and affirms itself; society is above all an active cooperation" (Durkheim 1995b, 421; 1991, 696). Indeed, it is precisely
because society is the source of religion that action is the core of
religious life (Durkheim 1995b, 421; 1991, 696).

The usual Durkheimian argument concerning the social
sources of religion is here coupled with the notion that it is only in
action that society's power is fully experienced. I take these references to copresent collective action to be decisive for his theory. The
social forces and energy mentioned above, the true "substance" of
society, are only allowed to loosen themselves in such settings of
intensely emotional assembly, association and, by implication,
breakdown of established social barriers and structures. That new
collective representations may, and usually do, result from these
social concentrations is a secondary outcome of their operation, and
is neither their cause nor their central aspect.

While the notion of "collective effervescence" is certainly central to Durkheim's analysis, it is by no means alone in his sociological rhetoric. It is matched, and sometimes eclipsed, by other terms
used to describe the outcomes of collective assemblies. Even in the
Forms, the notion of social concentration continues to be central
(Durkheim 1995b, 313, 443). As we have shown in previous chapters, Durkheim regularly employs such notions as moral density,
concentration, and others in his earlier work. Such terms as heat,
light, energy, forces, sentiments, emotions, contagion, delirium, and
others are also regularly (and rather indiscriminately) employed by
Durkheim, whose use of them, as Robert Alun Jones (1984) notes,
borders on the "obfuscatory." Many times the emphasis is placed on
the moral quality of these forces, although it is characteristic of
Durkheim that he frequently uses "moral" and "force" together,
without any hint that they might be viewed as contradictory terms,
drawn from rather different rhetorical arsenals. Here, the idealist
language seems to take center stage. Yet, in the very same paragraph, Durkheim is likely to use terms like energy, force, heat, light,
and so forth to describe the results of collective assemblies and
strongly imply that he is describing actual physical forces generated. He even uses a term such as "intensity" often enough to suggest that he thinks (as he did in *Suicide*) that these forces might possibly be measurable quantities. However, these "forces" are never
given separate theoretical treatment as "forces," that is, as a variety
of natural "physical" process, although they seem to form the very
"substance" of society itself, one of its most distinguishing characteristics as an natural entity. In addition, the terms collective senti-

ment and emotion are regularly employed to describe the core of the ritual process. Yet, once again, the line between the "moral" and the "physical" is not clearly drawn. How can "moral" phenomena be "physical?" Only because, when society is fully assembled and in action, it generates a type of "force" distinctive to human society, a "force" which is a part of the realm of nature, but is also moral, since it is exercised by humanity on humanity. There is certainly considerable tension here among Durkheim's central motifs.

At least some of the confusion can be cleared up if we assume that this varied terminology is meant to convey Durkheim's sense that these realms are, in fact, to be equated with one another. Society is a system of real forces, "free forces" as well as ones bound into traditions and institutions (Durkheim 1995b, 242); sentiments and emotions are forces or energies; periodic group assemblies and periods of intense social concentration gestate such energies and create ideas and ideals in the process; "moral force" is not an oxymoron, but an accurate expression of Durkheim's theory.

In my view, these seeming inconsistencies in Durkheim's language point to a deeper implied unity in his theory. This unity centers around his notion of "society," and, especially, society when it is actually assembled, for it is only at such times that it is truly and wholly society. Indeed, social differentiation and social process in Durkheim's mature work is understood primarily in relation to society in this active, creative, energizing sense of a "power."

Here, we also find one of the clearest points at which Durkheim modified his earlier work on *Division* in light of his new theory. In his earlier work, increased dynamic or moral density played a central role in explaining increased division of labor and organic solidarity, as well as the shift in the composition of legal sanctions. However, the concept itself was poorly developed and, in the end, seemed to rest on the notion of population density (and, to some extent, even on volume). As Durkheim's work proceeds, moral density appears to be largely disconnected from the issue of population volume, and, in effect, is used to explain the experience of force or power, although it is still clearly related to the social location and dynamic movements of people. The quantitative simplicity of his first theory, with its ultimate recourse to total social volume, is replaced by a more subtle, yet perhaps vaguer conception of the relationship between social concentrations in assemblies and the experience of power. However, in both instances, the bodily copresence and concentration of individuals remains crucial. On this point, Durkheim never wavered.

Durkheim's distinction between the sacred and the profane needs to be brought into the analysis again at this point. Like other terms in his theory, they are not altogether unambiguous. We have already noted some of its spatial connotations. At times, the sacred/profane distinction seems equivalent to the social group/egoism distinction (Durkheim 1995b, 321–22; 1991, 538–39). At other times, the notion of the profane refers to the "ordinary" or "mundane" social life of the group when it is not assembled for collective rites (Durkheim 1995b, 353; 1991, 587). Here, it seems to shade off into a "residual category," that is, everything which is not sacred is therefore profane. Indeed, this is probably the most helpful usage, and the one most congruent with the view of Durkheim which I am elaborating (for another view see Pickering 1984).

While the profane activities of the group are defined largely by opposition to the sacred ones, Durkheim by no means discounts the idea that sacred moral forces can be found in seemingly "routine" settings. Exceptional circumstances are not the only settings which generate the great collective passions. Society makes itself felt on a more regular, frequent basis. At "no instant" in life do we fail to experience a "certain rush" from outside ourselves (Durkheim 1995b, 213; 1991, 373). Society perpetually raises the level of our moral being. The level of group activity and the differences among the groups involved create variations in the precise character of this "moral toning," but in all instances the cause is found in external conditions (Durkheim 1995b, 213; 1991, 373).

These passages point to the notion that the forces of society-in-action, which engender the sense of the sacred in the special settings of religious ritual, also do so, perhaps to a more limited degree, in mundane, or profane ones. Durkheim had made similar remarks about the power of the school class to gestate experiences of a "sacred" type (Durkheim 1956, 112). The suggestion sometimes made by students of Durkheim, that he sees religion as a social product, but does not see all social groups as religious, requires rethinking (Parsons 1937). Society in all of its processes has the potential to engender experiences of the sacred. This notion is particularly central when one ties it to Durkheim's idea of the origin of organized society from the horde. It is during this transition, as well as in other fundamental transitions from one societal type to another, that the dynamic movement of peoples and concentration of energies takes place which can generate new religions and categories.

In general, Durkheim sees society and religion as necessarily implicated ideas, a notion which has been explored in different ways by several recent thinkers (Swanson 1966; R. Collins 1988, 187–229). In particular, Randall Collins has expanded on his reading of Erving Goffman's (allegedly Durkheimian) theory of interaction ritual to develop a perspective on religion which even recognizes the centrality of "emotional energy" in such processes. However, his theory operates primarily at an empirical level and fails to recognize either the monistic strand in Durkheim's theorizing or the closer rappprochement of his own emerging theory to earlier forms of "social energetics" (Sorokin 1928, chap. 1). However, I cannot now comment further on these alternate readings and extensions of Durkheim.

My interpretation of Durkheim's notions of the sacred and the profane should not be taken to imply that he was not in some key respects a dualistic thinker. Durkheim's work is, indeed, shot through with dualisms: within human nature, between the individual and society; the sacred and profane; two types of the sacred (the propitious and the unpropitious); empiricism and rationalism; egoism and altruism, anomie and fatalism; and so forth. On the contrary, it is meant to suggest that his evident attachment to dualistic ways of thinking was coupled with strong tendencies toward a more comprehensive sociological monism. The foregoing analysis of the *Forms* has aimed at demonstrating this.

10

THE PROBLEM OF TOTALITY IN DURKHEIM'S LAST WRITINGS

The Lectures on Pragmatism

Durkheim's lectures on pragmatism were delivered in 1913–14, before the beginning of World War I. According to Marcel Mauss, they were intended to introduce students to a current of thought of growing influence in France. In particular, they were for his son André Durkheim, who was to die in the war. Mauss remarks that the manuscript of the lectures, "the high point of Durkheim's philosophical work," was lost (Durkheim 1983, xi; 1955, 7). The lectures had to be reconstructed from two sets of student notes. The editor, Armand Cuvillier, emphasizes that what remains is "only a *reconstituted text*" (Cuviller's emphasis) (Durkheim 1983, 12; 1955, 8). As such, it poses many of the same problems currently generating debate over the value of Max Weber's *General Economic History*. While the work is interesting, it can hardly qualify as Durkheim's most important positive statement of the relationships between philosophy and social theory, despite Mauss's laudatory remark. This is especially true of the very philosophical issues of central concern to us in this work. Indeed, these lectures strike me as a disappointment when compared with the genius displayed in the *Forms*. Although we receive a much fuller account of his attitude toward pragmatism, my main aim is not to assess Durkheim's relationship to that school of thought.

Despite these limitations, Durkheim's lectures on pragmatism do confirm Durkheim's continued interest in philosophical issues and his need to analyze and combat an influential philosophical current which rivaled his own emerging standpoint. They also contain some strong hints which confirm the suspicions we have already voiced about his own intellectual lineage, in particular, his relationship to Spinoza. Finally, they tell us something about issues treated in the *Forms*, especially the categories and, in general, allow us to confirm many of the emphases already noted in his theory. Let us discuss these points in turn.

We have already seen Durkheim, early in his career and several times after, gesture to Spinoza's work in a fashion that would lead us to believe that he thought him to be an important and congenial thinker. In the lectures, Durkheim notes that William James's radical empiricism involved an open criticism of Spinoza's distinction between seeing nature as creating or created, in Spinoza's terms, *natura naturans* (nature naturing) and *natura naturata* (nature natured). While Durkheim does not directly criticize James (or defend Spinoza) at this particular point, his wide-ranging critique of him throughout the lectures would lead us to believe that he also thinks James in error on this issue. Indeed, Spinoza's double way of conceiving the key idea of his monistic philosophy is remarkably similar to Durkheim's own dualism-within-monism. As we have already seen, Durkheim thinks that nature as a whole is united and brought "within" society, through the intermediaries of religion and the categories, especially the category of totality. Within this overall conception, he argues for a dualism of human nature, one thoroughly grounded in society (a problem to be examined further in the next section). For the moment, I would merely reiterate the fact that Durkheim conceives the relationship between body and mind along Spinozist lines. He writes that the Pragmatists err in denying the specific nature of knowledge, thought, and consciousness. "The role of consciousness is not to direct the behavior of a being with no need of knowledge: *it is to constitute a being who would not exist without it.* (emphasis in original text) . . . This is what caused Spinoza to say that the soul is the idea of the body. Consciousness is . . . the organism knowing itself . . ." (Durkheim 1983, 82; 1955, 170).

Davy already had called attention to the parallels between Spinoza's conception of the mind/body problem and Durkheim's view (Davy 1911). Both adopted a species of parallelism. This conception of the relationship between body and mind (or soul) was presented by Durkheim immediately after he introduced another set of distinctions which also directly mirror Spinoza.

Durkheim argues that knowledge ascends in a series of stages from sensation to images to concepts. As knowledge moves from sensation to concepts, it also moves from a mode of thought (sensation) closely entangled with action to one most devoid of connections with emotion and action (concepts). Images form an intermediary stage in which representation gives the appearance of taking on an independent existence (Durkheim 1983:82; also 42–43; 1955, 169, 96–98). As we have already seen, Durkheim implicitely adds a fourth stage of knowledge with his distinction between concepts and categories, the latter being of a greater abstraction and inclusiveness as well as being molded more directly by society's structure than the former. Finally, among the categories, there is the preeminence of the category of totality. This set of stages is strongly reminiscent of the fourfold conception of knowledge developed by Spinoza in his early *Treatise on the Emendation of the Intellect* (Spinoza 1985, 12–13). While the correspondence is not perfect, since Durkheim actually has five "levels" (sensations, images, concepts, the categories, and totality), the parallels are suggestive.

Durkheim also reiterates the "circular" character of human thought, as opposed to the notion of thinking in linear series, although, in doing so, he does not explicitly mention the whole/part problematic which accompanied his discussion of the circle imagery in his other writing (Durkheim 1983, 67; 1955, 142–43).

In disputing the pragmatist emphasis on the idea that truth is always a human good, Durkheim notes that truth can often be painful. It can disturb the serenity of the mind, disabling and disconcerting the individual, and even require him to change his entire way of thinking. He adds a hypothetical instance. If an adult "suddenly realizes that all his religious beliefs have no solid basis, he experiences a moral collapse and his intellectual and affective life is in a sense paralyzed" (Durkheim 1983, 74; 1955, 155). May we imagine that this example is, in part, autobiographical and refers back, rather obliquely, to Durkheim's own "revelation" of 1895 about religion and his need to begin his studies over again? This is purely speculation, but the example remains oddly evocative. Equally suggestive in this same context is Durkheim's approving reference to Jouffroy's mid-nineteenth-century essay on how ideals die as a description of this process (Jouffroy 1924).

Durkheim discusses the pragmatist attitude toward the rationalist conception of truth and toward monism and offers his critique of their radical pluralism. The dynamic pragmatist conception of truth does point to the role played by humankind in the creation of new truth, and is especially confirmed by the role played by social change in gestating new realities. However, the pragmatists overlook the fact that, in a larger sense, truth still remains stable and the laws of nature are unchanging. In a related vein, it is interesting that Durkheim defines monism in the following terms: "If the universe is actually *one* (emphasis in original text) in the sense that it forms a closely linked system, all of the elements of which imply each other, a system where the whole commands the existence of the parts and where individuals are appearances that in sum constitute only one being, then change is impossible; for the place of each element is determined by the whole and the whole, in its turn, is determined by the elements. This is the monist point of view" (Durkheim 1983, 25; 1955, 70–71). Durkheim then briefly summarizes James's critique of this religion of the number one, but wonders whether pragmatism has captured what is essential in rationalism and returns to a discussion of the issue of truth (Durkheim 1983, 27).

It is difficult to interpret Durkheim's uneven and rather disjointed treatment. However, his general reservations about the pragmatist critique of rationalism might be thought to spill over into the pragmatist critique of monism (since the pragmatists tended to identify monism and rationalism). As I have already shown, the core rhetoric of monism, as described by Durkheim, has something in common with his own central images and analyses. Here, a certain caution is required. Durkheim surely would not subscribe to some of the elements of his own definition of monism, for example, that change was impossible and that individuals are only appearances (although, at times, he comes parlously close to the latter view). However, as I have argued in earlier sections of this work, Durkheim does exhibit a strong tendency to view the universe as a "linked system," where society plays a central role as its lynchpin. Society is one of the world's greatest forces and actually gives coherence to this system, folding the universe "within" society.

The presence of the whole/part rhetoric in his discussion should also give pause. As we have seen, Durkheim's repeated gesture to this analogy throughout his writings, whenever he needs to make a fundamental argument in support of his theorizing, places its importance in his system beyond dispute. Here he uses it in his characterization of monism and in a chapter which contains a reaffirmation of the creative role of society in gestating new truths and changing reality. This same chapter also ends with a qualified support of rationalism (or, at least, a claim that the pragmatists have not really grasped what is essential in rationalism). All of this certainly gives us reason to think that Durkheim might be expressing a qualified support for a modified monist position. Indeed, it is precisely Durkheim's support (whether entirely explicit or even fully acknowledged) of a sociological monism for which we have been arguing in these pages. However, I would also reinterate my cautionary remarks, since we discover Durkheim later suggesting that the pragmatists' "continuist" thesis about the universe is itself a form of monism. If any certain conclusion can be drawn from Durkheim's suggestive (and confusing) comments, it is that he remained preoccupied with the issues connected with philosophical monism (among other philosophical positions) late into his career.

A related issue is developed by Durkheim in a brief discussion of the problems of continuity and discontinuity. This issue had exercised philosophers since Zeno's paradoxes and was then being subject to new treatments in the work of Henri Bergson and William James (among others). James hoped to demonstrate that rationalism ended by implying the existence of an infinite number of things. Durkheim suggests that he has not proven his case against rationalism. In one of his only references to Renouvier's key notion of number, he writes:

> The greatest contemporary rationalist, Charles Renouvier, who demonstrated the impossibility of an actual infinity of parts, takes up Zeno's arguments. Thus, to insist on this impossibility is not necessarily to ruin intellectualism. (Durkheim 1983, 30; 1955, 76; Renouver 1875; Hamelin 1927)

This rather odd argument does tell us something: Durkheim thought Renouvier to be the "greatest contemporary rationalist" and also thought Renouvier had "demonstrated" that an infinity of parts was impossible.

In this same lecture, Durkheim refers to Octave Hamelin's analysis of the categories. He notes the latter's argument that there are links between the categories. For Hamelin, reality manifests an "immanent unity." The elements composing reality exist only through the relationships which unite them (Durkheim 1983, 35; 1955, 86). The pragmatists did not see this solution to the problem of the continuity or discontinuity of elements in the universe provided by "radical Idealism" (i.e. Hamelin's position). While it is clear from remarks made elsewhere that Durkheim does not fully accept the details of Hamelin's system, this passage again demonstrates Durkheim's willingness to entertain a conception of reality which includes the postulate of "immanent unity," a position at the center of Spinoza's work.

The remarks about Renouvier also suggest that this willing-

ness was linked to his acceptance of Renouvier's demonstration
that infinite plurality was impossible as well as to other elements
in Renouvier's philosophy. Durkheim's emphasis on the idea that
the relationships which unite the categories are as central as the
elements themselves recalls the central place occupied by the category of relation in Renouvier's philosophy. Durkheim similarly
locates relation in a privileged place among the categories and does
so in a fashion congruent with his overall stress on the whole/part
relation and totality. It is also of the greatest interest that the
notion of relation is not developed by Durkheim in connection with
the problems of association or collective representations, as a basis
for what has been called his "associational realism," but as a way of
uniting the categories into a larger totality. Indeed, Durkheim concludes his lectures by remarking that "we remain firmly in the
Kantian tradition" by emphasizing (as Renouvier had) that logical
necessity is a form of moral necessity and theoretical certainty is
rooted in practical certainty (Durkheim 1983, 102; 1955, 202). The
emphasis on practical reason, shared by Renouvier and Durkheim
is striking, even if Renouvier moved more towards a personalist
and Durkheim a collectivist version of this perspective.

The image of concentration also appears in modified form in
these lectures. Durkheim argues that the conditions of thought and
action are entirely different. In a rather obscure discussion,
Durkheim envisions thought as a "hyperconcentration of consciousness" and argues that the more thought is concentrated, "the
smaller the circle of reflection" (Durkheim 1983, 80; 1955, 166).
Reflection also requires time. On the other hand, action involves
"externalizing oneself." The individuals cannot be simultaneously
within and outside of themselves. It is not clear that this notion of
concentration, uncoupled as it is from action, has much to do with
Durkheim's other frequent uses of the concentration imagery in
connection with societal processes. Indeed, this image seems to be
quite contrary to his usual argument that only through the concentration of social energies in actual settings of social assembly that
the highest levels of thought are created and disengaged. The
image of an increasingly concentrated thought process pinpointed
into a ever shrinking circle is certainly difficult to reconcile with
Durkheim's social theory, unless we assume that such concentrated
individual thought is the residue of a prior state of social concentration.

The notion of concentration is also developed in a more familiar way, when Durkheim suggests that monotheism is the expres-

sion of the group's tendency toward greater concentration. He then immediately remarks: "Just as 'coenaesthetic' sensations are the central core of consciousness for the individual, collective truths are the basis of the common consciousness for society" (Durkheim 1983, 87; 1955, 177). Durkheim had referred earlier in his lectures to such "coenaesthetic" sensations in connection with his remarks about Spinoza's notion that the soul is the idea of the body. Here, we find him extending the discussion, quite logically, in the context of a consideration of the problems of myth, religion, and truth, to a parallel with social consciousness. This discussion evokes his remarks, both in his lectures on socialism and his contemporaneous letter to Gaston Richard, about the role of religion as a "common sensorium." For Durkheim, religion and the fundamental categories of knowledge do provide a kind of collective sensorium for society itself. In Spinozist language, they are the idea of the social being or body.

Another facet of this view is mentioned later, when Durkheim refers to primitive religious life as a whole which gathers up all the other forms of understanding (e.g. science, poetry, law, morality, other beliefs) and which is a "concentration of all kinds of energies, undivided in the sense that they are only various aspects of one and the same thing" (Durkheim 1983, 94–95; 1955, 192). Durkheim rejects the view that this state is the highest one. Indeed, he views it as the most basic, undifferentiated one, subject to later evolution and development, and, by implication, perfection. However, it remains interesting that he sees the origins of human culture's most important creations in terms of a setting of undivided concentration of energies. For Durkheim, this was a prominent rhetorical figure to describe all creativity. Creativity is linked to the whole, or some form of undifferentiated, concentrated social energies found there.

Pragmatism was becoming increasingly influential in France. The similarities between sociology and pragmatism were sufficient and confusing enough to drive Durkheim to clarify their fundamental differences. The role of action seems especially critical. Pragmatism placed action at the center of its conception of human experience. Durkheim's sociology had also given collective action, especially religious ritual, but group processes generally, a central role in the gestation of knowledge. It was therefore necessary to distinguish between this collectivistic sociology of the categories and the pragmatist image of truth and conduct, which Durkheim viewed as individualistic and subjectivistic. As he had recently stated, the individual was not the *finis naturae*, but perhaps society was. In sum, these lectures offer added evidence about Durkheim's mature standpoint and its relationship to our themes.

The Dualism of Human Nature

Durkheim's thesis of the dualism of human nature is well known. His main essay on this theme, "The Dualism of Human Nature and Its Social Conditions," was published in 1914, two years after the *Forms,* and meant to clarify one of its main theses. It is one of his most important brief statements not only of this problem, but of his overall perspective. It appears to pose difficulties for any interpretation of Durkheim's work which argues that there are strong monistic elements in his thought.

It is a remarkable fact that Durkheim's famous essay begins and ends with references to the whole/part problem. These references frame his study and give it a quality which has not always been fully appreciated. Indeed, it is odd to see Durkheim returning to this rhetorical motif, after having just given a sociological account of the category of totality in his most recent book. At the very opening of the essay, he argues his familiar case that society exists only by penetrating the individual consciousness and that many of our important mental states are of social origin. Durkheim thinks "the whole . . . in a large measure produces the part" and, as a result, "it is impossible to attempt to explain the whole without explaining the part, at least by counterposing it" (Durkheim 1964, 325; 1970, 314). Durkheim moves rapidly to introduce the notion of "civilization," that collection of moral, intellectual goods, the highest outcome of collective activity. He explains that this phenomenon can only be studied historically, suggesting at the same time that his recently published book on religion can be taken as an instance of this fact. I want to return to Durkheim's opening remarks on the whole/part issue, but first skip to the essay's conclusion where these comments are taken up again. At the close of his entire discussion, Durkheim argues that, if society were nothing but the "natural and spontaneous development of the individual," there would be no conflict between the two facets of the individual. But the dualism of human nature is, in fact, a painful condition which involves "perpetual sacrifices" on the part of the individual. Society's distinctive nature has requirements different from those resulting from the individual's nature. "The interests of the whole are not necessarily those of the part" (Durkheim 1964, 338; 1970, 331). These two sets of quotations frame the essay's central theme. They require our attention.

The first quotation is rather opaque. It should not confuse us into thinking that Durkheim is arguing that we need to understand "the part" (i.e. the individual) before we can understand "the whole" (i.e. society). Instead, Durkheim is saying (as always) that the whole produces the part. To understand the whole we need to understand that aspect of the part which is the direct result of the whole. If we have not accounted for the way in which the whole penetrates and molds the part, we have not understood the manifestation of the whole in its various instantiations. We will not be able to understand the seeming duality of the part, its division into two attributes, the one deriving from its own biological individuality and existential differentiation, the other deriving its preponderance of mental apparatus from the whole itself.

The concluding reference to the whole/part problem makes it clear that Durkheim sees the part as subordinate to the interests of the whole and even suffering from the demands of the whole. He suggests that increased sacrifices may be demanded of the individual in the future, thus adopting a position which some have claimed has parallels with Freud's theory (Meštrović 1988). I cannot now compare Durkheim and Freud on this (or any other) question. However, in all of his mature writings, Durkheim insists repeatedly on the idea that society serves as a moral authority for the individual and is the provider of all the good things valued and desired by the individual. It is not merely a question of increasing historical constraint and sacrifice. Both moral constraint and the good are merged in society. Durkheim's remarks at the essay's beginning on the social origins of "civilization" should be warning enough not to equate his "society," and the price it exacts from individuals, with Freud's "culture," whose advantages hardly "compensate" for the instinctual renunciations it demands. Moreover, it is not clear that Durkheim laments the increased sacrifices which may go with the advance of society, since he views them as necessary for any further moral "progess." For my present purposes, it is more important to note Durkheim's assertion that "the interests of the whole are not necessarily those of the part." Having framed the problem as a problem of the relationship between whole and part, how does he develop the discussion?

Durkheim offers a sociological resolution to the dualistic religious and philosophical problems inherited from the Western European tradition. This seems clear enough from the essay. This tradition has perennially identified a distinction within the person between body and soul and has seen the individual as embodying a contradiction, indeed, being a "monster of contradictions," both "angel and beast," in Pascal's phrases, both of which are quoted by Durkheim (Durkheim 1970, 321, 329; Pascal 1966). This intuition cannot be entirely illusory. We are, in fact, divided by two forces, those sensory experiences tied to the individual organism and the concepts and moral ideas which come to us from society. One part of our being makes us see everything from our own particular standpoint and is concerned only with ourself. The other being within us "knows things *sub specie aeternitatis*, as if it were participating in some thought other than ours . . ." (Durkheim 1964, 327–28; 1970, 318). We are this homo duplex.

The efforts to explain this fact have been inadequate. It is of considerable interest that Durkheim begins by rejecting "empirical monism" and "idealistic monism" (Durkheim 1970, 321). Both eliminate the problem rather than solve it. Only then does he go on to discuss, yet ultimately also reject, those explanations which "merit examination," but which do little more than reaffirm the facts to be explained without accounting for them. The most important examples of the latter standpoint are Plato's ontology and Kant's philosophy (Durkheim 1970, 324–26). Plato divides the world into "nonintelligent and amoral matter" and "Ideas, the Spirit, and the Good," both of which meet in and divide the individual. This view merely restates the problem in ontological terms and fails to explain either how the good would deign to emanate into matter or how matter could ever rise up from its dumb state into spirit. Kant's distinction between the two faculties of "reason" and "sensibility," between rational activity and sensory activity, also provides a good set of descriptive terms, but fails to show how they can both be found combined in the same individual. From this rejection of the inherited explanations, Durkheim goes on to recount the theory from the *Forms* and suggest that it offers a true resolution to the problem.

Several interesting things emerge from this text. First, there is Durkheim's reference to the Spinozist formula, *sub specie aeternitatas*, to describe that part of us which is "impersonal." I find it suggestive that Durkheim should once again use a phrase associated with one of the premier monistic, even pantheistic philosophers of the modern world at the very moment when he is about to reject monistic accounts of his problem. Durkheim is nothing if not ambiguous. Second, Durkheim rejects the available theories (at least all those he considers) and starts by disposing of two monistic philosophies, both of which eliminate the problem. Despite his disclaimer that they are worth examining, it is not clear that he thinks much more highly of Plato's and Kant's resolutions of the issue. Although they restate the problem clearly, they do little else. The fact that Durkheim spills more ink refuting the two monistic theories than the two allegedly meritorious ones should give us pause. Empirical monism is roughly identical (or so Durkheim thinks) with the pragmatist philosophy he is examining and criticizing in his contemporaneous lectures. Idealistic monism absorbs everything into a system of absolute concepts, yet is unable to explain why, despite the continued advance of our conceptual abilities, human malaise persists. Our inner contradictions (which Durkheim assumes to exist from his earlier discussion) must emerge from a different source. In the end, neither type of monism accounts for the move from the "inferior" to the "superior" in our natures, a distinction which Durkheim interjects into his critique (in rather circular fashion) as a presupposition about human duality.

In line with my earlier discussion, I would suggest that Durkheim is attempting two things simultaneously: to retain the notion of the dualism of human nature, which he has inherited from the intellectual tradition, and, at the same time, to construct a new type of theory within which to encompass this dualism. The position which emerges might be characterized as a modulated dualism set within an implicit monism. Since he rejects both empirical and idealistic monism (just as he criticizes the limits of "empiricism" and "idealism" generally), Durkheim's position is best designated as sociological monism. We need clarify this monistic resolution of dualism. To do so, let us return to his essay.

His solution to the problem of dualism is clear enough and, on first glance, seems to have little to do with monism. It is the argument already reviewed from the *Forms*. Durkheim develops his problem on both the moral and the cognitive fronts. He distinguishes between those ideas which emerge from individual sensory experience and those which develop out of the collective processes of society. The unaided individual could never develop the categories out of his own individual perceptions and experiences. They are a product of collective thought and have society as their model. The same holds true morally. The concepts of morality, especially the notions of duty and the good, but also the religious ideas intertwined with morality, transcend the individual. Only the collectivity can invest them with authority and evoke the emotional attachment to them which makes them desirable. In sum, the basic notions of both intellectual and moral life come only from society. Philosophers down the ages have had an intimation of this problem, but been unable to offer an explanation of the sources of their own dualistic philosophies. They have registered the problem and divided existence into body versus soul, reality versus appearance, reason versus sensibility. In doing so, they have merely substituted one or another name for the experience. Sociology alone can truly explain why we conceive of ourselves as double, as living in two worlds, so to speak. It does so through its analysis of how society gestates the experience and distinction of the sacred versus the profane. As usual, Durkheim asserts both the truth as well as the falsity of the inherited formulae. It is unthinkable they could have been wrong in their central experience and intuition, but they were mistaken in their explanations of it.

Does Durkheim really argue for the duality of human nature? While he appears unambiguous on this point, I would suggest that Durkheim's theory does not permit a thoroughgoing dualism. To the extent that he did hold to such an absolute dualism, his position was internally inconsistent. In truth, Durkheim greatly mutes the individual side of his individual/society dualism and lays all the emphasis on the societal. The key operating dualism in Durkheim is not between a presocial or non-social individual and society, but between a socialized individual as an individuated part of a society and society itself as a whole. Indeed, this is precisely how Georges Davy, one of Durkheim's close collaborators, characterized the Durkheimian position in an essay published after Durkheim's death (Davy 1931, 164–65; also Dumont 1980, 4–10, 231–34). In fact, there is a double dualism in Durkheim's theory: the opposition between the individual human organism and society and the opposition between the socialized person and society. But as I have already noted, the latter is not a full duality at all, since the social person is merely a limited "incarnation" of society's total forces, a "part" of them. The former seems to be a more uncompromising dualism. Yet on closer inspection, it also fails to have a fully symmetrical, dualistic character, since the unsocialized organism is entirely outside of society and opposed to it, but therefore hardly a "part" of it at all. Durkheim's dualism of human nature turns out to be either a pre- or a post-socialized opposition between highly unequal forces. In either case, his radical dualism collapes into a monistic assertion of society's unalterably unifying impulses.

At this point, it is worth recalling the comparison with Aristotle. His conception of the *polis* included citizens as parts of the whole, but excluded certain noncitizen groups (e.g. freedmen, merchants, etc.) as conditions (but not true parts). Aristotle's historical, cultural location made it difficult for him to conceive of anyone but the citizen as a part fit by nature for life in the *polis*. He did not share our equalitarian prejudices and quite logically treated noncitizens as conditions, but not parts.

Durkheim's modern view disallows the possibility of excluding any group or individual from society as unfit by nature for social life. Society is not only all inclusive, it is itself coterminous with our humanity. Here, Durkheim and Aristotle share the view that humankind is by nature made for life in society, however they differ in their senses of how universally this formula is to be applied.

For Aristotle, only humankind in the *polis* is truly and fully human, while for Durkheim, several types of society fit humankind for a human existence. Durkheim's intensely sociological theory requires an individual who is either social and human or mere animal, barely human at all. There is no pre- or non-social humanity in Durkheim, only a individuated part of society, a part which takes shape around the individual organism. Of course, the organism exists apart from society and, in some sense, before its impact is felt. Durkheim never says otherwise. But this individual is only an organism, not a individual person in any other meaningful sense. If it remains merely an organism, it also cannot be a human being, but only an animal (see Durkheim 1975, III:222). In Aristotle's language, the individual organism is a condition of society, but not a part. It is perhaps ironic that this condition for society's existence (the human body), unhuman in its animal, unsocialized form, is made so vitally important at another level in Durkheim's theory, in the various forms of social concentration which are at the center of his notion of society's creative "power."

In effect, Durkheim devalues individual bodily existence to a condition of the dualism of human nature, inferior in comparison with the higher, socially derived dimensions of civilization which are infused in the individual, yet which rely on the very physico-social combination of such bodies in collective assemblies to create and constantly renew these very same civilizational ideals. It is as if Durkheim really wanted an actual collective body. Indeed, all his metaphors of the social being, the social body, the universal sensorium, social substance, and so forth point in this direction. As metaphors, they both disguise and reveal the deeper wish.

This interpretation of Durkheim requires that we view him less as a strident dualist, but as the proponent of a theory which repeatedly encompasses dualities within a more inclusive monistic framework. Individuals are parts of the larger whole in several different senses. First, they are biological units of a social substance which itself absorbs and embraces them, draws them into varying degrees of mutual concentration, communication, and aggregation. Adapting a term from Marx's language, their "species being" is social (Marx 1977). Second, they are differentiated parts of a social whole in the sense of biological occasions for the individation of societal processes or the "incarnation" of social ideals. Third, they are parts of a whole of society for which they are by nature fitted, but without which they are not human. Fourth, they are the "transmitters" within the "social sensorium" without which it could not exist, but which, in turn, provides the collective mental and moral materials passing through them and otherwise unavailable to them. Only society can provide the true "collective sensorium" linking individuals who are, only by physical necessity, isolated monads. As we have seen, it accomplishes this especially through religion. Fifth, they provide the only sensory links, however inadequate, between society and the wider physical world. Society expends great energy improving upon the sensory inputs of these parts, by molding them to social purposes through the development of religious ideas, the categories and, ultimately, the various sciences. None of this requires that Durkheim be a fundamental dualist. Instead, it all implies that his monistic assumptions throughly control, permeate, and override the dualistic elements in his thinking.

11

SOCIOLOGICAL MONISM
AND THE ENCOUNTER BETWEEN
TRADITION AND MODERNITY

The discussion of Durkheim's final writings completes our chronological study of Durkheim and his earlier school. The main reconstructive aims of this book have been accomplished in our account of Durkheim's shifting usage of the whole/part metaphor, his developing conception of totality, his theory of religion, and the ways in which he weaves his account of the categories into his conception of society as a dynamic reality and a force of nature. Indeed, it might be thought possible, perhaps even desirable, to stop at this point and let the chronological analysis stand on its own, a display of fragments from Durkheim's evolving philosophical perspective and rhetoric. However, this would leave a misleading impression as well as a part of the task undone. It would give the false impression that Durkheim's sociological monism was somehow fragmentary. It can and needs to be stated more systematically. Although Durkheim himself was reluctant to fully compose the system, as we have seen, his formulations already move decisively toward a systematic philosophical view of the world. Moreover, we have also not fully accounted for some of the historical, civilizational sources of Durkheim's remarkable perspective. Although we have discussed several important intellectual antecedents of his conception of totality, we need to examine the civilizational confluences which led to his sociological monism. This task requires that we examine Durkheim's effort to square his attachment to Western European science and philosophy with elements in his formative Jewish experience and Western European religious traditions more generally.

In this final chapter, I would like to take up these two tasks. The first section will present a more systematic reconstruction of his sociological monism as a philosophical system. The second section will offer some reflections on the role played in his thought by the civilizational encounter between his formative Judaism and the modernizing, Western currents of thought on which he also drew so heavily. Let us turn to the first task.

Durkheim's Sociological Monism: A Systematic Reconstruction

I have referred intermittently to "sociological monism" as a general characterization of Durkheim's emerging position. What is meant generally by monism? What meaning can be attached to the phrase "sociological monism?" What is the overall system of sociological monism inherent in Durkheim's work and what are some of the philosophical and religious implications of this perspective? At this point, a definition of monism needs to be introduced and Durkheim's perspective related to it. The various components of the following summary statement have already been examined, as they have emerged and been modified throughout Durkheim's writings. The following discussion will provide a more integrated account of Durkheim's view. It should be clear that this more systematic theory or philosophy does not appear in precisely this form in Durkheim's own writings. I have argued that it is implicit in his work, almost from the beginning, and certainly is increasingly elaborated and opened to view as his ideas develop. It reaches the closest thing to systematic form in his last book. However, I would maintain that it is a monistic system in substance and perhaps in intent (although the latter question is difficult to determine, and, in any case, is of little relevance to my conception of the problem, which relies less on an interpretation of Durkheim's "intentions" than on his actual accomplishments).

The term monism is generally used to describe a philosophy which argues that there is actually only one thing, or one type of thing in the world. It is usually opposed to dualism and pluralism, which argue respectively that there is a fundamental gulf in the world between two realms of being, or that the world is actually made up of a variety of things, or kinds of things. Monism is often associated with the concept of totality and takes the form in metaphysics of a belief in a the fundamental unity of reality (Hall 1967). While monism can be merged with dualism, as in Spinoza's philosophy, such mergers involved the predominance of the unifying over the polarizing features.

I cannot now examine the history of monistic philosophies, or relate Durkheim to this tradition. A full discussion of modern monistic philosophies would require an examination of the impact of Spinoza's work (Yovel 1992, vol. II) as well as the writings of other major figures such as Hegel. It would also necessitate a study of monisitic systems of religious thought (Worsley 1907). For now, I would like to relate Durkheim's theory to this provisional "definition" of monism. One of my central arguments has been that Durkheim does believe in the fundamental unity of reality, in a particular sense of that phrase. His work is a form of sociological monism. Durkheim was critical of "anthropocentric" thought, yet his system is highly "sociocentric." In particular, it assigns to society the role of synthesizing all knowledge of nature and bringing nature itself "within" the confines of society. From one standpoint, it is a new "metaphysics of knowledge" and, as such, reflects a critical response to the earlier effort of Renouvier to accomplish this task with his "neo-criticism." It places the collective knowledge gestated by human societies at the center of reality as a whole. It gives humanity in its socialized form, therefore society, a privileged place in the larger scheme of nature. Its religious and philosophical implications are considerable.

Durkheim is keenly interested in the whole, or the notion of totality. This is the prime unifying category, the one enveloping all other categories. He equates this notion with both divinity and society. Divinity, or, more generally, religion is, in turn, seen as a product of society, both in a "weak" as well as, more importantly, a "strong" sense. Religion is not only a social institution, related to other social institutions. It is also an expression of society's essential nature, and, in fact, symbolically captures that nature better than any other form of representation. Society, in turn, is the *fons et origo* of both religion and the category of totality. Society's dynamic forces gestate religion. It is also a variously differentiated entity to whose central processes and structure correspond, as we have shown above, the various categories of the human spirit, including those of substance, genre, time, space, causality, number, and the person. This "correspondence" has a double character.

First, the categories, including that of totality, originate in the enthusiasms connected with religious processes, particularly religious assemblies. They are therefore expressions or emanations of divinity. However, divinity, religion itself, is merely a disguised form of society (even when it "transfigures" society). In reality, society finds it deepest nature expressed in "social dynamics," real forces, powers and energy, which are generated in the social processes of collective associations, concentrations and assemblies. These are the living reality of society, its "substance," as it were.

The categories also correspond to society in a second sense. They receive the impress of society's organization. They express in abstract form the structure of society and its social differentiations. At the same time, the categories provide a logical classification of the wider realities of nature, indeed, all reality. They bring all the objects composing this reality, the entire cosmos, "within" society, into society's interior, so to speak, through the overall processes of classification. The categories serve to unify all reality into one entity. This entity is society. This is particularly true of the notion of totality, which comprehends all the others. The categories emanate from society, yet comprehend nature. Such knowledge is possible because society itself is a facet of nature and nature is potentially self-consistent in its various facets. Human society— especially, but not only, the collective process of human beings co-present in action—is, in the end, the one central reality to which all others may be reduced, or within which all others are unified. Therefore, Durkheim is a sociological monist, since he argues that society, ". . . the most powerful combination of physical and moral forces which we can observe in nature" (Durkheim 1995b, 447), is the single force capable of unifying the world, and the one in which all things have been, are being, or will in the future be synthesized.

It is useful to repeat Durkheim's suggestion that totality, society and deity are three different faces of one idea (Durkheim 1995b, 443, fn.18). What notion corresponds to the three ideas of society, divinity and totality? This is an incompletely resolved issue in Durkheim's theory. The answer seems to be the notion of substance, perhaps more specifically, social substance. Society and divinity are explicitly identified by Durkheim at various points in his career. Totality and society are also identified, where society figures as the whole composed of, but not entirely identical with, various sets of parts. Totality and divinity come to be identified by implication in the *Forms* and explicitly in the crucial footnote. If social forces are the core of the idea of substance, then substance must also be identified with totality and divinity. The circle of these three terms closes around the notion of substance and, in Durkheim's theory, this substance can be nothing but social life itself in its true reality as power, force, energy, and concentration of human social life. These powers of social substance are, in turn, radiated out systolically into religion, the categories, and nature itself, all of which, in a second phase, are disastolically absorbed back into society. In Durkheim's social metaphysics, as Gaston Richard suspected, society is both the subject and object of knowledge, the beginning and the end.

This identification has interesting consequences. Society becomes the object which itself must ultimately be known in order to understand reality and only sociology can provide this knowledge. Society in its primitive beginnings creates religion and the fundamental frames of knowledge, but only through a future historical transformation of society will the fullest realization of knowlege of the whole of reality become possible. The analysis of the whole and its parts, assumed in a variety of ways in Durkheim's earlier work, has now been integrated into and explained by a complex philosophy which can be characterized best as a sociological monism. Spinoza's *Deus sive Natura* has been supplanted by Durkheim's *Deus sive Societas* and, ultimately, *Deus sive Natura sive Societas*, where the categories now substitute in Durkheim's system as a summary of nature. This position might as easily be called a variant of "sociological Spinozism." Indeed, Durkheim can plausibly be grouped with those others who have variously fallen within Spinoza's orbit and who Yirmiyahu Yovel has described as proponents of the philosophy of "immanence" (Yovel 1992, vol. II).

This statement of Durkheim's position is rather condensed, perhaps even cryptic, but no more so than the statement of any other metaphysical philosophy. However, it is precisely what Durkheim appears to maintain, although the key aspects of his argument are not as systematically articulated in his own texts as they would need to be to fully constitute the position he, in fact, seems to hold. In line with Durkheim's own preferred metaphors, it might be possible to diagram the general structure of Durkheim's mature philosophy. It takes the form of a circle, one of Durkheim's favorite ways of imagining the whole/part relation. The circle's innermost sphere represents the dynamic vital center of concentrated social energies or powers, the social substance. Within this circle are found the individuals, organized into mutually related groups, who form the active modes of the social substance, society, without which it could not sense, act, feel, or enter into contact with the wider reality. It is through their bodies that society acts and is instantiated in the world. But they are only the sensory elements of the social substance and can be nothing alone. Even their ability to act as "receptors" in a sensory system depends on their fusion into a "universal sensorium" by religion and the "incarnation" within them of the universalizing categories. Without both of these processes, the individual would be nothing but animal matter.

Beyond the perimeter of this circle lies the infinite expanse of nature, the rest of the physical world, separate from society, yet also dependent for its existence on society. Existence is only possible for an entity insofar as it is known. While society is itself a part of nature, it is the most powerful part. The remainder of the world is known through its collectively elaborated categories, which bring nature within the circle of society. These categories are the various modes of representation of the social substance. The adequacy of these categories for the understanding of nature comes precisely from their collective, social quality. It is because they are products of society, itself part of nature, that they can comprehend the rest of nature in turn. Despite his frequent qualifications of this assertion, Durkheim evidently sees nature only through the collective lens of society. He not only says that nature can only be known and have a meaning through the medium of human society, he says it does not exist except through collective human mediation. Durkheim gives the strong impression that the physical world exists, is "created" only for social humanity.

One might imagine, as did Richard in one of his later writings, a sort of "sociological Berkeleyism" (Richard 1943, 156–57), until we recall that the categories are not merely Kantian forms of perception, understanding, or representation, but forms of being crystallized out of society, predicates of society as a social substance, to use a more Aristotelian language. We need to recall Durkheim's repeated refrain that society is a "reality" in its own right. The categories "touch" the society of existing and acting groups at every point and, in fact, are molded on their model. In some sense, the groups are these categories, they physically embody them. As such, a category is a sort of "concrete universal" (in a very Durkheimian sense). As linguistic entities, they are parts of the system of collective representations whose existence parallels that of society, just as their existence within individuals parallels their personal bodily capacity to instantiate these categories and other collective representations. The categories do not have any of the "relative autonomy" of those intellectual "products of the second degree," to which Durkheim occasionally refers. Categories structure our thought and express reality *sub specie aeternitatis*, as Durkheim repeatedly tells us. They are the product of society, and are linked to its fundamental structure and dynamics. Other intellectual conceptions, "products of the second degree," may develop in any number of different directions depending upon how they are combined with one another and are not so closely tied to society. As society develops, so must the categories. Conversely, only when society itself has expanded and developed in new and more universal forms will a set of categories emerge which are truly adequate to the whole of nature in all of its aspects. The limits of society are the limits of our categories and, thus, also the limits of our knowledge of nature. Indeed, the categories demarcate the limits of nature's existence, at least, as far as humanity is concerned, and it is "socialized humanity" which is ultimately decisive from Durkheim's standpoint. The more globally comprehensive the society, the fuller our understanding of nature. Only a future society which has expanded itself socially to the whole of humanity (and perfected itself morally) can hope to develop those categories which will provide a fundamental understanding of nature, ones which will bring the entirely of the knowable world within society, until the two are truly merged into one.

The use of the circle as the image which best captures Durkheim's position is in keeping with his own work. As we have seen, it is found frequently enough in his writings and is strongly implied every time he uses the whole/part image. The two are connected in his thinking. Sociologists might be reminded of Simmel's work, especially his notion of the "intersection of social circles," perhaps even his overall geometrical metaphor in his study of forms of sociation (Simmel 1971, 23–40). I would hesitate to identify the approachs of Simmel and Durkheim, at least, on this score. Durkheim's method and Simmel's use of the image of intersecting circles and geometrical forms are quite different, as Durkheim himself argued in some detail. The resemblance between the two authors, if there is any, is not to be found in this area. However, it may be located elsewhere. It is precisely in the monistic, even pantheistic thrust of their work that we can see the similarity between them (although it is far from complete). Simmel's *The Philosophy of Money* is strongly monistic or pantheistic. His book is a philosophy of money, not primarily an analytical economics or sociology. I would emphasize the "methodological" quality of Simmel's monism. He states that its method reflects only one "value sensibility," the "pantheistic" (in my terminology, "monistic"). It is indebted to Spinoza, a fact hinted at by Simmel and already noted by Alfred Vierkandt upon its publication (Simmel 1990, xviii, 118, 526). Everything in culture and society is related to the problem of money, like parts to a whole, ones comprehensible only in relationship to the whole. Each facet inheres in the overall crystal, and, as the latter is turned and examined in different ways, new light is refracted from each part and we are given a fuller illumination of the whole. However, this examination of reality through its immanence in the phenomenon of money is a more limited and focused conception of totality than the one developed in Durkheim's philosophy. It is closer to Mauss's later orchestration of the problem of totality around the topic of gift exchange (Mauss 1990). Both are "methodological," rather than "substantive" assertions of totality, although through rather different "media." I would place Simmel's standpoint somewhere between those of Durkheim and Mauss, since he shares some qualities with each, but is identical with neither.

On the other hand, Durkheim's philosophy finds the entire reality of God and Nature immanent in society and only in society. In the end, Durkheim is much more daring, as his own followers noted (see Davy's remarks on immanence in Durkheim 1957). Durkheim discards any transcendent conception of God, especially any notion of the "supernatural," in favor of a naturalistic conception of God's immanence in society. In this respect, he also follows Spinoza's philosophy of immanence (Yovel 1992, vol. II, who does not mention Durkheim; Nielsen 1987a). He also discards any notion that society (that is, collective human existence) and nature themselves are in any way alien realms or separated by some hierarchical barrier in a chain of creation. Society is the most powerful force of nature and everything else ultimately finds its realization within its bounds.

My reference above to the future synthesizing of knowledge and society, as a facet of Durkheim's theory, is conjectural, but not entirely fanciful. It is well established that there are strong "practical" dimensions to Durkheim's theories, although commentators differ about the precise nature and sources of his concern for social, moral, political, economic, and educational reform (Lukes 1973; Clark 1973; Jones 1986; Filloux 1977). However, seen as an emerging system of sociological monism, Durkheim's work implies broader goals. He aimed not only at immediate social reforms (e.g. education, professional groupings, etc.), but also at a philosophical vision of reality and an image of an unfolding future, one informed by a new sociological understanding of history, society, religion, and Nature. Durkheim never fully articulated this vision, and perhaps, in reaction to Auguste Comte's work, even had a horror of the philosophy of history, as Georges Davy once suggested (in Durkheim

1957). However, his wider view would surely have supplanted or, at least, greatly supplemented his ideas on societal transformation in *Division*, including those about occupational associations.

There are strong residues of Saint-Simon's pantheism and "internationalism" in Durkheim's position. For example, we have seen them not only in his portrayal of the Saint-Simonians in his lectures on socialism (Durkheim 1962), but also in the concluding pages of the *Forms*, where he envisions a richer religious life as well as philosophy emeging out of more international and universal social processes. These processes are capable of indefinite advance and ultimately aim at a condition in which ". . . logical organization . . . differentiates itself from social organization and becomes autonomous" (Durkheim 1995b, 446). The outcome of this process of social, religious and intellectual expansion can, in accordance with Durkheim's entire sociological conception, ultimately result in nothing less than a truer and fuller comprehension of reality. In the future, knowledge will be truer, for things will be "organized according to the principles which are their own," and fuller because as logical thought is differentiated from its former "social frames," its capacity increases to encompass new, hitherto unknown facets of reality. Science will truly become what it essentially is: a more perfect religious thought (Durkheim 1995b, 431). As such, it will see reality more clearly, and call things by their true names, a hope also expressed in the Jewish mystical theology which had influenced the Saint-Simonians (Bouglé and Halevy 1924) and which Mauss had also examined in the 1890s as part of his work on Spinoza (compare Benjamin 1978).

The fact that this fuller transformation will take place only when logical organization "becomes autonomous" seems to raise problems for my interpretation. Much depends on how we interpret the notion of the "autonomous." In my view, such autonomy still implies a certain dependence. If Durkheim were suggesting that logical organization (which I take to mean the fundamental categories) can ever become entirely free from any dependence on social organization, or ever cease, in some sense, to derive its energies from and be modeled on it, then he would be involved in a contradiction violating the central principles of his social philosophy. I think he means instead that only a certain sort of social organization can achieve this more autonomous logical organization. Autonomous thought itself does not become entirely divorced from society, but is dependent upon and mirrors a particular form of society in a peculiar fashion, in rather the same way that the cult of the

individual is a social creation and not identifiable with "individualism" in any other sense.

The logical categories can never cease to be collective products. However, it is perfectly coherent to argue that they can
become universal, "become autonomous," only under particular historical, social conditions. Universalizing categories must be deter-
minately related to some social order, otherwise they are merely
individual speculations, dialectical manipulations, a socially disconnected product of the sort of anarchic, intellectual "anomie"
which he so vigorously opposed in his early work. However, the
corollary to this is the impossibility of their autonomy without a
given set of social conditions. Remove these social conditions and
their autonomy also collapes.

It is worth adding that Durkheim makes no mention at the
close of the *Forms* of a socially differentiated cadre of workers in a
division of labor, that is, no mention of occupational specialization
which marked his earlier proposals for social reform. The focus is
entirely on religion, logic and society, but not the specific future
societal order which would be necessary for a more autonomous,
comprehensive and truer level of thought to emerge. Can we
assume that he viewed the solution to this problem in terms similar to those developed in *Division* and several of his other earlier
writings? Would a cadre of intellectual specialists operating within
professional groupings in a complex division of labor provide the
needed conditions? I think this would be part of the solution, as
Durkheim himself implies by his continued references to his first
book in his last one. However, it not the whole solution. We must
recall Durkheim's emphasis in his essay of 1909 on sociology itself
as an "encyclopedic" or synthetic science, one which will provide a
microcosm which reflects the macrocosm. Here, we find the true
solution to the problem. While the professional groupings of various
specialists can contribute their diverse categories of knowledge to
the whole, only sociologists can forge this whole and comprehend all
knowledge within a more synthetic system of thought, precisely
because they grasp the terms of social embeddedness of all thought
and conduct. They are ones who can speak for the whole. In a sense,
they are like Karl Mannheim's socially unattached thinkers
(Mannheim 1936) in their capacity to take all sides and adopt all
standpoints, although their role departs radically from that cast for
Mannheim's more politically oriented thinkers. Durkheim's sociologist is not merely a neutral party, capable of adopting all social and
political perspectives, or even mediating among them. He actually

synthesizes the whole, both of society in its self-understanding as well as of nature, insofar as the physical world is brought inside society through a comprehensive, universal system of categories. Such sociologists would be more Comtean in their daring and the scope of their synthesizing activities. Durkheim's emerging theoretical position might be placed closer to the work of Pierre Teillard de Chardin, whose philosophy also has "pantheistic" overtones (Teilhard de Chardin 1961, 309–10; Hughes 1969, 256–57). Teilhard's notion of humanity's role in an expanding "noosphere" of universal consciousness, but once again sociologically conceived, represents a position more congruent with Durkheim's emerging perspective than any version of his work which stresses only more narrow pedagogical, political, or even social reforms. However, given Durkheim's emphasis on the importance of social concentrations, it is unlikely that he would have looked very favorably on a purely "communicative" or electronic "virtual" global community, freed from the need for actual human assemblies.

Sociological Monism in Civilizational Perspective: Toward the Historical Location of Durkheim's Thought

My aims until now have been strictly analytic and synthetic, oriented especially to the analysis of Durkheim's texts, but also to the systematic reconstruction of his emerging position. However, the development of what I am calling Durkheim's sociological monism also depends ultimately on a complex set of historical realities. Many historical currents of thought went into the making of his theory. Some of them have been studied by other writers and I do not intend to review them here. The focus and method of this work suggest an examination of only those historical settings which are particularly relevant to the understanding of his sociological monism. In this final section, I would like to make some brief suggestions about his work from the standpoint of a sociology of knowledge working in civilizational perspective. From this perspective, Durkheim's thought is discovered to emerge from an encounter between traditional currents of religious thought, Jewish and Christian, and various "modernizing" philosophical and scientific ideas. It is within the context of this encounter that Durkheim's sociological monism needs to be placed.

The civilizational perspective requires that we examine the central rationales which go into the making of any cultural creation and the ways in which it is related to the longer term historical development and encounters of civilizations (Nelson 1981; also Eisenstadt 1992). We have done this in our preceeding examination of Durkheim's work. There we have unearthed his central, if shifting theoretical images and ideas and located them in relation to the work of selected precedessors. I have especially differentiated between the relatively short versus the longer term historical situation. Durkheim responds as much to the "deep structures" (Gouldner 1973, chap. 11) located in the cultural and intellectual context of the *longue durée* (Braudel 1980) as to the immediate historical events and environment of his lifetime. His thought is not focused only on contemporary France, but has wider Western European civilizational dimensions (Durkheim and Mauss 1971). To understand him, we have made reference to a wide range of historical figures from across the centuries, especially Aristotle, Bacon, Spinoza, Pascal, Kant, and Renouvier, in addition to those more recent writers who Durkheim himself discusses at length. Durkheim wanted to offer solutions to key problems posed by the inherited philosophical tradition, in particular, the nature of the central categories of thought, especially that of totality. I have argued that this represented a central aspect of the entire Durkheimian program of theory and research.

He also wanted to preserve, yet "naturalize" the reality of religion in his theory. In my view, his desire to preserve, yet transcend the form of truth found in religious representations emerges both from his wider encounter with the religious traditions of Western Christianity as well as his own originating experience of Judaism. Indeed, this latter experience, which seemed to have been entirely superceded early in his career by his devotion to Western European secular philosophy and science, was by no means eliminated. It provides another context (along with "primitive" religion) for the encounter of traditional religion and modern thought in Durkheim's thought. Durkheim wanted to retain both the realities of religion and philosophy in the form of modern social science. As I have demonstrated above, Durkheim repeatedly refers to this primary motive of his theorizing.

The specific conflict within Durkheim's thought between dualistic and monistic outlooks also emerges from this context of encounter. In this case, the encounter is more complex. On the one hand are found the strongly dualistic traditions of Western European civilization. Western philosophy, from Plato forward, but especially after Descartes and Kant, were strongly dualistic and a critical reconceptualization of this dualism was one of his main aims. He offers an implicit critique of Descartes' dualistic conception of extended and unextended substance, in favor of a more Spinozistic resolution of both into a single reality. Christianity had also introduced a strongly dualistic cast of thought in its distinction between the two natures of Christ, the human and divine. This religious duality was carried into its understanding of human nature. Pascal's thought reflects these ideas and, as we have already noted, Durkheim's conception of these problems is never far from Pascal's image of man as simultaneously "angel and beast." Durkheim also takes up and offers a sociological alternative to the Pascalian, and in general the Christian, answer to the question of why human nature is so constituted—their doctrine of the Fall of humankind. He explicitly envisions his sociological account as an alternative to this doctrine (Durkheim 1995b, 447). As I have noted elsewhere, he also wanted to offer a sociological account of religious dependence, in opposition to Protestant, individualisitic accounts of this experience (Nielsen 1987a). Finally, we must also mention a variety of real influences from modern culture in Durkheim's thinking, ones which emphasized reason and individualism, values to which Durkheim was clearly committed (Durkheim 1973). These also contributed to the dualistic orientations which his thought attempted to comprehend. His own theories expressed a variety of dualistic rationales of thought, some of them derived from these very historical traditions: between the sacred and the profane, the individual and society, types of social solidarity, and so forth.

On the other hand, equally central is Durkheim's evident commitment to unification, the whole, and totality. Philosophical monism lies at a deeper layer in his thought, less clearly on the surface, than dualism. Yet, as we have shown, it is a central part of his theorizing. It repeatedly escapes from and overarches the dualistic environments in which it is seemingly trapped. Even though Durkheim did not fully elaborate his monistic theory, many of the central tendencies of his final theory are inexplicable without reference to a monistic inspiration. As we have seen, Durkheim is seldom satisfied to retain a stark dualistic opposition without folding it into a more comprehensive framework or loading the dualistic values in asymmetrical fashion to overwhelmingly emphasize one side of the scale, thus tempering or erasing any meaningful dualism. What is the historical source of the monistic current in Durkheim?

I would suggest that we need to connect Durkheim's "revelation" of the mid-1890s, concerning the importance of religion in society, to elements of his originating Jewish experience. However, Durkheim's residual commitment to Jewish culture and religion is not to be unearthed by searching the Torah or Talmud for ideas which might, by ad hoc arguments, be made to parallel Durkheim's own mature formulations (e.g. Schoenfeld and Meštrović 1989, 121–25; in general Pickering 1984; Pickering and Martins 1994). As Ivan Strenski (1997) has noted, there is nothing "essentially" Jewish, in this sense, about Durkheim's philosophy. However, even the detailed study of the organization and values of his Alsacian community of birth or the immediate historical setting of French Judaism will not be of much help to us (Raphael and Weyl 1977; Marrus 1971; Strenski 1997). Durkheim's relationship to Judaism, at the most fundamental philosophical level, is not to be discovered in any of these quarters.

Durkheim was a modern Jew, interested ultimately in grafting Western European philosophical and scientific ideas and images onto a transfigured set of inherited religious commitments. He did so, not through the direct study of Judaism, even Ancient Judaism, but through the general medium of primitive and archaic cultures. The turning point of 1895 toward religion was crucial for him. It also saw him direct Mauss toward the study of religion, while Mauss was simultaneously examining the work of Spinoza. We must ask: what happened to the early balance Durkheim had achieved before 1895, between his residual commitment to his community of birth and the scientific ethos to which we had become deeply devoted, when the theoretical centrality of religion dawned upon him in the mid-1890s? This balance had found its fullest expression in *Division*, his first, yet ultimately unsatisfactory, attempt to understand totality scientifically through the study of morality and a reliance on the whole/part metaphor. The "revelation" of religion's importance for his intellectual problems was the very solution he needed to truly begin integrating his inherited religious culture, his Western European scientific and philosophical education, and his pressing practical concerns for the renewal of moral community. His sociological monism was precisely the sort of orientation he needed to develop in order to fully achieve this new integration. While Durkheim occasionally reminds us that he was the son of a Rabbi, it is clear that his social philosophy could not (and did not) retain a thoroughgoing connection to the traditional beliefs and practices of the Talmudic Jewish community in which he had been nurtured. However, he could like other Jewish thinkers from the recent, as well as the more distant past, retain many of Judaism's central religious elements in a more abstract, universalized form: its monotheism and emphasis on unified understanding of reality, its sense of nature as a potentially sacralized, humanly relevant creation, its highly integrated moral community, and its analytic bent and ability to absorb large infusions of Western European philosophy and adapt them to its own religious purposes.

Sociological monism, with a strong pantheistic undercurrent emerging from the emphasis on religion, was the best philosophical move for Durkheim. It allowed him to overcome the conflict emerging from the different cultural elements in his own experience and also to create a systematic theory which would integrate nature, divinity and society.

In this respect, his spiritual situation, if not its precise expression, was like that of earlier Jewish thinkers such as Philo of Alexandria, Maimonides, Spinoza, and others whose thought emerges within the shifting encounters between traditional religiosity and more modernizing currents of philosophy and science distinctive to the eras in which they wrote. Each faced a different set of modernizing cultural influences. Each related in a different way to the Jewish cultural community of his birth. Each found a way to merge ideas from both contexts and combine them into distinctive intellectual syntheses, new creations sui generis, which could be reduced to none of their component formative influences.

Philo defends ancient Judaism and the Torah against its critics (including Jewish apostates to Hellenistic culture) by encorporating Greek philosophy, especially the work of Plato and Greek mathematical images, into his emerging world view, including his allegorical exegeses of the Torah, its laws and narratives (Nielsen 1996a). In the process he helps to create "religious philosophy" as a new intellectual genre (Wolfson 1962).

Maimonides' work emerges more firmly within the Talmudic framework long established by his time. His commentaries on this corpus reflect a central part of his commitment to traditional cultural orientations. However, he also absorbed philosophical influences from the medieval Aristotle as well as Arabic philosophy and combined them with his devotion to Jewish scriptures. The resulting philosophical writings break new ground to be exploited by later medieval thinkers as well as Spinoza and others (Maimonides 1963; Roth 1924).

Spinoza operates within the modernizing currents of the early modern philosophical and scientific revolution and also the emerging sectarianism and religious liberalism of the post-Reformation in the Netherlands. Descartes and the geometrical method provide one central modern reference point in his work, although he is also critical of Descartes. He poses challenges to Judaism and Christianity through his new interpretations of Scripture. Despite his excommunication from his Jewish community of birth, he forges a monistic philosophy of a single substance which retains traditional religious dimensions of Jewish monotheism within new metaphysical frames (Woolhouse 1993).

Durkheim needs to be located within a similar context of conflict and encounter between traditional religiosity and modernizing culture. His break with his formative religious community comes early, but the rupture is not radical. He also becomes strongly attached to the secular science and culture of Republican France, where career opportunities are open to him. In addition to wide training in the deeper structures of philosophical and religious thought, he is particularly taken by Aristotle's discussions of the problem of the whole. Indeed, as with Philo's attachment to the ideas of Plato, the Pythagoreans, and other Hellenistic thinkers, Durkheim adopts Aristotle's ideas as tools with a thoroughly modern relevance. However, his first effort to forge a theory of totality founded on morality and law in *Division* is ultimately replaced, but not entirely rejected, under the influence of his renewed appreciation of religion and his new methodological discoveries of the mid-1890s. The result is a new emphasis on primitive religious origins and the creation of a more synthetic philosophy of religion, the categories and society's integral relationship to nature. His emerging sociological monism reintegrates many of the features of Judaism, including its image of religious community and nature, with a social metaphysics of totality which emphasizes the centrality of society as a force and a social substance.

Despite Durkheim's attachment to Aristotle, Renouvier, and others, the most helpful systematic comparison is with the work of Spinoza. As I have shown, there are similarities between the two authors' systems. Their overall intellectual strategies are also similar, especially their central commitments to the wholistic understanding of God, humanity, and Nature. Monism, even pantheism, in one or another form, is the logical outcome in each case, because it is the best resolution to the common theoretical, practical, and historical dilemmas facing them. Spinoza's critique and transcendence of Descartes' dualism is matched by Durkheim's critique of Kantian dualism (as well as others before it). Spinoza's conception of a single substance with infinite attributes is parallelled by Durkheim's sense of society's substantial character and its ability to unite all things inside itself. Spinoza's deterministic view of the individual and his parallelism of body and soul is matched by Durkheim's overwhelmingly sociologistic sense of society's moral superiority over the individual and his parallelism between collective representations and their incarnation in individuals. At a more practical level, both share a common commitment to the political liberalism of their respective eras (Feuer 1958). In these and other respects, Durkheim and Spinoza forge monistically oriented philosophies within contexts of civilizational encounter, philosophies which retain their dual commitments to both tradition and modernity.

Why Durkheim should have created a sociological solution to his problem, as opposed to a more purely philosophical one, is a question which cannot be easily answered, except perhaps by reference to the varying importance of the different elements in the mix of his experience. He chose to integrate his thinking about nature, divinity, and society around a sociological core. In the process, he created a daring and suggestive theory, one whose scope and implications have not yet been fully appreciated. In this respect, he took a different path from the vitalism of his contemporary Henri Bergson, with whom he otherwise shared many cultural roots (Greenberg 1976). Ultimately, we need to explain Durkheim's sociological orientation itself. Why did a social philosophy alone satisfy Durkheim's evidently wide-ranging theoretical sensibility?

It is helpful to recall the role played by the concept of Nature in Durkheim's thought and relate it to his ideas of God and society. Durkheim's monism emerges out of an attempt to see society and divinity as part of Nature, an immanent manifestation of its powers, but also to see the ways in which a series of "transfigurations" take place among society, religion, and Nature (seen now through the summarizing lens of the categories, especially the notion of totality). Durkheim's philosophy emerges at the meeting point of these three concepts and from his sense that the three are somehow unified as aspects of another notion (Durkheim 1995b, 443, fn.18).

I think it important to note the implications of this identification. In the end, society itself is not the highest unifying concept (even if he frequently suggests that society is the ultimate source of the experiences expressed in the other two notions). What more inclusive notion could express the unity of totality, divinity, and society? Durkheim does not tell us in any direct way. Whatever answer may be suggested, his final system does maintain, in effect, that God has three faces: one reflected in society, another in religion, and the third in Nature, via its comprehension through the categories. For Durkheim, God is preeminently immanent in society, is brought to an exterior life and expression through religious beliefs and especially religious practices, and generates a divine aura overarching nature itself through the categories of true human knowledge. Yet, these three faces are, in some sense, different visions of a single reality.

I have suggested above that the notion of substance, even that of social substance, lurks about Durkheim's writings as a undeveloped premise. It may provide part of the resolution to the enigma of his identification of society, divinity, and totality. However, at a metaphorical level, it is the notion of the whole itself which is the primary image enveloping all the other three distinctions. Durkheim persistently identified this whole with society or social substance. His social philosophy, perhaps more than any other, is strongly committed to this image of unity. This is puzzling only if we fail to see how deeply rooted this image and metaphor was in his thinking, and how many other commitments it implied. The notion of the whole seems to be the tie that binds his sociological monism to the past, both philosophically and religiously. The philosophical notion of totality, mediated through Renouvier, takes Durkheim back to Aristotle's discussions of this problem and, at the same time, to Spinoza's philosophy of a single substance. The religious notion of totality, with its impulse to transcend all dualisms, takes Durkheim back to his own religious origins, where he must often have heard the words spoken: "Hear, Oh Israel, the Lord our God; the Lord is one" (Deut. 6:4). It is from this confluence of civilizational currents that his social philosophy ultimately flows.

BIBLIOGRAPHY

Alexander, Jeffrey C. 1982. *Theoretical Logic in Sociology Vol.2, The Antinomies of Classical Thought: Marx and Durkheim*. Berkeley: University of California Press.

Alpert, Harry. 1939. *Émile Durkheim and His Sociology*. New York: Columbia University Press.

Aristotle. 1941. *The Basic Works of Aristotle*. Edited by Richard McKeon. New York: Random House.

———. 1955. *The Politics of Aristotle*. Translated with Intro. and Notes by Ernest Barker. New York: Oxford University Press.

———. 1995. *Aristotle: Selections*. Translated with an Intro., Notes, and Glossary by T. Irwin and G. Fine. Indianapolis, Ind.: Hackett.

Bacon, Francis. 1955. *Selected Writings of Francis Bacon*. Edited with Intro., and Notes by Hugh Dick. New York: Modern Library.

Barker, Ernest. 1959. *The Political Thought of Plato and Aristotle*. New York: Dover Press.

Bellah, Robert N. 1970. "Christianity and Symbolic Realism," *Journal for the Scientific Study of Religion* 9, no. 2: 89–99.

Benjamin, Walter. 1978. *Reflections*. Translated by E. Jephcott, Intro. by P. Demetz. New York: Schocken Books.

Bennett, Jonathan. 1984. *A Study of Spinoza's Ethics*. Indianapolis, Ind.: Hackett.

Benrubi, J. 1933. *Les Sources et les Courants de La Philosophie Contemporaine en France*. 2 vols. Paris: Félix Alcan.

Berger, Peter. 1967. *The Sacred Canopy*. Garden City, N.Y.: Doubleday.

Bergson, Henri. 1911 (1907). *Creative Evolution*. Authorized Translation by Arthur Mitchell. New York: Henry Holt.

————. 1960 (1889). *Time and Free Will: An Essay on the Immediate Data of Consciousness.* Authorized Translation by F. L. Pogson. New York: Harper Torchbooks.

————. 1988 (1896). *Matter and Memory.* Authorized Translation by Nancy M. Paul and W. Scott Palmer. New York: Zone Books.

Berthelot, Jean-Michel. 1995. *1895 Durkheim: L'Événement de la Sociologie Scientifique.* Toulouse: Presses Universitaires du Mirail.

Besnard, Philippe, ed. 1983. *The Sociological Domain.* New York: Cambridge University Press.

Bloor, David. 1982. "Durkheim and Mauss Revisited: Classification and the Sociology of Knowledge." In *Society and Knowledge*, edited by N. Stehr and V. Meja, 51–75. New Brunswick, N.J.: Transaction Books.

Bouglé, Célestin. 1899. *Les Idées Égalitaires: Étude Sociologique.* Paris: Félix Alcan.

————. 1935. *Bilan de la Sociologie Française Contemporaine.* Paris: Félix Alcan.

————. 1969 (1908). *Essais sur le régime des castes* Préface de Louis Dumont. Paris: Presses Universitaires de France.

Bouglé, Célestin and Élie Halévy. 1924. *Doctrine de Saint-Simon* Exposition Premier Année, 1829. Publiée avec introduction et notes par C. Bouglé et E. Halévy. Paris: Marcel Rivière.

Boutroux, Émile. 1949. *De L'Idée de Loi Naturelle dans La Science et la Philosophie.* Cours de M. Émile Boutroux, Professée à la Sorbonne en 1892–93. Paris: Librairie Philosophique J. Vrin.

Braudel, Fernand. 1980. *On History.* Translated by Sarah Matthews. Chicago: University of Chicago Press.

Brunschvicg, Léon. 1927. *Le Progrès de la Conscience dans la Philosophie Occidentale.* 2 vols. Paris: Félix Alcan.

Cahnman, Werner J., ed. 1973. *Ferdinand Tönnies, A New Evaluation: Essays and Documents.* Leiden: E. J. Brill.

Carrithers, Michael, Steven Lukes, and Steven Collins, eds. 1985. *The Category of the Person: Anthropology, Philosophy, History.* New York: Cambridge University Press.

Challenger, Douglas. 1994. *Durkheim Through the Lens of Aristotle. Durkheimian, Postmodernist and Communitarian Responses to the Enlightenment.* Lanham, Md.: Rowman and Littlefield.

Cladis, Mark. 1992. *A Communitarian Defense of Liberalism; Émile Durkheim and Contemporary Social Theory*. Stanford, Calif.: Stanford University Press.

Clark, Terry. 1973. *Prophets and Patrons: The French University and the Emergence of the Social Sciences*. Cambridge, Mass.: Harvard University Press.

Collins, Randall. 1988. *Theoretical Sociology*. San Diego, Calif.: Harcourt, Brace, Jovanovich.

Collins, Steven. 1985. "Categories, Concepts or Predicates? Remarks on Mauss' Use of Philosophical Terminology." In *The Category of the Person*. Edited by Michael Carrithers, Steven Lukes, and Steven Collins, 46–82. New York: Cambridge University Press.

Comte, Auguste. 1975. *Auguste Comte and Positivism*. Edited by G. Lenzer. New York: Harper Torchbooks.

Cornford, Francis M. 1912. *From Religion to Philosophy*. Cambridge, England: Cambridge University Press.

———. 1957. *Plato's Theory of Knowledge: The Theaetetus and The Sophist*. Translated with Intro., and Notes by F. M. Cornford. Indianapolis, Ind.: Bobbs-Merrill.

Couchoud, Paul-Louis. 1902. *Bénoit de Spinoza*. Paris: Félix Alcan.

Davy, Georges. 1911. *Émile Durkheim: Choix de Textes avec étude du système sociologique*. Collection: Les Grands Philosophes Français et Étrangers. Paris: L. Michaud.

———. 1922. *La Foi Jurée*. Paris: Félix Alcan.

———. 1931. *Sociologues d'Hier et d'aujourd'hui*. Paris: Félix Alcan.

Dennes, William Ray. 1924. "The Method and Presuppositions of Group Psychology." *University of California Publications in Philosophy* 6, no. 1. Berkeley: University of California Press.

Deploige, Simon. 1938 (1911). *The Conflict Between Ethics and Sociology*. Translated by Rev. C. C. Miltner. London: B. Herder.

Douglas, Jack. 1967. *The Social Meanings of Suicide*. Princeton, N.J.: Princeton University Press.

Dumont, Louis. 1980. *Homo Hierarchicus: The Caste System and Its Implications*. Rev. English Edition. Translated by M. Sainsbury, L. Dumont, and B. Gulati. Chicago: University of Chicago Press.

Durkheim, Émile. 1933 (1893). *The Division of Labor in Society*. Translated by George Simpson. New York: Free Press.

————. 1950. *Lecons de Sociologie: physique des moeurs et du droit*. Introduction de Georges Davy. Paris: Presses Universitaires de France.

————. 1951 (1897). *Suicide*. Translated by John Spaulding and George Simpson. New York: Free Press.

————. 1955. *Pragmatisme et Sociologie*. Edited by A. Cuvillier. Paris: J. Vrin.

————. 1956. *Education and Sociology*. Translated by S. D. Fox. Intro. by P. Fauconnet. New York: Free Press.

————. 1957. *Professional Ethics and Civic Morals*. Translated by C. Brookfield. Intro. by Georges Davy. New York: Routledge.

————. 1961. *Moral Education*. Foreword by P. Fauconnet. Translated by E. K. Wilson and H. Schnurer. New York: Free Press.

————. 1962. *Socialism*. Translated by C. Sattler. Preface by M. Mauss. Intro. by A. Gouldner. New York: Collier.

————. 1963. *Incest: The Nature and Origin of the Taboo*. Translated by E. Sagarin. New York: Lyle Stuart.

————. 1964 (1914). "The Dualism of Human Nature and Its Social Conditions." In *Essays on Sociology and Social Philosophy by Émile Durkheim et. al.* Edited by K. Wolff, 325–40. New York: Harper Torchbooks.

————. 1965. *Montesquieu and Rousseau: Forerunners of Sociology*. Intro. by Henri Peyre. Ann Arbor: University of Michigan.

————. 1966a. *Montesquieu et Rousseau: Précurseurs de la Sociologie*. Note Introductive de Georges Davy. Paris: Marcel Rivière.

————. 1966b. *Éducation et Sociologie*. Préface de Maurice Debesse. Introduction de Paul Fauconnet. Paris: Presses Universitaires de France.

————. 1967. *Sociologie et Philosophie*. Préface de C. Bouglé. Paris: Presses Universitaires de France.

————. 1969a. *L'Évolution Pédagogique en France*. Intro. de M. Halbwachs. Paris: Presses Universitaires de France.

————. 1969b. *Journal Sociologique*. Edited by J. Duvignaud. Paris: Presses Universitaires de France.

————. 1970. *La Science Sociale et L'Action*. Edited by Jean-Claude Filloux. Paris: Presses Universitaires de France.

―――. 1973. *Émile Durkheim on Morality and Society*. Edited with an Introduction by R. N. Bellah. Chicago: University of Chicago Press.

―――. 1974a. *Sociology and Philosophy*. Translated by D. F. Pocock. Preface by C. Bouglé. New York: Free Press.

―――. 1974b. *L'Éducation Morale* Avertissement de Paul Fauconnet. Paris: Presses Universitaires de France.

―――. 1975. *Textes*. 3 vols. Présentation de V. Karardy. Paris: Éditions de Minuet.

―――. 1977. *The Evolution of Educational Thought*. Translated by P. Collins. New York: Routledge.

―――. 1978. *Émile Durkheim on Institutional Analysis*. Translated and Edited by Mark Traugott. Chicago: University of Chicago Press.

―――. 1979. *Durkheim: Essays on Morals and Education*. Translated and Edited by W. H. C. Pickering. London: Routledge.

―――. 1982. *The Rules of Sociological Method and Selected Texts on Sociology*. Translated by W. D. Halls. Intro. S. Lukes. New York: Free Press.

―――. 1983. *Pragmatism and Sociology*. Translated by J. C. Whitehouse. Intro. by J. B. Allcock. New York: Cambridge University Press.

―――. 1984 (1893). *The Division of Labor in Society*. Translated by W. D.Halls. Intro. by L. Coser. New York: Free Press.

―――. 1985 (1902). "On Totemism." Translated by R. A. Jones. *History of Sociology* 5, no. 2 (Spring): 91–121.

―――. 1986. *Durkheim on Politics and the State*. Edited by A. Giddens. Translated by W. D. Halls. Stanford: Stanford University Press.

―――. 1988 (1895). *Les Règles de la méthode sociologique*. Précédes de "Les Règles de la Méthode Sociologique ou l'instauration de raisonnement experimental en sociologie" par Jean-Michel Berthelot. Paris: Flammarion.

―――. 1991 (1912). *Les Formes Élémentaires de la vie religieuse: Le système totémique en australie*. Présentation par M. Maffesoli. Paris: Le Livre de Poche, Classique Philosophique.

―――. 1992. *Le Socialisme*. Introduction de Marcel Mauss. Préface de Pierre Birnbaum. Paris: Quadrige, PUF.

―――. 1993 (1887). *Ethics and the Sociology of Morals*. Translated with an Intro. by Robert T. Hall. Buffalo: Prometheus Books.

———. 1994a. *Durkheim on Religion*. Translated and Edited by W. H. C. Pickering. Boston: Routledge.

———. 1994b (1893). *De la division du travail social*. Paris: Quadrige, PUF.

———. 1995a (1897). *Le Suicide: Étude de Sociologie*. Paris: Quadrige, PUF.

———. 1995b (1912). *The Elementary Forms of Religious Life*. Translated with an Intro. by K. Fields. New York: Free Press.

Durkheim, Émile and Marcel Mauss. 1963 (1903). *Primitive Classification*. Translated with an Intro. by R. Needham. Chicago: University of Chicago Press.

———. 1971 (1913). "Note on the Notion of Civilization." Translated by B. Nelson. *Social Research* 38: 808–13.

Eisenstadt, S. N. 1992. *Jewish Civilization*. Albany: State University of New York Press.

Evans-Pritchard, E. E. 1965. *Theories of Primitive Religion*. Oxford: Clarendon Press.

Fauconnet, Paul. 1928. *La Responsabilité*. Deuxieme Ed. Paris: Félix Alcan.

Feuer, Lewis. 1958. *Spinoza and the Rise of Liberalism*. Boston: Beacon Press.

Filloux, Jean-Claude. 1977. *Individualisme, Socialisme et Changement Social Chez Émile Durkheim*. Thèse Présentée Devant L'Université de Paris V, Le 29 Novembre 1975. Lille: Service de Reproduction des Thesès.

Fournier, Marcel. 1994. *Marcel Mauss*. Paris: Fayard.

Frances, Madeleine. 1937. *Spinoza dans les pays Neerlandais de la seconde moitié du XVII Siècle*. Paris: Félix Alcan.

Freud, Sigmund. 1954. *The Origins of Psychoanalysis*. Translated by E. Mosbacher and J. Strachey. New York: Basic Books.

Gane, Mike. 1988. *On Durkheim's Rules of Sociological Method*. New York: Routledge.

Garrett, Don, ed. 1996. *The Cambridge Companion to Spinoza*. Cambridge: Cambridge University Press.

Gehlke, C. E. 1915. "Émile Durkheim's Contributions to Sociological Theory." *Studies in History, Economics and Public Law* 63, no. 151. New York: Columbia University Press.

Giddens, Anthony. 1971. *Capitalism and Modern Social Theory*. New York: Cambridge University Press.

Gouldner, Alvin. 1973. *For Sociology*. New York: Basic Books.

Granet, Marcel. 1934. *La Pensée Chinoise*. Paris: Éditions Albin Michel.

Greenberg, Louis M. 1976. "Durkheim and Bergson as Sons and Assimilators: The Early Years." *French Historical Studies* 9:619–34.

Gurvitch, Georges. 1971. *The Social Frameworks of Knowledge*. Translated by M. A. Thompson and K. A. Thompson. New York: Harper Torchbooks.

Halbwachs, Maurice. 1971 (1941). *La Topographie Légendaire des Évangiles en Terre Sainte: Étude de Mémoire Collective*. Paris: Presses Universitaires de France.

———. 1980. *The Collective Memory*. Translated by F. J. Ditter and V. Y. Ditter. Intro. by Mary Douglas. New York: Harper Colophon.

———. 1992. *Maurice Halbwachs on Collective Memory*. Translated and Edited by Lewis Coser. Chicago: University of Chicago Press.

Hall, Robert T. 1987. "Émile Durkheim: Ethics and the Sociology of Morals." *Contributions to Sociology*, no. 69. New York: Greenwood Press.

Hall, Roland. 1967. "Monism and Pluralism." In *Encyclopedia of Philosophy*, vol. 5. Edited by Paul Edwards, 363–65. New York: MacMillan.

Hamelin, Octave. 1925. *Essai sur les Éléments Principaux de la Représentation*. 2nd ed. Paris: Félix Alcan.

———. 1927. *Le Système de Renouvier*. Publié par P. Mouy. Paris: Librairie Philosophique J. Vrin.

Hertz, Robert. 1922. "Le Péché et L'Expiation dans les Sociétés Primitives." *Revue de l'Histoire des Religions* 86: 1–60. Paris: Éditions Ernest leRoux.

———. 1970. *Sociologie Religieuse et Folklore*. Préface de G. Balandier. Intro. par Alice Robert Hertz. Préface de Marcel Mauss. Paris: Presses Universitaires de France.

———. 1973 (1909). "The Preeminence of the Right Hand: A Study in Religious Polarity." Translated by R. Needham. In *Right and Left: Essays on Dual Symbolic Classification*. Edited by Rodney Needham, 3–31. Chicago: University of Chicago Press.

Hester, William. 1947. *A Critical Examination of the Philosophy of Charles Renouvier* With particular reference to his Metaphysics. Ph.D diss. Durham, N.C.: Duke University.

Hirst, P. Q. 1975. *Durkheim, Bernard and Epistemology.* London: Routledge.

Hubert, Henri and Marcel Mauss. 1929 (1909). *Mélanges d'Histoire des Religions.* Deuxième Éd. Paris: Félix Alcan.

———. 1964 (1899). *Sacrifice: Its Nature and Functions.* Translated by W. D. Halls. Chicago: University of Chicago Press.

———. 1972 (1904). *A General Theory of Magic.* Translated by R. Brain. Chicago: University of Chicago Press.

Hughes, H. Stuart. 1969. *The Obstructed Path: French Social Thought in the Years of Desperation.* New York: Harper Torchbooks.

Hulme, T. E. 1924. *Speculations.* Edited by H. Read. New York: Harvest Books.

Huvelin, Paul. 1907. "Magie et Droit Individuel." *L'Année Sociologique* 10: 1–47.

James, William. 1890. *Principles of Psychology.* 2 vols. New York: Henry Holt.

Jay, Martin. 1984. *Marxism and Totality.* Berkeley: University of California Press.

Jones, Robert Alun. 1986. *Emile Durkheim: An Introduction to Four Major Works.* Beverly Hills, Calif.: SAGE.

Jouffroy, Théodore. 1924. *Le Cahier Vert.* Comment Les Dogmes Finissent. Lettres Inédites, Publiés par Pierre Poux. Paris: Les Presses Françaises.

Kant, Immanuel. 1968. *Critique of Pure Reason.* Translated by Norman Kemp Smith. New York: MacMillan.

Kneale, William and Martha Kneale. 1962. *The Development of Logic.* Clarendon: Oxford University Press.

LaCapra, Dominick. 1972. *Émile Durkheim: Sociologist and Philosopher.* Ithaca, N.Y.: Cornell University Press.

LaCroix, Bernard. 1981. *Durkheim et le Politique.* Montréal: Presses de l'Université de Montréal.

Lalande, André. 1962. *Vocabulaire Technique et Critique de la Philosophie.* Paris: Presses Universitaires de France.

LeBon, Gustave. 1960 (1895). *The Crowd: A Study of the Popular Mind.* New York: Viking Press.

Lehman, Jennifer. 1993. *Deconstructing Durkheim, A Post-Post-Structuralist Critique.* Boston: Routledge.

———. 1994. *Durkheim and Women.* Lincoln: University of Nebraska Press.

Lester, David, ed. 1994. *Émile Durkheim: Le Suicide, One Hundred Years Later.* Philadelphia: Charles Press.

Levine, Donald. 1995. *Visions of the Sociological Tradition.* Chicago: University of Chicago Press.

Lévi-Strauss, Claude. 1963. *Totemism.* Translated by R. Needham. Boston: Beacon Press.

———. 1987. *Introduction to the Work of Marcel Mauss.* London: Routledge.

Lévy-Bruhl, Lucien. 1910. *Les Fonctions Mentales dans les Sociétés Inférieures.* Paris: Félix Alcan.

Lloyd, G. E. R. 1992. *Polarity and Analogy.* Indianapolis, Ind.: Hackett.

Logue, William. 1993. *Charles Renouvier, Philosopher of Liberty.* Baton Rouge: Louisiana State University Press.

Lovejoy, Arthur O. 1936. *The Great Chain of Being.* Cambridge: Harvard University Press.

Lukes, Steven. 1973. *Émile Durkheim, His Life and Work.* London: Allen Lane, Penguin Press.

Maimonides. 1963. *Guide for the Perplexed.* 2 vols. Translated by Shlomo Pines. Intro. by Leo Strauss. Chicago: University of Chicago Press.

Mannheim, Karl. 1936. *Ideology and Utopia.* Translated by L. Wirth and E. Shils. London: Routledge.

Marrus, Michael R. 1971. *The Politics of Assimilation.* Oxford: Clarendon Press.

Marx, Karl. 1977. *Karl Marx: Selected Writings.* Edited by D. McClellan. New York: Oxford University Press.

Mauss, Marcel. 1966. *Sociologie et Anthropologie.* Troisième Édition. Augmentée, Présentation par C. Lévi-Strauss. Paris: Presses Universitaires de France.

———. 1968. *Oeuvres.* 3 vols. Présentation de V. Karardy. Paris: Éditions de Minuet.

———. 1979a. *Sociology and Psychology*. Translated by Ben Brewster. New York: Routledge.

———. 1979b. *Seasonal Variations of the Eskimo: A Study in Social Morphology*. Translated by J. J. Fox. New York: Routledge.

———. 1990. *The Gift: The Form and Reason of Exchange in Primitive and Archaic Societies*. Translated by W. D. Halls. Foreword by Mary Douglas. New York: Norton.

Mead, George Herbert. 1934. *Mind, Self and Society*. Chicago: University of Chicago Press.

Merton, Robert K. 1968. *Social Theory and Social Structure*. Enlarged Ed. New York: Free Press.

Merz, John Theodore. 1965 (1904–1912). *A History of European Thought in the Nineteenth Century*. 4 vols. New York: Dover.

Meštrović, S.G. 1988. *Émile Durkheim and the Reformation of Sociology*. Totowa, N.J.: Rowman and Littlefield.

———. 1991. *The Coming Fin-de-Siècle: An Application of Durkheim's Sociology to Modernity and Postmodernism*. New York: Routledge.

Nandan, Yash, ed. 1980. *Émile Durkheim: Contributions to L'Année Sociologique*. Translated by J. French, Andrew Lyons, John Sweeney, Kennerly Woody. New York: Free Press.

Nelson, Benjamin. 1981. *On the Roads to Modernity*. Edited by T. Huff. Totowa, N.J.: Rowman and Littlefield.

Nielsen, Donald A. 1986. "Robert Hertz and the Sociological Study of Sin, Expiation and Religion: A Neglected Chapter in the Durkheim School." In *Structures of Knowing*. Edited by Richard Monk, 7–50. Lanham, Md.: University Press of America.

———. 1987a. "Auguste Sabatier and the Durkheimians on the Scientific Study of Religion." *Sociological Analysis* 47, no. 4: 283–301.

———. 1987b. "A Theory of Communicative Action or a Sociology of Civilizations?: A Critique of Jürgen Habermas." *International Journal of Politics, Culture and Society* 1, no. 1: 159–88.

———. 1988. "The Natural Law Concept of 'Community' and 'Society' and Their Relevance for the Comparative Study of Civilizations: A Note on Ferdinand Tonnies' Theory." *Sociologia Internationalis* 26, no. 2: 223–36. .

———. 1989. "Sects, Churches and Economic Transformations in Russia and Western Europe." *International Journal of Politics, Culture and Society* 2, no. 4: 493–522.

———. 1990. "The Inquisition, Rationalization and Sociocultural Change in Medieval Europe." In *Time, Place and Circumstance: Neo-Weberian Essays in Comparative Religious History*. Edited by William H. Swatos, 107–22. New York: Greenwood Press.

———. 1991. "Natural Law and Civilizations: Images of 'Nature', Intracivilizational Polarities, and the Emergence of Heterodox Ideals." *Sociological Analysis* 52, no. 1: 55–76.

———. 1996a. "La Misura divina: creazione e retribuzione nel libro della Sapienza e in Filone. Aspetti dell'incontro fra giudaismo ed ellenismo." Translated from the English by E. Stein. *Religiona e Societa* 11, no. 24: 9–21.

———. 1996b. "Pericles and the Plague: Civil Religion, Anomie and Injustice in Thucydides." *Sociology of Religion* 57, no. 4: 397–407.

———. 1996c. "Review of Émile Durkheim, *The Elementary Forms of Religious Life*. Translated by Karen Fields." *Sociology of Religion* 57, no. 3: 328–29.

———. 1996d. "Review of Stjepan G. Meštrović, *The Coming Fin-de-Siècle: An Application of Durkheim's Sociology to Modernity and Postmodernism*." *Social Forces* 75, no. 1: 347–48.

Nietzsche, Friedrich. 1968. *The Portable Nietzsche*. Translated by Walter Kaufmann. New York: Viking Press.

Nisbet, Robert. 1969. *Social Change and History*. New York: Oxford University Press.

———. 1974. *The Sociology of Emile Durkheim*. New York: Oxford University Press.

Orru, Marco. 1987. *Anomie*. Boston: Allen and Unwin.

Parkin, Robert. 1996. *The Dark Side of Humanity: The Work of Robert Hertz and Its Legacy*. Amsterdam: Harwood Academic Publishers.

Parodi, Dominique. 1930. *Du Positivisme a l'Idéalisme*. Paris: J. Vrin.

Parsons, Talcott. 1937. *The Structure of Social Action*. New York: Free Press.

———. 1957. "Malinowski and the Theory of Social Systems." In *Man and Culture*. Edited by Raymond Firth, 53–70. New York: Harper Torchbooks.

Pascal. 1966. *Pensées*. Translated by A. J. Krailsheimer. New York: Penguin.

Pearce, Frank. 1989. *The Radical Durkheim*. London: Unwin Hyman.

Picard, Roger. 1908. *La Philosophie Sociale de Renouvier*. Paris: Marcel Rivière.

Pickering, W. H. C. 1984. *Durkheim's Sociology of Religion*. London: Routledge.

Pickering, W. H. C. and H. Martins, eds. 1994. *Debating Durkheim*. New York: Routledge.

Pope, Whitney. 1976. *Durkheim's "Suicide": A Classic Analyzed*. Chicago: University of Chicago Press.

Raphael, Freddy and Robert Weyl. 1977. *Juifs en Alsace. Culture, Société, Histoire*. Toulouse: Privat, Editeur.

Renouvier, Charles. 1875. *Essais de Critique Générale, Premier Essai; Traité de Logique Générale et de Logique Formelle*. 2nd ed., 3 vols. Paris: Au Bureau de la Critique Philosophique.

———. 1896. *Introduction à la Philosophie Analytique de l'Histoire*. Nouvelle édition. Revue et Considerablement Augmentée. Paris: Ernest Laroux.

———. 1912a. *Essai de Critique Générale, Deuxième Essai. Traité de Psychologie Rationelle d'après Les Principes du Criticisme*. 2 vols. Paris: Armand Colin.

———. 1912b. *Essai de Critique Générale, Troisième Essai. Les Principes de la Nature*. Paris: Armand Colin.

Ribot, Theodule. 1896. *La Psychologie des Sentiments*. Paris: Félix Alcan.

Richard, Gaston. 1943. *Sociologie et Théodicée*. Paris: Presses Universitaires.

Rorty, Richard. 1979. *Philosophy and the Mirror of Nature*. Princeton, N.J.: Princeton University Press.

Ross, David. 1995. *Aristotle*. With a New. Intro. by J. L. Ackrill. New York: Routledge.

Roth, Leon. 1924. *Spinoza, Descartes, Maimonides*. Oxford: Clarendon Press.

Rousseau, Jean Jacques. 1911. *Émile*. Translated by B. Foxley. London: J. M. Dent.

———. 1978. *On the Social Contract*. Translated by J. R. Masters. Edited by R. D.Masters. New York: St. Martin's Press.

Scheler, Max. 1992. *On Feeling, Valuing and Knowing: Selected Writings*. Edited with an Intro. by Harold Bershady. Chicago: University of Chicago Press.

Schmaus, Warren. 1994. *Durkheim's Philosophy of Science and the Sociology of Knowledge*. Chicago: University of Chicago Press.

Schoenfeld, Eugen and S. Meštrović. 1989. "Durkheim's Concept of Justice and Its Relationship to Social Solidarity." *Sociological Analysis* 50, no. 2: 111–27.

Scott, John A. 1951. *Republican Ideas and the Liberal Tradition in France*. New York: Columbia University Press.

Séailles, Gabriel. 1905. *La Philosophie de Charles Renouvier*. Paris: Félix Alcan.

Seger, Imogene. 1957. *Durkheim and His Critics in the Sociology of Religion*. New York: Columbia University, Bureau of Applied Social Research Monographs.

Simmel, Georg. 1971. *On Individuality and Social Forms*. Edited by D. Levine. Chicago: University of Chicago Press.

———. 1990. *The Philosophy of Money*. Translated by T. Bottomore and D. Frisby, from a First Draft by K. Mengelberg. 2nd Ed., enlarged. New York: Routledge.

Simpson, George. 1933. "Émile Durkheim's Social Realism." *Sociology and Social Research* 18: 3–11.

———. 1963. *Émile Durkheim*. New York: Thomas Y. Crowell.

Skorupski, John. 1976. *Symbol and Theory: A Philosophical Study of Theories of Religion in Social Anthropology*. New York: Cambridge University Press.

Sorokin, P. A. 1928. *Contemporary Sociological Theories*. New York: Harper and Row.

Soustelle, Jacques. 1940. *La Pensée Cosmologique des Anciens Mexicains: Le Temps et l'Espèce*. Paris: Hermann.

Spade, Paul Vincent, trans. and ed. 1994. *Five Texts on the Medieval Problem of Universals*. Indianapolis, Ind.: Hackett.

Spencer, Baldwin and F. J. Gillen. 1968 (1899). *The Native Tribes of Central Australia*. New York: Dover Press.

Spinoza, Baruch. 1985. *The Collected Works of Spinoza*. Vol. 1. Translated by Edwin Curley. Princeton, N.J.: Princeton University Press.

———. 1991. *Tractatus Theologico-Politicus*. Translated by Samuel Shirley. Leiden: E. J. Brill.

———. 1995. *Baruch Spinoza: The Letters*. Translated by S. Shirley. Intro. and Notes by S. Barbone, L. Rice, and J. Adler. Indianapolis, Ind.: Hackett.

Strenski, Ivan. 1997. *Durkheim and the Jews of France*. Chicago: University of Chicago Press.

Swanson, Guy. 1966. *The Birth of the Gods*. Ann Arbor: University of Michigan Press.

Takla, Tendzin N. and Whitney Pope. 1985. "The Force Imagery in Durkheim: The Integration of Theory, Metatheory and Method." *Sociological Theory* 3: 74–88.

Tarde, Gabriel. 1969. *Gabriel Tarde on Communication and Social Influence*. Translated and edited by Terry Clark. Chicago: University of Chicago Press.

Teillard de Chardin, Pierre. 1961. *The Phenomenon of Man*. Translated by B. Wall. New York: Harper Torchbooks.

Tiryakian, E. A. 1962. *Sociologism and Existentialism*. Englewood Cliffs, N.J.: Prentice-Hall.

Turner, Stephen P. 1986. *The Search for a Methodology of the Social Sciences. Durkheim, Weber and the Nineteenth Century Problem of Cause, Probability and Action*. Dordrecht, The Netherlands: D. Reidel.

Vialatoux, Joseph. 1939. *De Durkheim à Bergson*. Paris: Bloud and Gay.

Wallwork, Ernest. 1972. *Émile Durkheim: Morality and Milieu*. Cambridge, Mass.: Harvard University Press.

———. 1985. "Durkheim's Early Sociology of Religion." *Sociological Analysis* 46, no. 3: 201–17.

Webb, Clement, C. J. 1916. *Group Theories of Religion and the Individual*. London: George Allen and Unwin.

Weber, Max. 1975. *Roscher and Knies: The Logical Problems of Historical Economics*. Translated with an Intro. by Guy Oakes. New York: Free Press.

Wolff, Kurt, ed. 1964. *Essays on Sociology and Social Philosophy by Emile Durkheim et al*. New York: Harper Torchbooks.

Wolfson, Harry A. 1934. *The Philosophy of Spinoza*. Cambridge, Mass.: Harvard University Press.

————. 1962. *Philo*. 2 Vols. Cambridge, Mass.: Harvard University Press.

Woolhouse, R. S. 1993. *Descartes, Spinoza, Leibniz: The Concept of Substance in Seventeenth-Century Metaphysics*. London: Routledge.

Worsley, Arthington. 1907. *Concepts of Monism*. London: T. Fisher Unwin.

Yovel, Yirmiyahu. 1992. *Spinoza and Other Heretics*. 2 Vols. Princeton, N.J.: Princeton University Press.

INDEX